Toward a Unified Criminology

Integrating Assumptions about
Crime, People, and Society

Robert Agnew

NEW YORK UNIVERSITY PRESS
New York and London

NEW YORK UNIVERSITY PRESS
New York and London
www.nyupress.org

References to Internet websites (URLs) were accurate at the time of writing.
Neither the author nor New York University Press is responsible for URLs
that may have expired or changed since the manuscript was prepared.

Library of Congress Cataloging-in-Publication Data

Agnew, Robert, 1953–
Toward a unified criminology : integrating assumptions about crime, people and society /
Robert Agnew.
p. cm. — (New perspectives in crime, deviance, and law series)
Includes bibliographical references and index.
ISBN 978-0-8147-0508-7 (hardback) — ISBN 978-0-8147-0509-4 (pb) —
ISBN 978-0-8147-0527-8 (ebook) — ISBN 978-0-8147-0790-6 (ebook)
1. Crime. 2. Criminologists. 3. Criminology. I. Title.
HV6025.A38   2011
364—dc23   2011028152

New York University Press books are printed on acid-free paper,
and their binding materials are chosen for strength and durability.
We strive to use environmentally responsible suppliers and materials
to the greatest extent possible in publishing our books.

Manufactured in the United States of America

c   10 9 8 7 6 5 4 3 2 1
p   10 9 8 7 6 5 4 3 2 1

Contents

Preface

This book has its origins in an earlier book I wrote, *Why Do Criminals Offend? A General Theory of Crime and Delinquency* (Agnew, 2005). I have long felt that each of the major theories in criminology has something useful to say about the causes of crime, and this book was my effort to integrate them into a general theory. The theory I developed is quite solid, but I have since come to realize that it is built on a weak foundation. While the general theory does a good job of pulling together the core arguments from several theories of crime, it does not devote sufficient attention to such foundational issues as the nature of crime, people, and society. For example, the theory barely discusses the nature of crime; instead, it focuses on the street crimes that dominate mainstream research in criminology. As a result, there is some uncertainty about whether the theory applies to other types of crime (and what those types of crime might be). The theory implicitly assumes that crime is determined by forces beyond the individual's control; it does not discuss whether people exercise free will and, if so, how that might affect the arguments that are made. Likewise, the theory says little about human nature, despite the fact that the causes it examines are derived from theories that make different assumptions about the nature of people. And the theory devotes little attention to the nature of societies and how variation in societal characteristics affects the causes that are described. Like many mainstream criminologists, I ignored or took a lot for granted in my attempt to better explain crime.

As a result, I started to think and read about the underlying assumptions on which crime theories are based, particularly assumptions about the nature of crime, people, society, and reality. For example: Are people naturally self-interested, socially concerned, or "blank slates" shaped by the environment? Is society characterized by consensus over core values and interests or by conflict, with some groups oppressing others? And is there an objective reality that can be accurately measured, or are there multiple subjective realities? It quickly became apparent that the assumptions that criminologists make in these areas have a fundamental impact on their work: they largely determine what criminologists study, the causes they examine, the control strategies they recommend, and how they test their theories and evaluate crime-control strategies. Further, they are at the root of the division in criminology. There are many theories and perspectives in the discipline, and the differences between them usually derive from the different underlying assumptions they make. But despite the importance of the assumptions that are made, most are seldom discussed, particularly by mainstream criminologists.

Recent research in several disciplines, however, has taken a new look at many of these assumptions, including those regarding free will versus determinism, the nature of human nature, the nature of society, and how we perceive "reality." This research suggests that the different assumptions made by crime theories and perspectives have each captured a *part* of the truth. Drawing on this research, I offer a new set of underlying assumptions for criminology in this book. These assumptions integrate and extend the different assumptions made by current theories and perspectives. As such, they provide a more solid foundation on which to construct a general or unified theory of crime.

The construction of such a theory is critical for the success of criminology. As Weisburd and Piquero (2008) point out, criminologists are able to explain only a small portion of the variance in crime. And the amount of variance explained has not increased in recent years. In my view, the problem is not a lack of theories or explanations; the discipline is blessed (cursed?) with scores of theories. Rather, the problem is the inability of criminologists to create a general theory that captures the essential insights of the different theories and perspectives. It is my hope that this book helps pave the way for such a theory.

The intended audience for the book ranges from upper-level undergraduates to professional criminologists. It is important to reach out to students who are embarking on the study of crime before they have had a chance to internalize a particular set of underlying assumptions. At the same time, graduate students and professionals will find the book both useful and challenging: useful because of the overviews of the underlying assumptions and the research on them that it provides; challenging because it likely questions certain of the assumptions on which they rely. Also, it suggests several new directions for research, some quite different from current research—particularly in mainstream criminology.

I of course recognize that many may not agree with my interpretations of the research literature or the new assumptions I propose. But I will consider the book a success if it stimulates criminologists to devote more attention to the assumptions that guide their work, to familiarize themselves with certain of the literatures outside of criminology that bear on these assumptions, and to engage in constructive dialogue with those who make different assumptions about crime, people, society, and reality.

This book would not have been possible without the help of numerous people. I especially want to thank Ilene Kalish, criminology editor at NYU Press, and John Hagan, editor of the NYU Press New Perspectives in Crime, Deviance, and Law Series. I am also most appreciative of the comments provided by several anonymous reviewers on the book proposal and manuscript. And, as always, I am indebted to Mary, Willie, and Jenny for their love and support.

A Divided Criminology

Most criminologists would agree that there are too many theories in criminology. All of the standard theories have been around for at least twenty-five years. . . . In addition, new theories appear on the scene with astonishing frequency. . . . Most criminologists would agree that the abundance of theories does not enrich the field but impedes scientific progress. . . . Theory is supposed to direct research and to accumulate its product into a coherent, understandable framework. . . . The failure to accomplish this is one reason why criminology research has tended toward a million little modest studies.

—Bernard and Snipes, "Theoretical
Integration in Criminology"

Introduction

This book is about the underlying assumptions that criminologists make about the nature of crime, people, society, and reality. I describe the assumptions that different groups of criminologists make in each of these areas, noting that they are often opposed. For example, some criminologists assume that people are naturally self-interested; others that they are socially concerned; and still others that they are "blank slates," shaped by their social environment. This opposition makes it impossible to integrate the different approaches in criminology or develop a unified criminology. I draw on recent work from several disciplines to suggest an alternative set of underlying assumptions. These alternative assumptions incorporate the essential insights from a range of approaches in criminology and so lay the foundation for a unified criminology that can more fully explain a broader range of crimes. I begin this book, however, with a brief overview of the divisions in criminology, the problems that these divisions create, and the assumptions that I will examine.

A Divided Criminology

Criminology is a divided discipline. The most prominent division is between "mainstream" and "critical" criminologists, who tend to focus on different types of crime, employ different explanations for these crimes, test their explanations using different methods, and make different recommendations for controlling crime. Mainstream criminologists focus on acts that are in violation of the criminal law, particularly individual acts of violence, theft, and drug use. Such acts are partly explained by individual characteristics, such as low self-control and beliefs favorable to crime. And they are partly explained by characteristics of the individual's immediate environment, such as poor parental supervision, negative school experiences, delinquent peer association, and residence in disorganized communities. These ideas are usually tested by conducting surveys, with the survey data being analyzed using sophisticated statistical techniques. Such analyses control for race/ethnicity, sex, and class; but there is often little consideration of how these factors shape life experiences and outcomes. Based on such analyses, mainstream criminologists recommend that crime be controlled by rehabilitating offenders, preventing crime among at-risk individuals and, in some cases, punishing criminals in a more effective manner.

There are many versions of critical criminology, including Marxist, feminist, critical race, left-realist, constructionist, and postmodernist approaches (see DeKeseredy, 2011; Einstadter and Henry, 2006; MacLean and Milovanovic, 1997 for overviews). These approaches differ from one another in important ways, but they also share much in common. Critical criminologists focus on a much broader range of "crimes" than mainstream criminologists, including many acts that are not in violation of the criminal law. These acts are frequently committed by organizations, especially corporations and states. And they are explained in terms of larger social forces, particularly the efforts of certain groups to maintain their privileged position, oppressing others in the process (e.g., the oppression of workers by capitalists). Variables such as race/ethnicity, gender, and class play a central role in such explanations; they define the larger social conflicts that result in crime. Survey research is seldom employed to test critical theories; it is felt that the brief responses provided in surveys cannot adequately capture the complex forces that result in crime. Rather, critical criminologists rely on techniques such as historical and comparative analysis, observation, and intensive interviews. Based on their analyses, they recommend that crime be controlled by altering the larger social environment in ways that reduce oppression.

To be sure, some mainstream criminologists are sympathetic to critical criminology and have been influenced by it. For example, some mainstream researchers do not limit their focus to individual acts of theft and violence, but study topics such as corporate crime (e.g., see Simpson and Weisburd, 2010). Many have become more sensitive to the critical role that gender, race/ethnicity, and class play in explaining crime (e.g., Steffensmeier and Allan, 1996; Unnever et al., 2009). And many have supplemented their statistical analyses of survey data with more qualitative approaches, such as the analysis of observational and interview data (e.g., Giordano et al., 2002; Sampson and Laub, 1993). Likewise, some critical criminologists have been influenced by mainstream research. For example, some argue that it is important to examine the individual acts of violence and theft that dominate mainstream research (e.g., Young and Matthews, 1992). Some make use of survey research (e.g., Barkan, 2009; DeKeseredy, 2011). And while critical criminologists focus on larger social forces, many recognize that such forces affect crime partly through their impact on the social-psychological factors examined by mainstream researchers (e.g., Colvin, 2000; Currie, 1997, 1998).

Nevertheless, there remains a large gulf between mainstream and critical criminology. Most mainstream criminologists ignore the contributions of critical criminologists (see Rafter, 2010). And some mainstream criminologists go so far as to reject critical criminology as unscientific (see Chambliss, 1989). They claim that critical criminologists let their values influence their definition of crime, fail to follow the scientific method when studying crime, and make policy recommendations based on their political agendas (e.g., Akers and Sellers, 2008; Toby, 1979). At the same time, critical criminologists claim that mainstream criminology is misguided, serving the interests of the state and major power holders. In particular, they argue that mainstream criminologists let the state define their subject matter, overlook the larger social forces that cause crime, and—despite their claims of scientific neutrality—conduct analyses and make policy recommendations that reinforce existing social arrangements. Ferrell et al. (2008, 204) express the views of many critical criminologists when they state that "mainstream criminology is an abject failure" (also see Chambliss, 1989; DeKeseredy, 2011; Lynch and Michalowski, 2006; Social Justice, 1999)

As a result, there appears to be little prospect for the integration of mainstream and critical approaches. And mainstream and critical criminologists often work in largely separate worlds (see Chambliss, 1989; Pemberton, 2007; Rafter, 2010). Mainstream criminologists dominate the field; their work fills the leading criminology journals and texts, is regularly taught in college courses, and is frequently supported by government grants. Critical criminologists occupy a marginal place in the discipline, particularly in the United States. Their work tends to be published in a few second-tier journals (in the eyes of mainstream criminologists), is sporadically taught in college classes, and is rarely supported by government grants. Further, mainstream criminologists dominate the leading professional organizations, such as the American Society of Criminology (ASC). Critical criminologists belong to these organizations, occasionally occupying leadership positions in them, but they generally present their work in separate sessions and participate in separate subgroups, such as the Division of Critical Criminology of the ASC. As DeKeseredy (2011, 15) states, "to this day, many American critical criminologists experience hostility, academic isolation, and marginalization."

The division that characterizes criminology, however, is not limited to that between mainstream and critical criminology. There are also deep divisions within mainstream criminology. Perhaps the major division is between those who focus on the motivation for crime and those who focus on the controls against crime.[1] Strain, social learning, and certain other theorists argue that individuals will not engage in crime unless they are strongly motivated to do so. They therefore focus on those factors that pressure individuals into crime, such as strains or stressors, or on those factors that entice individuals into crime, such as anticipated rewards. Certain control, deterrence, and classical theorists, however, argue that *all* individuals are strongly motivated to engage in crime. They therefore focus on those factors that restrain individuals from engaging in crime, such as self- and social controls.

Likewise, there are deep divisions within critical criminology. For example, the different approaches within critical criminology focus on different causes; some assume that class conflict is the primary cause of crime, others give primacy to gender conflict, and still others to race and ethnic conflict. Critical criminologists also employ different methods. Some attempt to objectively describe the manner in which one group oppresses another. Others argue that such objective description is impossible, and they instead examine the subjective views of different groups, particularly those views that are seldom heard by others. This strategy is said to foster a deeper understanding of crime, contribute to a reduction in oppressive practices, and promote a more humane response to crime (see Arrigo, 2006; Einstadter and Henry, 2006; Henry and Lanier, 2006).

Still other divisions can be described, but the central point is clear: there are a variety of criminologies that differ from one another in fundamental ways. As a final demonstration of this point, consider the survey that Cooper and associates (2010) conducted in 2007. Members of the American Society of Criminology were asked the following question: "Overall, which theory do you consider the most viable with respect to explaining variations in serious and persistent criminal behavior." Only about half of the respondents listed a theory, with twenty-four theories being listed. And the top-ranked theory was selected by only 13 percent of the respondents.

There have been several attempts to develop integrated theories of crime that bridge certain of the divisions in criminology, particularly the divisions between mainstream theories.[2] I am the author of one such attempt at integration (Agnew, 2005). None of these integrations has attracted a significant following, however. This stems at least partly from the fact that these integrations ignore certain prominent theories and perspectives. Also, some claim that these integrations violate the core assumptions of certain of the theories they do consider (see Hirschi, 1969; Messner et al., 1989). So despite the earnest efforts of some, criminology remains a divided discipline.

This book is motivated by the belief that this division has hurt the field and the larger society. As Bernard and Snipes suggest in the quote at the start of this chapter, this division undermines efforts to develop a "coherent, understandable framework" for the analysis of crime. And the absence of such a framework likely explains why criminologists are unable to explain most of the variation in the crime (Weisburd and Piquero, 2008). This division prevents criminologists from agreeing on recommendations for controlling crime. As an example, the American Society of Criminology, unlike many other professional organizations, generally avoids making policy recommendations. They have tried doing so in the past, but stopped because of the discord that it provoked. Relatedly, this division leads criminologists to speak in many voices, reducing the likelihood they will be heard by policymakers and others.

As I suggest in the chapters that follow, an integrated or unified criminology has the potential to overcome these problems. I believe that each of the major theories and perspectives has something of value to offer to the study of crime. This should come as no surprise: each theory and perspective reflects the work of talented criminologists who have studied crime for many years. It would be surprising if these theories and perspectives did *not* capture something of value regarding crime. Combining the key insights of these theories and perspectives should therefore allow us to better explain and control crime. Unfortunately, the construction of such a unified criminology is not easily accomplished.

The Roots of Division:
The Underlying Assumptions of the Different Criminologies

The divisions that characterize criminology have deep roots. They are based on the different assumptions that theories and perspectives make about the nature of crime, people, society, and reality. Before there can be any hope for a unified criminology, these assumptions must be confronted and the differences between them resolved. Only then will there be a sufficient foundation to build the type of unified criminology capable of attracting wide support and advancing the study of crime. The underlying assumptions on which the different criminologies are based are briefly described below, with these assumptions organized into five areas. I state the assumptions in pure form, which facilitates their description, comparisons between them, and the evaluation of them. I recognize, however, that many criminologists do not fully embrace certain of the "purified" assumptions I list. I elaborate on this point in the chapters that follow. At the same time, I believe that most criminologists favor one or the other of the assumptions listed in the five areas. Further, these assumptions are reflected in their work, as described below:

A. *The Definition of crime.* Mainstream criminologists assume that crime is best defined in terms of violations of the criminal law. Critical criminologists strongly challenge this assumption, arguing that mainstream criminologists let the state define their subject matter for them. As a result, mainstream criminologists ignore many harmful behaviors that are not in violation of the law. Critical criminologists propose several alternative definitions of crime, most of which focus on acts that are "blameworthy" and harmful, although developing precise definitions of harm and blameworthiness has been a challenge. Mainstream criminologists claim that critical criminologists draw heavily on their own values and political agendas when defining crime, undermining the scientific status of the discipline.

B. *Determinism versus agency.* Most mainstream criminologists assume or act as if crime is fully determined by forces beyond the individual's control. These forces include a range of biological, psychological, and social factors. Critical criminologists and certain others place great stress on agency or the ability of people to exert some independent influence on their thoughts and behavior. These criminologists do not deny that people are influenced by a range of factors, but they claim that people are sometimes able to transcend the forces to which they are subject.

C. *The nature of human nature.* There is much disagreement regarding human nature among criminologists. Some argue that people are self-interested; they seek to satisfy their needs and desires in the most expedient manner, with little concern for others. Others claim that people are socially concerned; they desire close ties to others, are quick to conform, and are reluctant to harm innocent others. Still others state that people are "blank slates"; they have few natural inclinations, and are instead shaped by their social environment.

D. *The nature of society.* Many, perhaps most mainstream criminologists assume that society is characterized by consensus. People hold similar values, with everyone agreeing that certain behaviors are wrong and should be punished. People have compatible goals, such that goal achievement by some fosters goal achievement by others. And when people do compete, they agree on the rules of competition. Most critical criminologists, however, argue that society is characterized by conflict. The members of different groups disagree over core values, particularly which behaviors are wrong and should be punished. And groups have conflicting goals. Most notably, the members of more-privileged groups want to maintain or enhance their privileged position. The members of less-privileged groups want to improve their position. Conflict is the result, with the more-privileged groups oppressing those in less-privileged groups.

E. *The nature of reality.* Most mainstream criminologists and certain others believe that there is an objective reality "out there" that can be accurately measured. They focus on developing the single best measures of this reality. Many critical criminologists argue that different people hold different views of the world, and they focus on measuring these different views since they exert the major effect on behavior—including crime. In fact, some critical criminologists claim that there is no objective reality "out there," rather there are multiple subjective realities.

These assumptions are the foundations upon which mainstream and critical theories of crime are built. They define the scope of the field; that is, the types of acts that criminologists should and should not study. Mainstream criminologists focus on violations of the criminal law, while critical criminologists consider many acts that are not technically in violation of the law. In particular, critical criminologists devote much attention to the harmful acts committed by states, corporations, and powerful actors as they seek to maintain or enhance their privileged position.

These assumptions influence the causes of crime that are examined. Most mainstream criminologists focus on those individual problems that lead people to violate the social consensus, committing acts that are widely condemned. For example, individuals are said to engage in crime because they have personality defects or were raised in dysfunctional families. Critical criminologists focus on the efforts of some groups to oppress others and on the consequences of such oppression. For example, they argue that discrimination, poverty, and inequality are at the root of much crime. These assumptions also influence the causes examined *within* mainstream and critical criminology. For example, control theorists focus on those factors that restrain self-interested individuals from engaging in crime. Strain theorists focus on those factors that pressure socially concerned actors to engage in crime. And social-learning theorists focus on the manner in which individuals—viewed as blank slates—learn to engage in crime.

These assumptions influence the methods that criminologists employ. Most mainstream criminologists rely on survey research and sophisticated statistical techniques to develop what they believe are the best measures of objective reality. Many critical criminologists go to great lengths to determine how individuals view the world and interact with one another. In doing so, they employ qualitative methods such as intensive interviews and field observations. Finally, these assumptions influence the crime control strategies that are recommended. Mainstream criminologists focus on correcting individual problems, altering the immediate social environment, and/or increasing social control. Critical criminologists focus on reducing group conflict and its negative consequences, such as poverty.

Clearly, the underlying assumptions made by criminologists have a fundamental impact on their work. But despite their importance, these assumptions are seldom discussed in detail, particularly by mainstream criminologists. Rather, these assumptions are part of the "taken-for-granted world" of many criminologists; regularly relied upon, but rarely examined. There are several reasons for this. Criminologists come to internalize these assumptions as socialized by their mentors and others. Further, challenging these assumptions would undermine their work and that of their colleagues. Also, mainstream criminologists would jeopardize certain of the benefits they reap from their assumptions, such as employment, government grants, and prestige in the discipline (see Henry and Lanier, 2001; Hillyard and Tombs, 2004). Finally, many of these assumptions are seen as difficult or impossible to evaluate. For example, how does one determine the "true" nature of people or whether there is an objective reality that can be accurately measured?

Critical criminologists, however, have devoted significant attention to many of these assumptions. Their marginal status in the discipline puts them under greater pressure to justify the approach they take.[3] Also, a few mainstream criminologists have begun to challenge *certain* of these assumptions. Gottfredson and Hirschi (1990), for example, reject the use of legal definitions of crime and instead build their theory of crime around the explanation of "acts of force and fraud undertaken in the pursuit of self-interest." And several prominent theorists have recently questioned the assumption that crime is fully determined by forces beyond the individual's control (e.g., Giordano et al., 2002; Laub and Sampson, 2001; Wikstrom, 2005). I draw heavily on the work of these critical and mainstream criminologists in my own examination of the underlying assumptions of criminology.

The Goals of This Book

The first goal is to explicitly *describe* the assumptions made by criminologists in each of the above areas and their impact on crime theory and research. These assumptions typically receive little attention in criminology texts (for a prominent exception by two critical criminologists, see Einstadter and Henry, 2006). Describing these assumptions and their impact will make both students and professionals better aware of the foundations on which the discipline is built. Further, describing the differences in assumptions across theories and perspectives will shed much light on the sources of division in criminology. But most importantly, I hope that the discussion of these assumptions undermines their taken-for-granted status, prompting (mainstream) criminologists to devote increased attention to them.

The second goal is to *evaluate* the different assumptions made by criminologists in each of the above areas. I do not argue that any of the assumptions are wrong; rather, I argue that the assumptions are incomplete, describing only a part of the larger world. For example, I do not claim people are self-interested *or* that they are socially concerned *or* that they are blank slates. I argue that the evidence suggests that they are self-interested, socially concerned, *and* learn much from others. Further, the extent to which they exhibit these traits varies across individuals and social circumstances. You may recall the parable of the several blind people, each examining one part of an elephant and so developing incomplete descriptions of the animal. This parable is a recurring theme throughout the book.

My evaluations of the assumptions draw not only on the research in criminology but also on recent research in biology, psychology, anthropology, sociology, and political science. Certain of this research is quite innovative, addressing topics that were previously thought to be beyond the scope of empirical research, such as issues of determinism and agency. The fact that I can draw on this research allows me to move beyond the work of my predecessors in the field, since this research provides a firmer foundation on which to evaluate the assumptions listed earlier. At the same time, the recent and often tentative nature of this research should always be kept in mind. The conclusions I draw will likely be refined and in many cases revised as additional research is completed.

A third goal is to *reformulate* the underlying assumptions of criminology. My reformulations are integrative in nature, reflecting the fact that the existing assumptions each capture a part of the truth. In particular, the reformulated assumptions I propose capture the key insights of both mainstream and critical criminology; as well as the different theories and perspectives within both mainstream and critical criminology. One might ask how assumptions that are seemingly opposed can be integrated. The answer, as well as a second recurring theme in this book, is that the world is complex and variable. For example, the three leading assumptions about human nature each have some truth; individuals are self-interested, socially concerned, *and* (partly) blank slates. Further, the relevance of each of these components of human nature varies across individuals and social environments.

Since the reformulated assumptions are integrative in nature, they will hopefully have some appeal to both mainstream and critical criminologists. These assumptions do not require that we reject either mainstream or critical theory and research; instead, they incorporate and extend the essential insights of both. These assumptions are based to varying degrees on empirical research of the type carried out by mainstream criminologists, something that should increase their appeal to mainstream researchers (although perhaps make certain critical criminologists leery). And, most importantly, these assumptions provide a foundation for a unified criminology, capable of more fully explaining a broader range of crimes.

I do not attempt to build a unified theory of crime; something that would be both premature and far beyond the scope of this book. The reformulated assumptions I propose need to be discussed further, empirically examined, and refined before serious work begins on a unified theory of crime. To that end, I propose numerous recommendations for further research. At the same time, I do sometimes provide suggestions for a unified theory. For example, I provide an outline for an integrated consensus/conflict model of society. My focus, however, is on the underlying assumptions. If an effort is made to build a unified theory based on these assumptions, it will likely be a long-term endeavor involving the work of numerous criminologists with expertise in various areas.

The following chapter begins the process of describing, evaluating, and reformulating the underlying assumptions of criminology, with a focus on the assumptions regarding the nature of crime. Subsequent chapters address the assumptions regarding determinism and agency, human nature, the nature of society, and the nature of reality. These chapters are organized in a similar manner. I describe the underlying assumptions in more detail, beginning with the assumptions made by mainstream criminologists and moving onto alternative assumptions, typically those made by critical criminologists. The impact of these assumptions on the discipline is made clear, particularly their impact on the types of crime that are considered, the causes of crime that are examined, the control strategies that are recommended, and/or the methods that are employed. The evidence regarding the utility or accuracy of these assumptions is considered, sometimes as I am discussing the assumptions and sometimes in a separate section. Finally, I present a reformulated assumption or set of assumptions, which integrate and extend those previously discussed. The implications of this reformulated assumption(s), including the implications for empirical research, are discussed. Later chapters also discuss the relationship between the various reformulated assumptions I have proposed. These assumptions do not stand in isolation from one another; rather, many are intimately related.

2

The Scope of the Discipline

What Is Crime?

Simon Pemberton (2007:27–28), a critical criminologist, discusses his visit to the American Society of Criminology (ASC) meetings in the following quote, with the ASC being the leading organization for academic and research criminologists in the world.

It was my first visit to the ASC, as well as my first visit to Los Angeles. . . . The ASC meetings should not have surprised me—I had been forewarned. However, there is probably no better place than the discipline's largest annual conference to confirm your suspicions about its parlous condition . . . . During the conference one afternoon, I took the time to visit some of the sights adjacent to Downtown LA . . . some colleagues and myself decided to walk the edges of "skid row" in the heart of Downtown LA, the city's central business district. "Skid Row" covers an approximate area of a mile square consisting of several blocks of cardboard boxes and tents which are home to an estimated 7,000–8,000 people. Amidst the towering, gleaming skyscrapers of "Downtown" Los Angeles we witnessed the city's most vulnerable people—the mentally ill, those with drink and drug addictions, the poor—strewn across the sidewalks, abandoned. A striking example of social polarization and a damming indictment on a deeply individidialised society, the champion of "free-market" capitalism and residual welfarism. Not only is this an indictment of this specific form of social organization, but it struck me as we returned to the conference, arguably on criminology too! The irony was not lost; literally kilometers away from "skid row" is the Los Angeles Convention Centre where the ASC meetings were taking place. Yet, in the midst of the 1,000 plus papers and posters . . . not one paper addressed the mass social harms being conducted on the inhabitants of skid row. . . . This is unsurprising, the silence of [mainstream] criminology on such pressing social issues—in particular, the harm produced by current modes of social organization—and the contrasting noise it produces on the "low" level incivilities of the relatively powerless, has been extensively documented.

Criminology is distinctive among academic disciplines (see Reiman and Leighton, 2010). Most disciplines study a range of topics but do so from a common perspective. Sociologists, for example, study topics such as racism, music, and education, but they focus on the social dimensions of these topics. For example, sociologists examine the effect of social factors on racism but do not examine the effect of biological and psychological factors. Criminology, by contrast, focuses on the single topic of crime but examines this topic from a variety of perspectives—including sociological, psychological, and biological. A natural starting point when examining the underlying assumptions of criminology, then, is with the assumptions regarding the nature of crime. The manner in which criminologists define crime determines the scope of the discipline; what is and is not studied. And it has a major effect on the content of the discipline as well, including the causes of crime that are considered and the control strategies that are recommended.

This chapter begins with a description of the leading definition of crime. Mainstream criminologists define crime as acts that violate the criminal law, and they focus their research on what are sometimes called "street crimes," which include individual acts of violence, theft, and drug use. Next, I describe the major criticisms of the legal definition of crime and the associated focus on street crimes. I then examine and evaluate the major alternatives to the legal definition, most proposed by critical criminologists. I conclude by presenting an integrated approach to defining crime that draws on the legal definition and these alternatives. This integrated approach substantially expands the scope of criminology, directing attention to a range of new "crimes" and research questions.

The Mainstream Definition of Crime

Even though the discipline of criminology is built around the topic of crime, mainstream criminologists spend surprisingly little time discussing the actual definition of crime. The major criminology texts usually devote only one or a few pages to definitional issues, and crime is typically defined in terms of violations of the criminal law (Henry and Lanier, 2001; Kramer, 1982).[1] Consider, for example, these definitions of crime from three leading criminology texts:

We define crime as all behaviors for which a society provides formally sanctioned punishment (Hagan, 2008:15).

A crime is any human conduct that violates a criminal law and is subject to punishment (Adler et al., 2007:13).

Crime is a violation of social rules of behavior as interpreted and expressed by a criminal legal code created by people holding social and political power (Siegel, 2006:17).

Likewise, the research on crime is largely based on this legal definition. Research reports usually do not present a formal definition of crime, but the large majority focus on acts that are in violation of the criminal law. The failure to present a formal definition reflects the "taken for granted" status of the legal definition: this definition is so pervasive in mainstream criminology that it is no longer necessary to present or defend it.

It is important to note, however, that criminologists do not examine *all* violations of the criminal law. Hundreds of acts are in violation of the criminal law, including the laws of the federal government, the fifty states, and municipalities within these states. Criminologists tend to focus on individual acts of violence, theft, and drug use. These "street crimes" include homicide, rape, assault, robbery, burglary, larceny theft, vandalism, illicit drug use, and drug selling. An analysis of research reports appearing in three major criminology journals from 2000 to 2005 found that well over 90 percent of these reports focused on street crimes (Michalowski and Kramer, 2007).

The assumption that crime is best defined in terms of violations of the criminal law, and the associated focus on street crimes, is certainly understandable. Many people are victimized by such crimes. Data on the lifetime likelihood of victimization in the United States, for example, indicate that over 99 percent of the population will be the victims of theft and the large majority will be the victims of violence as well (Koppel, 1987). Most of these victimizations will be minor in nature, but the rates of victimization for serious crimes are sometimes high as well—both in the United States and elsewhere. Homicide, for example, is the leading cause of death among young African American men (Henry J. Kaiser Family Foundation, 2006). Likewise, rape is often common, particularly during periods of war and other mass violence. For example, it is estimated that 80 percent of Tutsi women were raped during the one hundred days of the Rwandan genocide in 1994 (Bijleveld et al., 2009; also see Hagan et al., 2005b). Further, street crimes cause much harm to victims, with these harms including death, physical injury, the loss and destruction of property, psychological trauma, medical and other costs, and the disruption of such daily activities as work and school (Shapland and Hall, 2007). These crimes also cause harm to the larger community; often disrupting ties between community members and consuming resources that might otherwise be invested in such things as education and health care (Garcia et al., 2007; Liska and Warner, 1991). Cohen and Piquero (2009) estimate that the street crimes committed by a single career criminal in the United States cost society between 3.2 and 5.7 million dollars.

Further, street crimes receive much attention from and are strongly condemned by politicians, government officials, the media, and the general public (Chambliss, 1999). In particular, these crimes are frequently at the center of political campaigns when crime rates are high (Chambliss, 1999). These crimes are the central focus of those organizations charged with controlling crime, including the police, courts, correctional agencies, and research/funding agencies such as the National Institute of Justice. The local media devote more attention to these crimes than to any other topic (you may have heard the expression, "if it bleeds, it leads"; see Beckett and Sasson, 2000). And these crimes are viewed as quite serious by most people in the United States and other societies (Piquero et al., 2008; Stylianou, 2003). Depending on such things as the crime rate, street crimes often emerge as the major or one of the major concerns of the general public (see Chambliss, 1999).

So street crimes are common, cause a great deal of harm, are widely condemned, and are the focus of crime control agencies. Beyond that, there are several practical advantages to employing the legal definition and focusing on street crimes. The legal definition is reasonably precise and provides criminologists with a ready-made list of crimes to examine (see Michael and Adler, 1933; Kramer, 1982; Tappan, 1947). Government organizations collect extensive data on these crimes and provide funding for research on them, greatly facilitating the work of criminologists. Related to this, many academic and research organizations are organized around the study of such crimes, again facilitating the work of criminologists, through employment, research support, training, and the provision of publication outlets. But despite the many advantages of the legal definition, not all criminologists have adopted it nor have they focused their research on street crimes.

Criticisms of the Legal Definition of Crime

While the legal definition of crime reigns supreme among mainstream criminologists, it has been heavily criticized by critical criminologists.[2] These criticisms often begin by echoing Sellin's (1938) point that a scientific discipline such as criminology should define its own subject matter, rather than letting the state do so (as happens when criminologists adopt the legal definition of crime). The legal definition is then criticized for the following reasons.

Failure to Identify the Core Characteristics of Crime

The legal definition fails to identify the core characteristics of crime. Instead, it simply lists a large number of behaviors that vary greatly on a range of dimensions (see Gibbons and Farr, 2001; Sellin, 1938). As Sutherland (1939:218) states, these behaviors "have very little in common, except that they are all violations of the law." They differ in terms of "the motives and characteristics of the offenders, the situations in which they occur, the techniques that are used, the damages which result, and the reactions of the victims and of the public." Further, the behaviors defined as crimes vary somewhat over time and across societies (Galliher, 1989; Meier and Geis, 2006). For example, few states prohibited the possession and sale of marijuana in the 1920s, but all states did so by the late 1930s (Auerhahn, 1999). Male homosexuality is legal in many societies but defined as a crime in many others (International Lesbian, Gay, Bisexual, Trans, and Intersex Association, 2010). The failure to identify the core characteristics of crime is said to impede the development of criminology. The subject matter of criminology appears to consist of a diverse and shifting set of behaviors; and criminologists lack a compelling answer to the question of *why* these behaviors are grouped together under the rubric of "crime." It is more difficult to explain and control crime when one lacks a clear conception of what it is.

Reflects the Interests and Values of Dominant Groups

The criminal law is said to at least partly reflect the interests and values of dominant groups, since these groups are able to exert more influence on the legislative process.[3] In particular, those behaviors that threaten the interests and values of dominant groups tend to be criminalized, while other harmful behaviors are less likely to be criminalized, particularly if they are committed by the members of powerful groups. Criminologists who adopt the legal definition of crime, then, effectively align themselves with the dominant groups in a society and against the less powerful groups. Criminologists seldom view themselves in this manner; in fact, those who adopt the legal definition of crime sometimes state that they do so in order to avoid drawing on their own values when defining crime (see Tappan, 1947). But as Schwendinger and Schwendinger (2001:83) state, this profession of value neutrality is a "great myth which prevent[s] principled scholars from being aware of the ideological character of their basic theoretical assumptions."[4]

The argument that the criminal law reflects the interests of dominant groups has been challenged. Some criminologists and legal scholars claim that many legally defined crimes—such as murder, assault, and theft—threaten the interests of virtually all individuals. It is therefore in the interests of all that they are criminalized. In perhaps the best statement of this position, Kornhauser (1978) argues that these behaviors threaten universal human needs, particularly the need for physical safety, and so threaten the existence of social groups. As Kornhauser (1978:40) states: "No human group could come into existence, let alone survive, that tolerated uncontrolled theft, assault, or murder. The protection of its members from force and fraud, and their agreement about what constitutes force and fraud, are minimum requirements for all collectivities." Reflecting this fact, we find that behaviors such as murder, rape, and theft are condemned by the large majority of people in the United States and other societies, and are in effect defined as crimes in the vast majority of societies (Brown, 1991; Pinker, 2002; Stylianou, 2003).

Many critical criminologists acknowledge these points (e.g., Young and Matthews, 1992; Reiman and Leighton, 2010). Box (1983:8), for example, states that:

> None of us wants to be murdered, raped, or robbed; none of us wants our property stolen, smashed or destroyed, none of us wants our bodies punched, kicked, bitten, or tortured. In that sense, criminal law against murder, rape, arson, robbery, theft, and assault are in all our interests, since in principle we all benefit equally from and are protected by their existence. Without them life would be "nasty, poor, solitary, brutish, and short."

But at the same time, Box (1983:9) goes on to state that it is important to note that there are many types of violence, property loss, and property destruction that are *not* defined as crimes.

The criminal law defines only some types of avoidable killings as murder; it excludes, for example, deaths resulting from acts of negligence, such as employers' failure to maintain safe working conditions in factories and mines; or deaths resulting from an organization's reluctance to maintain appropriate safety standards, or deaths resulting from governmental agencies giving environmental health risks a low priority, or deaths from drug manufacturers failure to conduct adequate research on new chemical compounds before embarking on aggressive marketing campaigns. (Also see Bronitt, 2008)

Further, certain acts that do *not* involve theft, property destruction, or violence are sometimes defined as crimes. This is the case, for example, with acts such as drug use, homosexuality, and prostitution. Case studies of the origin of the laws against such acts suggest that they often emerge out of conflict, with more powerful groups having their views translated into law (e.g., Box, 1983; Chambliss and Zatz, 1993; Kubrin et al., 2009). And data suggest that individuals and groups are *not* united in their condemnation of such acts (Stylianou, 2003).

In sum, parts of the criminal law do appear to reflect the interests of all people. Specifically, it is in the interests of all to define acts involving interpersonal violence, the destruction of property, and theft as crimes. Such acts are sometimes referred to as *mala in se* offenses (offenses that are intrinsically bad or "bad in themselves"). But at the same time, many harmful acts are not defined as crimes, and certain relatively harmless acts are defined as crimes. These later acts, such as homosexuality, are sometimes referred to as *mala prohibita* offenses (wrong only because the law prohibits them). So taken as a whole, there is reason to believe that the law *partly* reflects the interests and values of dominant groups.

Excludes Many Harmful Behaviors/Includes Some Behaviors That Cause Little Harm

If the criminal law partly reflects the interests and values of dominant groups, it follows that certain harmful behaviors may not be defined as crimes, particularly those behaviors that serve the interests of dominant groups. Those harmful acts committed by corporations and states figure prominently here. And critical criminologists have pointed to a range of harmful behaviors that are not in violation of the criminal law.

Reiman and Leighton's (2010) popular text, *The Rich Get Richer and the Poor Get Prison,* points to the great harm caused by unsafe conditions at work, a range of health care practices (e.g., unnecessary surgery, the overuse of antibiotics), smoking, and poverty. Reiman and Leighton, for example, estimate that each year approximately 55,000 deaths and 2,100,000 other physical harms result from work-related diseases and injuries, compared to about 17,000 deaths and 860,000 physical harms from the street crimes of homicide and aggravated assault (2006 data). This difference is especially compelling when one considers that only about half of the population is employed. To give another example, Reiman and Leighton estimate that unnecessary surgery and medication cost the nation between 28 and 34 billion dollars each year, versus the 17 billion-dollar cost from street-variety property crimes.

In the book *It's Legal but It Ain't Right* (Passas and Goodwin, 2004), several researchers describe the tremendous harm caused by the legal or quasi-legal behaviors associated with the tobacco industry, arms trade, gambling industry, pesticide industry, agricultural industry, pharmaceuticals industry, and the corporate world more generally. The activities and products associated with these industries have large physical costs (death, injury, and illness); financial costs (e.g., the health care costs associated with smoking, the large financial losses associated with gambling and certain business practices); environmental costs (e.g., the pollution from "factory farming"); and social costs (e.g., undermining the democratic system, as sometimes occurs when corporations exert pressure on foreign governments). Passas and Goodwin (2004:3) refer to the behaviors described in their book as "lawful but awful."

Green and Ward (2004) begin their book, *State Crime*, by stating that "modern states kill and plunder on a scale that no 'robber band' could hope to emulate" (2004:1). They then cite Rummel's (1994) estimate that 169 million people were murdered by governments from 1900 to 1987, excluding deaths in wars (also see Maier-Katkin et al., 2009). But they note that since "states define what is criminal," most deaths caused by states are *not* defined as crimes (and so are rarely studied by criminologists). Several other criminologists have likewise pointed to the enormous harm that results from many *legal* behaviors, and all conclude that there are a range of legal behaviors—committed for the most part by corporations and states—that cause far more harm than the street crimes which are the focus of mainstream criminology.[5]

At the same time, it is argued that certain relatively harmless behaviors are defined as crimes. These are often behaviors that powerful individuals and groups find morally offensive, such as homosexuality and certain forms of drug use (see Meier and Geis, 2006; Stylianou, 2003: 43). Beyond that, certain other behaviors are defined as crimes not because they cause harm to individuals but because they threaten the interests of the state or powerful others. For example, repressive states may use the legal system to prohibit free speech or restrict the rights of women.

Sometimes Does Not Reflect Public Views about What Should Be Defined as a Crime

Proponents of the legal definition of crime justify this definition not only by claiming that it provides a good indicator of harmful behaviors but also because it reflects public views about what should and should not be defined as a crime (see especially Tappan, 1947). That is, the law is said to be based on a social consensus or agreement. A good number of studies have asked people in the United States and other societies to rate the "seriousness" of various behaviors—including a variety of street crimes (homicide, rape, robbery, theft), "victimless" crimes (drug use, homosexuality, prostitution), and white-collar offenses (factory pollution, fixing prices on products). Such studies suggest that people agree that behaviors involving bodily injury, property damage, and property loss are *relatively* serious (see the review in Stylianou, 2003). At the same time, there is significant disagreement regarding the seriousness of other offenses, particularly victimless crimes such as marijuana use, homosexuality, and gambling. Further, critical criminologists point out that while there may be consensus regarding the seriousness of certain crimes today, that does not mean that the law emerged out of consensus. The law may have emerged out of conflict, with certain groups using their power to get acts defined as crimes, and the consensus may have come later. Case studies and historical analyses provide some support for this view (e.g., Box, 1983; Chambliss, 1999; Galliher, 1989).

In sum, the legal definition of crime has been criticized on several major points. And while there is some debate regarding the merit of certain of these criticisms, it seems clear that the legal definition is problematic: it fails to describe the core characteristics of crime; involves the tacit acceptance of a politically generated definition, one that sometimes favors the interests and values of powerful groups; excludes many acts that cause great harm; includes some acts that are relatively harmless; and only partly reflects public views about what should and should not be defined as a crime.

Contemporary Alternatives to the Legal Definition

It is one thing to critique the legal definition of crime and another to present a viable alternative. There have been several efforts to propose such alternatives, most by critical criminologists. The most popular alternative defines crimes as acts that result in harm and are "blameworthy," regardless of whether such acts are defined as crimes by the state. It has been difficult, however, to precisely define the term "harm." Partly as a result, this alternative definition has had little effect on mainstream criminologists. Critical criminologists, however, have increasingly turned to the international human rights law in an effort to better define harm.

Other criminologists claim that it is impossible to objectively define harm and blameworthiness. They argue that any definition of crime is a social construction, reflecting the values and interests of those who created it. That is why the definition of crime varies somewhat across societies and over time. Rather than attempt to develop an objective definition of crime, they argue that criminologists should acknowledge that crime is a social construction and focus on the legal definition of crime. Some also argue that criminologists should focus on public views regarding crime. Criminologists should focus on the legal definition and public views not because the acts they define as crimes are necessarily harmful and blameworthy—as many mainstream criminologists contend. Rather, they should focus on legal definitions and public views because they have important consequences. For example, the legal definition strongly influences who is sanctioned by the state, which has enormous consequences for individuals and communities. I discuss these approaches to defining crime in the following sections.

A Focus on Blameworthy Harms: Defining Harm

Many critical criminologists argue that one of the defining characteristics of crimes is that they result in harm. Further, this harm may be caused by both individuals and groups, particularly corporations and states.[6] Focusing on corporate and state crime is seen as critical since, as indicated earlier, such crime is far more harmful than street crime.[7] Efforts to define crime in terms of harm have been criticized, however. Definitions of harm are frequently quite general, thereby providing much room for criminologists to draw on their own values when deciding what is and is not a crime. As Hillyard et al. (2004:272) state, "harm appears to be a generalized, amorphous term, covering an enormous range of quite heterogeneous phenomena" (also see Goode, 1997; Tappan, 1947;

Tittle and Paternoster, 2000:8). Critical criminologists, however, have tried to develop a more precise definition of those harms that should qualify as crimes.

Harm Defined in Terms of Human Rights Violations. Schwendinger and Schwendinger (1970, 2001) state that there are two major strategies for defining harm. The first defines harms as acts that threaten the survival and effective functioning of existing social institutions (also see Tittle and Paternoster, 2000:6–7). The other focuses on the "historically determined rights of individuals," defining harms as those acts or omissions that violate human rights. Schwendinger and Schwendinger favor the later approach, given their view that existing institutions often serve the interests of dominant groups and frequently harm the members of less powerful groups (also see Reiman and Leighton, 2010). Human rights refer to "the necessary conditions for leading a minimally good life" (Fagan, 2009:1). In the words of Schwendinger and Schwendinger (2001:85):

> All persons must be guaranteed the fundamental prerequisites for well-being, including food, shelter, clothing, medical services, challenging work, and recreational experiences, as well as security from predatory individuals or imperialistic social elites. These material requirements, basic services, and enjoyable relationships are not to be regarded as rewards or privileges. They are rights!

Schwendinger and Schwendinger (2001:88) go on to state that there are certain "basic" rights, which are especially relevant to criminology, rights whose "fulfillment is absolutely essential to the realization of a great number of values." While they do not present a full list of such rights, they give as an example the right to "security to one's person," noting that "a danger to one's health or life itself endangers all other claims. A dead man can hardly realize any of his human potentialities." They further state that the same applies to the rights to racial, sexual, and economic equality. In particular, "the abrogation of these rights certainly limits the individual's chance to fulfill himself in many spheres of life." Individuals and states who deny these rights are said to be criminals, and racism, sexism, and poverty are said to be crimes. It is clear that defining harm in terms of human rights violations would substantially expand the scope of criminology. Schwendinger and Schwendinger (2001:89) further note that "in the process of redefining crime, criminologists will redefine themselves, no longer to be defenders of order but rather guardians of human rights." Many other critical criminologists have followed their lead, defining crime in terms of the violation of human rights.[8]

This focus on harm as a human rights violation is a significant advance, but it still falls short of providing a precise definition of those harms that should qualify as crimes. While certain human rights (and rights violations) are reasonably well defined, others are quite vague. For example, some criminologists speak of the rights to "autonomy, development, and growth" (Hillyard and Tombs, 2004:20–21). There is obviously much room for individual judgment when determining whether particular acts violate such broadly defined rights. Further, it is unclear how one determines what is and is not a human right. Many might object to certain of the rights advanced by Schwendinger and Schwendinger (1970) and others, claiming that they reflect the values or political agendas of those advancing them. It is therefore critical to more precisely describe human rights (and rights violations) and provide some justification for their selection.

A Focus on Acts That Violate the International Human Rights Law. Several criminologists have therefore argued that the discipline should rely on the international law to define rights and rights violations.[9] There has been a dramatic expansion in the international law over the last few decades, with a range of treaties and other documents providing reasonably precise descriptions of human rights and rights violations. This stems, in part, from the fact that many rights treaties contain monitoring requirements; necessitating the development of precise definitions of the rights described. Further, the United Nations, other governmental organizations, nongovernmental groups, and scholars are actively engaged in efforts to better define human rights and monitor rights violations.[10] This work, it should be noted, is having an increasingly large effect on nation-states; for example, principles from the international law have been incorporated into the constitutions of many nations (Blau and Moncada, 2009). There is every reason to believe that this "human rights revolution" will continue, since it partly reflects the rapid increase in globalization in recent decades.[11]

A further advantage of the international law is that it reflects a broad consensus among states regarding the nature of human rights and rights violations. The major documents defining the international law have been endorsed by representatives from a wide range of nations, usually after extensive deliberation. These nations differ in many ways, including their political and economic organization, level of development, religious composition, race/ethnicity, and value orientations (e.g., emphasis on individualism versus social cohesion). It is not surprising, then, that the international law reflects both a liberal emphasis on civil and political rights (e.g., the right to vote, to freedom of assembly), and a communitarian emphasis on economic, social, and cultural rights (e.g., the rights to adequate food and shelter). In sum, the international law represents the closest thing we have to a universal consensus regarding rights and rights violations. This provides compelling justification for its use and gives some moral force to the work of criminologists who draw on it (Blau and Moncada, 2009: Brooks, 2008; Normand and Zaidi, 2008).

This is not to claim that the international law is problem free. It is very much a political creation, as histories of the international law make abundantly clear (e.g., Normand and Zaidi, 2008; Rothe and Mullins, 2006). Nations often engage in vigorous lobbying to get their views translated into law. And, not surprisingly, more powerful nations typically exert a disproportionate influence on the law—although the views of less powerful nations do find expression in the law (see Blau and Moncada, 2009). Some nations have not ratified or have conditionally ratified major treaties, with the United States being notorious for its failure to fully ratify key documents (Barak, 1994; Blau and Moncada, 2009; Rothe and Mullins, 2006). In addition, there is an active debate over whether certain rights apply to individuals in *all* nations. Some argue that considerations of cultural diversity should limit the applicability of particular rights.[12] Finally, certain of the rights described in the international law are vaguely defined. But despite these problems, a good case can be made that the international law is the most promising vehicle for developing a reasonably precise, broadly agreed-upon definition of harm, which is generally applicable, transcending the politics of particular states.

Several criminologists have already drawn on the international law to identify harmful acts, some of which do *not* qualify as crimes according to the laws of particular nations (e.g., Green and Ward, 2000; Hagan et al., 2005b; Passas and Goodwin, 2004a). An example is Kauzlarich and Kramer's (1998) *Crimes of the American Nuclear State*. Drawing on several international treaties and the rulings of the International Court of Justice, they argue that the United States engaged in illegal acts involving the threat to use nuclear arms in Korea and Vietnam, environmental contamination associated with the production of nuclear arms, and the conduct of radiation experiments on human subjects. These acts were often legal according to laws in the United States. To give another example, Green and Ward (2004) examine several state "crimes" said to violate human rights, including state involvement in the precipitation of and inadequate response to natural disaster, police crime, torture, war crimes, and genocide (also see Maier-Katkin et al., 2009; Ward, 2004).

A Focus on Blameworthy Harms: Defining Blameworthy

Individuals and groups sometimes commit very harmful acts, but such acts are not defined as crimes by nation states or the international law. For example, an automobile driver may accidentally kill a pedestrian who stepped into the road without looking. Or soldiers may kill members of an invading army. So in defining crime, we must consider both the harm caused by the act *and* the circumstances surrounding the act. Most attempts to define crime by critical criminologists take this into account and stipulate that the harm be "avoidable," "preventable," "unnecessary," etc. (e.g., Box, 1983; Fletcher, 2007; Passas and Goodwin, 2004a:17). These qualifiers get at the notion of blameworthiness.

Criminologists draw heavily on the criminal law and legal theory in defining blameworthiness. Blameworthy harms have several key features, with these features reflected in a range of societies and in the international law.[13] They are *voluntary* and *intentional,* ranging along a continuum from acts, which are purposely committed to harm another to those committed not to harm but with the knowledge that harm is a highly likely outcome, to those committed not to harm but with the knowledge that there is a risk of harm (reckless behavior) to those committed not to harm and without knowledge of the risk of harm—even though a "reasonable person" should have been aware of the risk (negligent behavior). Further, the act is both *unjustified and inexcusable.* States differ somewhat in the justifications and excuses they allow, although there is much overlap in this area (Fletcher, 2007). Commonly accepted justifications and excuses include insanity, duress, necessity, reasonable mistake-of-fact, and self-defense in response to unjustified attacks. For example, someone who steals a boat in order to survive during a flood may justify this act through the defense of "necessity." Someone threatened with death if they do not steal from their place of employment may excuse this act by claiming that they acted under duress.

In sum, *blameworthy* harms are those for which individuals or groups bear some responsibility, are unjustified, and are inexcusable.[14] Researchers who employ these criteria for blameworthiness argue that many harmful acts, which are *not* defined as crimes in the United States, *should be* defined as crimes. For example, Reiman and Leighton (2010) and Daynard (2004) argue that the manufacture and sale of tobacco products should be a crime. There is little doubt that such products cause great harm; each year tobacco products cause about 440,000 deaths in the United States and more than 4 million deaths worldwide; about 100 million people were killed by tobacco products in the twentieth century; and tobacco may cause one *billion* deaths by the end of this century (World Health Organization, 2008). Many additional people are disabled by tobacco products, and the financial, psychological, and social costs of such products are enormous (see Sloan et al., 2004). Evidence suggests that corporate executives in the tobacco industry have been aware of the harm caused by their products for some time. Further, the commonly accepted justifications and excuses for crime do not apply in their case (see Daynard, 2004; Reiman and Leighton, 2010). Thus there is little doubt that the manufacture and sale of tobacco products is a blameworthy harm of great magnitude and therefore should be defined as a crime according to certain criminologists.

A Focus on Acts That Are Condemned and/or Sanctioned

The effort to define crime in terms of blameworthy harm reflects a position sometimes referred to as "essentialism," the view that "phenomena have inherent, unchanging 'essences' that remain with them under any and all circumstances" (Goode, 1997:35; also see Fagan, 2005; Tittle and Paternoster, 2000:6–8). It is assumed, in particular, that there are certain acts that are intrinsically harmful and blameworthy in all societies and at all times. The international law—reflecting a broad consensus among states on the nature of human rights and rights violations—is said by some to be the best vehicle for identifying these acts. This approach to defining crime, however, has been criticized by a subgroup of critical criminologists known collectively as "constructionists."[15]

Constructionists claim that there is no good basis for arguing that certain behaviors are intrinsically harmful and blameworthy. Views of what is and is not a blameworthy harm are said to be socially constructed. This is true of those blameworthy harms described in the international law, just as it is true of those described in domestic criminal law. That is why we find much variation in the definition of human rights over time and between societies (e.g., Blau and Moncada, 2009; Normand and Zaidi, 2008). Democratic societies in the West, for example, tend to define human rights in political and civil terms, focusing on such things as the right to vote; socialist societies define rights in economic and social terms, focusing on such things as the right to adequate housing. According to constructionists, there have been numerous attempts over the course of history to claim that certain acts are intrinsically harmful and blameworthy–with such attempts drawing on a variety of religious, philosophical, political, and most recently, scientific arguments (see chap. 4). In the final analysis, however, the definition of what is harmful and blameworthy cannot be viewed as anything more than a social construction, subject to change as social conditions change.

If there are no intrinsically harmful and blameworthy acts, how then might we define crime? Constructionists argue that we should acknowledge that crime is a social construction and define it in terms of the legal definitions employed by particular societies at particular points in time (see Kramer, 1982; Goode, 1999; Tittle and Paternoster, 2000). That is, criminologists should study those acts defined as crimes by the state. Related to this, constructionists argue that it is also important to examine how the criminal law is applied (the "law in action" as opposed to the "law on the books"). Some acts may technically be defined as crimes, but the laws prohibiting such acts may be rarely enforced or they may be selectively enforced. For example, some evidence suggests that certain laws are more likely to be enforced against the members of less powerful groups (see Reiman and Leighton, 2010, for an overview).

While constructionists argue that criminologists should examine legally defined crimes, they differ from most mainstream criminologists in important ways. They do not assume that legally defined crimes are necessarily harmful or that they reflect a social consensus about what should be defined as a crime. Constructionists, in fact, argue that groups compete with one another to get their views translated into law, with the more powerful groups winning out. And as social conditions change, so does the criminal law. Sellin (1938:23) provides the classic statement of this position; stating that because of changing social conditions, "everything the criminal law of any state prohibits today, it will not prohibit at a given future time." Further, constructionists devote much attention to those factors that influence the development and enforcement of the criminal law, factors such as the competition between groups seeking to advance their interests, media portrayals of crime and criminals, and religious views.[16]

Constructionists argue that it is critical to examine the legal definition of crime, even though it is a social construction, because social constructions have important consequences. Most notably, the criminal law influences how the state responds to a range of behaviors; with some acts being severely sanctioned and others ignored. This response, in turn, has a dramatic impact on individuals, communities, and the total society. In the United States, for example, approximately one out of every thirty adults is under the control of the criminal justice system at any given time, with certain groups being especially likely to experience criminal sanction (Office of Justice Programs,

2007). Approximately one-third of all black males will serve time in prison at some point during their lives, for example (Bonczar, 2003). These experiences with the criminal justice system are quite consequential; for example, a criminal record dramatically reduces one's employment prospects (Bernburg and Krohn, 2003). And the concentration of people with criminal records in certain communities may undermine the level of social control in such communities (Clear, 2007).

Some constructionists also argue that criminologists should examine acts that are condemned and sanctioned by the general public and groups within the public, even if these acts are not in violation of the criminal law. Public condemnation and sanction also have important consequences; among other things, they have a strong effect on those who are condemned and sanctioned, including whether they engage in state-defined crimes (Agnew, 2009; Matsueda, 1992). This idea is at the heart of labeling theory, particularly recent efforts to focus on informal labeling—or labeling by family, friends, neighbors, and others.

Perhaps the best example of a constructionist approach to defining crime is that of Hagan (1985).[17] Hagan argues that criminologists should examine both state-defined crimes and noncriminal forms of deviance. He further proposes that each act—criminal as well as deviant—be ranked on three dimensions:

1. the degree of public agreement about the *wrongfulness of the act*, which can range from general apathy to disagreement to general agreement that the act is wrong;
2. the societal evaluation of the *harm inflicted by the act;*
3. the severity of the *social response to the act*, ranging from polite avoidance to public execution.

Acts can then be classified according to their standing on these three dimensions (which Hagan refers to as the "pyramid of crime").

Hagan states that these dimensions are closely associated in most modern societies, so that acts viewed as very wrong tend to be seen as harmful and tend to be subject to severe penalties by the state. Those acts rated as high on the three dimensions are referred to as "consensus" crimes, and include murder, forcible rape, and kidnapping for ransom ("mala in se" crimes). Those acts rated as low on all three dimensions involve noncriminal forms of deviance, such as nonconformist dress. The association between the three dimensions, however, is not perfect. For example, some acts that are subject to strong sanction may be viewed as relatively harmless (e.g., marijuana use in certain areas and at certain times). Also, there may be disagreement among the public regarding the standing of an act on a dimension; for example, a criminal act may be viewed as very wrong by some but not so wrong by others. Such acts are referred to as "conflict crimes"; they include drug use, euthanasia, and some white-collar offenses.

In sum, Hagan's approach to defining crime does not state that there are certain acts that are intrinsically harmful and blameworthy; rather, it follows a constructionist approach and proposes that criminologists examine acts that are defined as crimes by the state *and* those that are condemned by the public (viewed as wrong and/or harmful). It further recognizes that such acts may differ across societies and over time (although see Greer and Hagan, 2001:222–25).

An Attempt to Integrate the Essentialist and Constructionist Approaches

There have been some attempts to develop definitions of crime that integrate the essentialist and constructionist perspectives (e.g., Green and Ward, 2000). The most sophisticated is that of Henry and Lanier (1998, 2001; also see Lanier and Henry, 2004). Henry and Lanier's "prism of crime" incorporates the three dimensions identified by Hagan: (a) the perceived wrongfulness of the act, (b) the perceived harmfulness of the act, and (c) the severity of the societal response to the act. Henry and Lanier also argue that one should consider the certainty or likelihood of punishment, a dimension that allows one to more fully describe "the law in action" or how the law is enforced.

Henry and Lanier also argue that crime should be defined in an essentialist as well as constructionist manner, so they classify acts according to the extent and severity of the harm they cause. The most harmful acts have a large number of victims and are "those in which the victims are killed and those in which they become permanently injured and maimed; [followed by acts] that are harmful through some temporary loss of capability, money, or property; to those that might offend moral sensibilities but do not result directly in personal loss" (2001:232). Henry and Lanier recognize that the public is often unaware of the harm that results from many crimes, especially state and corporate crimes, whose effects "may be so slow and diffused that no one notices any harm" (2001:228). For example, pollution by a corporation may increase the number of cancer deaths over a broad area several years into the future. This fact makes it is important for criminologists to rate the harmfulness of acts independently of public perceptions.

The prism of crime developed by Henry and Lanier has six dimensions, and acts are classified into various categories based on their standing on these dimensions. Consequently, their classification scheme is quite complex, a fact that may partly account for its limited use by criminologists. Also, their definition of harm is more limited than that adopted by those employing the human rights approach, which focuses on a broader range of harms. Further, there is no essentialist measure of the blameworthiness of an act. Nevertheless, their incorporation of both the constructionist and essentialist approaches provides a useful model for others to follow.

An Integrated Definition of Crime

The integrated definition of crime presented in this section attempts to capture the advantages of the definitions discussed above, while minimizing their disadvantages. The integrated definition assigns a central place to violations of the criminal law and street crimes. As mainstream criminologists point out, street crimes are common, quite harmful, widely condemned, and the focus of the criminal justice system. The integrated definition also focuses on a range of harmful acts that are not legally defined as crimes, including acts committed by states and corporations. As critical criminologists point out, many such acts are far more harmful than street crimes and they meet the legal criteria for blameworthiness. In addition, the international human rights law has developed to the point where it provides a solid foundation for the precise definition of such acts. Finally, the integrated definition focuses on those acts that are sanctioned by the state and condemned by the public—even if such acts do not qualify as human rights violations. As constructionists point out, such condemnation and sanction have major effects on individuals, the criminal justice system, and the larger society. Criminologists cannot ignore such effects and, related to this, cannot ignore the mechanisms by which acts are socially constructed as crimes.

These definitions are integrated using the approach developed by Hagan (1985) and Henry and Lanier (1998), among others. Rather than stating that acts are "crimes" if they possess a single core characteristic, such as being illegal or a human rights violation, I state that acts are crimes if they possess one or more of the several core characteristics identified by the different definitional approaches. Further, acts can be classified according to their standing on these characteristics, with several major types of crime being identified. These types include the street crimes that dominate mainstream criminology, the state and corporate crimes that many critical criminologists examine, and socially constructed crimes. As discussed in the following section, taking account of the different definitional approaches and distinguishing between different types of crimes has several major advantages.

It is important to note, however, that the integrated definition is a work in progress; the core characteristics of crime that I describe need to be refined and the strategies for their measurement better developed. Such work will likely be an ongoing part of criminology; just as other disciplines regularly work to refine the definition and measurement of their dependent variables. Psychologists, for example, continually refine the definition and measurement of mental disorders as reflected in the ongoing revisions of the Diagnostic and Statistical Manual of Mental Disorders (DSM). At the same time, the integrated definition does identify a range of acts that clearly qualify as "crimes," many of which are not defined as crimes according to the laws of particular nations.

The Core Characteristics of "Crime"

As suggested earlier, a few core characteristics are routinely mentioned in definitions of crime. Many critical criminologists argue that criminal acts are harmful and blameworthy, with these characteristics being defined in a universally applicable way. Constructionists argue that criminal acts are condemned and sanctioned by the state and/or public (at least partly because they are believed to be harmful and blameworthy). Mainstream criminologists focus on state sanction, believing it to be a good indicator of both public condemnation and harm (see especially Tappan, 1947). The integrated definition focuses on each of these core characteristics.

1a. Harmful. There are two avenues for defining social harm in a universally applicable and reasonably precise way. First, there is a core set of acts that threaten physical security and are viewed as harmful across the vast majority of societies. These acts involve killing and injuring others, rape, theft, and the damage and destruction of property without the owner's voluntary consent. These acts, then, can be classified as harmful. Second, the international law identifies a range of human rights violations that can also be viewed as universally harmful. The international law has expanded dramatically since World War II, and numerous treaties and related documents provide descriptions of human rights and rights violations. The international law is especially useful for identifying harms committed by states and, increasingly, groups within and across states—including corporations. In drawing on the international law, criminologists are of course letting others define their subject matter for them. But any definition of harm beyond direct threats to physical well-being is necessarily a social construction, reflecting the value judgments of individuals and groups. As indicated earlier, the international law represents the best available attempt to reach a broad consensus regarding those behaviors that are universally harmful.

It is not possible to present a full description of the international law in this chapter. I leave it for others to provide a comprehensive guide for criminologists.[18] A rough sense of the relevant international law, however, can be provided by briefly describing the key documents dealing with international humanitarian and human rights law. Humanitarian law focuses on those rights that apply during armed conflicts, with individuals being held responsible and sanctioned for violations; while human rights law focuses on rights during peacetime (see ICRC, 2003; Blau and Moncada, 2007, 2009). States and, increasingly, groups within and across states are held accountable for human rights violations (although certain human rights may be violated by individuals, just as states may engage in humanitarian violations; see Blau and Moncada, 2007).

The *Rome Statute of the International Criminal Court,* adopted in 1998, is a key treaty focusing on humanitarian law, particularly genocide, crimes against humanity, war crimes, and the crime of aggression (see the United Nations website at http://untreaty.un.org/cod/icc/index.html). The first three crimes are defined in some detail, with the fourth to be defined shortly. As an example, crimes against humanity involve "a widespread or systematic attack directed against any civilian population, with knowledge of the attack, [and involving such acts as] murder, extermination, enslavement, deportation or forcible transfer of population, imprisonment or other severe deprivation of liberty, torture, rape, sexual slavery, enforced prostitution, forced pregnancy, enforced sterilization, and apartheid." Many of these terms, such as "torture," are further defined.

Another major set of documents are the *Universal Declaration of Human Rights* (UDHR) and the two covenants that flowed from this declaration: the *International Covenant on Civil and Political Rights* and the *International Covenant on Economic, Social, and Cultural Rights* (see Office of the United Nations High Commissioner for Human Rights, 2008; the United Nations website at http://www.un.org/en/rights/index.shtml). The UDHR, adopted in 1948 by the member states of the United Nations, is widely regarded as the seminal declaration of human rights (Blau and Moncada, 2009; Normand and Zaidi, 2008). The two covenants, adopted in 1966, elaborate on and extend the rights described in the UDHR, as well as describe (weak) mechanisms for monitoring and enforcing these rights (Blau and Moncada, 2009; Normand and Zaidi, 2008). These documents list both negative rights (freedom from X) and positive rights (the right to X). As illustrations, these rights include:

- Freedom from torture or cruel, inhuman or degrading treatment or punishment
- Right not to be arbitrarily deprived of property
- Right to freedom of thought, conscience and religion
- Right to freedom of peaceful assembly and association
- Right to periodic and genuine elections which shall be by universal and equal suffrage and shall be held by secret vote or by equivalent free voting procedures
- Right to work, free choice of employment, to just and favorable conditions of work, and to protection against unemployment
- Right to equal pay for equal work (applies to everyone, "without any discrimination")
- Right to a standard of living adequate for health and well-being, including food, clothing, housing and medical care and necessary social services, and the right to security in the event of unemployment, sickness, disability, widowhood, old age or other lack of livelihood in circumstances beyond the individual's control
- Right to education

Many of these rights are stated in general terms; however, there has been much effort to specify them. Most notably, the *International Covenant on Economic, Social, and Cultural Rights* establishes certain "minimum core obligations" or "obligations considered to meet the minimum essential levels of each of the rights." Examples include "access to the minimum essential food which is nutritionally adequate and safe, to ensure freedom from hunger for everyone; access to basic shelter, housing and sanitation, and an adequate supply of safe drinking water; and free and compulsory primary education for all." Further, the UN Committee on Economic, Social and Cultural Rights has described the meaning of each economic, social, and cultural right—such as the right to education—in some detail. In addition, numerous examples of rights violations have been identified, including: contaminating water, failure to ensure a minimum wage sufficient for a decent living, failure to prevent starvation in all areas and communities in a country, systematically segregating children with disabilities from mainstream schools, failure to prevent employers from discriminating in recruitment (based on sex, disability, race, political opinion, social origin, HIV status, etc.), and banning the use of minority or indigenous languages (see Office of the UN High Commissioner for Human Rights, 2008). (A more recent set of UN treaties focus on the rights of special groups, including minorities, children, indigenous peoples, and women. Also, there has been a recent focus on the rights to development and to a sustainable environment [Blau and Moncada, 2009; Normand and Zaidi, 2008; Office of the UN High Commissioner for Human Rights, 2008]).

Certain of the above rights, such as the rights to housing and medical care, may strike many U. S. residents as extreme given the strong emphasis on individualism in this country (i.e., the belief that individuals should pursue their own interests, with limited involvement by the state (see Blau and Moncada, 2009)). These rights are viewed differently in other countries, however; with the residents of these countries often being shocked at the extensive poverty in the midst of plenty in the United States. Further, these rights are starting to be viewed differently in the United States, as reflected in recent movements to provide both housing and health care to all in need. Other rights, such as the right to safe drinking water, may be taken for granted by many in the United States. Unfortunately, this is not the case in other parts of the world. The United Nations Children's Fund, for example, estimates that diarrheal dehydration caused by a lack of safe drinking water kills nearly 2 million children each year and "has killed more children in the past ten years than all people lost to armed conflict since the Second World War" (Office of the UN High Commissioner for Human Rights, 2008:4).

In sum, the international human rights law allows for the identification of a range of harmful behaviors. Certain of the harms identified involve the further specification of those behaviors that threaten physical well-being (e.g., torture, the contamination of drinking water), but others move beyond direct physical threats (e.g., discrimination, threats to religious freedom).[19] The international law has several advantages: it reflects a broad consensus among states with a range of interests and values; it encompasses the large share of harms identified by both mainstream and critical criminologists; it is reasonably precise; and it allows criminologists to draw on the work of numerous organizations and scholars who are involved in efforts to better define rights and monitor rights violations. That said, I do not believe that criminologists should accept the international law without question, just as few would argue that criminologists should accept the laws of particular nations without question. The international law is still an imperfect and evolving creation, and criminologists should contribute to its further development. Criminologists have a range of contributions to make in this area. To give a few examples: "Green" or environmental criminologists are raising questions about the definition of *human* rights, particularly the manner in which we balance human rights against the rights of nonhuman animals and the larger biosphere (White, 2008). The work of critical criminologists on the harms resulting from "lawful but awful" acts can certainly inform efforts to better define and identify rights violations. Criminologists of course have much experience with strategies for monitoring harmful acts (e.g., Mosher et al., 2002). And certain criminologists are beginning to examine the policy implications of a focus on human rights, including the factors that affect the response to rights violations and the merits of different types of responses— such as criminal prosecutions, civil proceedings, and truth commissions (Hagan and Levi, 2007). (See Smith, 2006, for a discussion of how criminologists might play a more active role in United Nations discussions of crime).

1b. Blameworthy. There is much agreement across countries and in the international law about assigning blameworthiness. As indicated above, blameworthiness involves voluntary and intentional behavior, with intention broadly defined; in particular, it includes purposeful, knowledgeable, reckless, and negligent behavior (see earlier and Reiman and Leighton, 2010). Also, individuals and groups should be held responsible for the failure to prevent harm when they have a specific duty to intervene (see n14). There is the question of who imposes the duty to intervene, but the international law is again of some use. The international law, in particular, indicates that states and certain individuals within states sometimes have a duty to (a) protect the rights of individuals and groups, and/or (b) to ensure that these rights are satisfied. For example, the Covenant on Social, Political, and Economic Rights states that each nation that is a party to the Covenant must undertake "steps, individually and through international assistance and co-operation, especially economic and technical, to the maximum of its available resources, with a view to achieving progressively the full realization of the rights recognized in the present Covenant by all appropriate means, including particularly the adoption of legislative measures." This is followed by a more specific discussion of the steps that must be taken and how to determine if adequate progress is being made.[20]

Also, blameworthiness involves behavior that is unjustifiable and inexcusable. As indicated earlier, there are certain widely recognized excuses and justifications that negate blameworthiness. I do not mean to imply, however, that that the assignment of blameworthiness is easily accomplished in all cases. For example, there is some debate over the acceptability of certain excuses and justifications for crime (see Fletcher, 2007). Also, applying the criteria for blameworthiness in particular cases is sometimes problematic. That is why we have judges and juries, including the International Criminal Court. And criminologists have a role to play here as well. In this area, there are several excellent case studies that have convincingly applied the criteria of blameworthiness to particular types of behavior, such as unsafe working conditions (e.g., Reiman and Leighton, 2010), and to particular acts, such as the manufacture of an unsafe car (e.g., Cullen et al., 1987). So while certain issues regarding blameworthiness remain to be resolved, there is much agreement about the major criteria for blameworthiness and many acts can be readily classified as blameworthy.

2. *Condemned by the Public.* Drawing on constructionist approaches, criminologists should also examine acts that are condemned by the general public and groups within the public. The degree of condemnation can be measured through surveys. At one extreme, a behavior will be strongly condemned by the large majority of people, regardless of group membership. At the other extreme, a behavior will not be condemned by anyone. Between these extremes, behaviors will be moderately condemned by most people or strongly condemned by some and less strongly condemned by others. It is of course important to distinguish between these two states. Criminologists usually measure the degree of public condemnation by asking people to rank behaviors from "least serious" to "most serious" or to assign behaviors a number indicating their level of "seriousness." There is, however, some uncertainty over what is meant by "seriousness," and researchers should explore alternative ways of measuring condemnation (see the overview in Stylianou, 2003).

Condemnation may better be conceived as having several dimensions, including beliefs, values, emotions, and behavioral intentions. To what extent do individuals *believe* that an act is harmful *and* blameworthy? To what extent do they *evaluate* the act as wrong or immoral? To what extent do they experience a negative *emotional reaction* to the act (e.g., anger, disgust)? And how strongly are they *inclined to sanction* those who commit the act (with sanctions ranging from polite avoidance to death)? In measuring these dimensions, information should be provided about the circumstances surrounding the act, with researchers manipulating the justifications and excuses for crime.

These dimensions should be correlated, such that acts believed to be harmful *and* blameworthy are seen as wrong, provoke negative emotional reactions, and elicit a strong inclination to severely sanction. Researchers, however, should explore the relationship between these dimensions; there may be circumstances where the correlations are weak. Most notably, certain acts—such as sodomy—may be seen as blameworthy harms of a minor nature, but very wrong by some (see Stylianou, 2003). The overall level of condemnation might be measured by combining the ratings on these dimensions, assuming that they are strongly correlated with one another. If these dimensions are not strongly correlated, they should of course be considered separately.

3. *Sanctioned by the State.* Finally, criminologists should examine acts that are subject to state sanction. This characteristic draws on both mainstream criminology and the constructionist approach. Three dimensions should be considered here. First, how serious is the act defined by the law; that is, is the act defined as a major versus minor felony, a misdemeanor, or a "crime-like" civil violation (i.e., a civil violation where the act is described as harmful and there is an effort to punish) (see Sutherland, 1944). Second, how severe are the actual penalties administered for the offense. And third, what is the certainty of punishment. These later dimensions allow us to distinguish the "law in action" from the "law on the books." This is critical when examining the consequences of state definitions. At one extreme, behaviors will be defined as serious offenses and subject to a high certainty and severity of punishment. At the other extreme, behaviors will not be defined as crimes or civil violations and not subject to state sanction. There are several possibilities between these extremes; for example, behaviors may be defined as less serious felonies and have a moderate certainty and severity of punishment; or behaviors may be defined as serious felonies, have a high severity of punishment, and a low certainty of punishment.

Application of the Integrated Definition of Crime

In sum, behaviors can be classified according to their standing on three general characteristics; the extent to which they are (a) blameworthy harms; (b) condemned by the public; and (c) sanctioned by the state. While this scheme draws on Hagan's (1985) crime pyramid and Henry and Lanier's (1998) crime prism, the characteristics are somewhat different. The most significant difference is that this scheme draws on the critical criminology literature and the international law to present essentialist definitions of both harm and blameworthiness. I would argue that any behavior classified as a blameworthy harm, subject to at least modest condemnation by a significant portion of the public, or classified as a crime or "crime-like" civil violation by the state should be viewed as a proper part of the subject matter of criminology.[21] This is an admittedly broad conception of "crime" and includes many behaviors that are not in violation of the criminal law of particular nations. But as argued later, this broad definition has several advantages.

Once acts are roughly ranked on these characteristics, criminologists can classify them into several categories. It is not possible to list all such categories in this chapter, but a simple classification is presented—based on whether acts score high or low on each characteristic. More complex classifications are possible, particularly if one takes account of the varying levels and different dimensions of each characteristic. For example, the categorization simply classifies behaviors according to whether they are generally condemned by the public: it does not consider that middle level where some people condemn the behavior and others do not, nor does it separately consider dimensions such as the perceived harm and wrongfulness of the behavior. It should be noted that this categorization is not intended as the ultimate scheme for classifying crimes; it is simply meant to illustrate the range of acts that criminologists should examine and provide one possible scheme for classifying crimes when studying such things as their correlates, consequences, causes, and control (other schemes may prove to be more productive).

- *Core Crimes.* These behaviors are blameworthy harms, are strongly condemned, and are severely sanctioned by the state. They include murder, robbery, rape, burglary, theft, and vandalism. Mainstream criminology is largely devoted to the study of such behaviors.
- *Unrecognized Blameworthy Harms.* These are blameworthy harms that are not strongly condemned and sanctioned. Such harms may not be condemned and sanctioned because (a) the harm they cause is [inappropriately] justified, excused, or minimized (e.g., the victims of discrimination are said to "deserve" it because of their negative traits or behavior); (b) the harm is hidden (e.g., the negative health consequences that result from pollution, the higher prices that result from corruption); and/or (c) the blameworthiness is hidden, as is often the case with corporate negligence. Much state and corporate harm falls into this category, since the power of state and corporate actors makes it easier for them to justify and excuse harm, hide harm, hide blameworthiness, and prevent state sanction. In such cases, criminologists can play an important role in making the harm and/or blameworthiness apparent through their research and advocacy (a central recommendation of critical criminologists).

- *Public-Only Recognized Harms.* These are blameworthy harms that are condemned but not subject to meaningful state sanction. There are two subcategories here. In one case, the harms are legal. In the other, they are technically defined as crimes by the state, perhaps in an effort to satisfy public demand, but the certainty and/or severity of state sanction are quite low. (As indicated earlier, the "law in action" is sometimes quite different than the "law on the books"). Examples of such harms include the manufacture and sale of cigarettes, and state/corporate corruption in certain countries (see Green and Ward, 2004; Passas and Goodwin, 2004b). Even though such behavior is harmful and condemned, powerful interests prevent the imposition of meaningful state sanctions. Many behaviors in this category are in a transitional stage, however. The harm they cause has become increasingly apparent, to the point where they now elicit widespread condemnation, and efforts are being made to impose meaningful state sanctions.
- *State-Only Recognized Harms.* These are blameworthy harms that are sanctioned by the state but not widely condemned by the public. We would not expect such harms to be common. Public condemnation is a major force in eliciting state sanction and, conversely, state sanction often fosters public condemnation. Behaviors in this category may involve blameworthy harms with low visibility; perhaps the harm caused is indirect and not well publicized (e.g., certain corporate offenses). Nevertheless, such harms attract the attention of the state. The harms may involve conflicts between the state and corporate actors or between corporate actors, with the state acting as mediator. Less commonly, "progressive" states might criminalize harms that have widespread cultural support (e.g., female genital mutilation, see Blau and Moncada, 2009). This may be done as a result of pressure from other states or international organizations.
- *Constructed Crimes.* These are behaviors that cause little blameworthy harm but are condemned by the public and sanctioned by the state. While behaviors are frequently condemned and sanctioned because they cause "real" harm, certain behaviors may be mistakenly thought to cause harm or simply viewed as "wrong" or immoral. Powerful groups may foster the mistaken impression that certain acts are harmful as they seek to promote their interests. Also, certain "objectively" harmless acts may threaten core values (thus the condemnation and sanction of homosexuality in many societies). In some cases, the condemned and sanctioned behaviors may actually involve the assertion of human rights, as when peaceful efforts to resist discriminatory treatment are condemned and sanctioned. This category encompasses many *mala prohibita* crimes (see page 18).

- *Constructed Deviance.* These behaviors cause little blameworthy harm and are not subject to state sanction but are widely condemned by the public. Such behaviors frequently violate core values, but the violation may not be considered severe enough to justify state sanction or the state may decriminalize the behavior in response to pressure from powerful groups. An example is sodomy in the contemporary United States.
- *Repressive State Crimes.* These behaviors cause little blameworthy harm and are not widely condemned but are subject to state sanction. Such behaviors are common in states that seek to maintain power through repressive measures, such as the prohibition of free elections. This category illustrates a central point regarding the definition of harm; the focus is on the violation of *human rights* rather than on threats to the state (although there is some overlap between the two).

Advantages of the Integrated Definition of Crime

The integrated definition has several major advantages over other definitions, particularly the legal definition that now dominates mainstream criminology.

1. It Identifies Core Characteristics of Crime That Are Universally Applicable. The legal definition of crime fails to identify the core characteristics of those behaviors defined as crimes; rather, it simply lists a wide variety of illegal acts, with these acts varying somewhat across societies and over time. The integrated definition draws on several literatures to argue that "crimes" are distinguished by the fact that they involve blameworthy harms, are condemned, and/or are subject to state sanction. These characteristics, as defined, are universally applicable. Blameworthy harms are the same in all societies and at all times. The specific behaviors that are sanctioned and condemned do differ somewhat across societies and over time; but the focus is not on these specific behaviors but rather on those behaviors that are condemned and sanctioned, whatever those behaviors may be. For example, when constructing a theory of crime, the focus would be on explaining why individuals commit acts that are condemned by others and carry a significant risk of sanction, *not* on explaining why they engage in the specific behaviors that are condemned and sanctioned.

The identification of core characteristics is critical since it provides direction to criminologists seeking to explain and control crime, giving them a better idea of what they are trying to explain and control. To illustrate, the characteristics of *harm* and *blameworthiness* suggest certain explanations for crime. Individuals may commit blameworthy harms because they deny or are ignorant of the harm caused (this is especially likely for "unrecognized blameworthy harms"), do not care about the harm caused (e.g., psychopaths), justify the harm (e.g., "the victim deserved it"), excuse their behavior-denying blameworthiness (e.g., "I was forced to do it"); or are pressured or enticed into committing such acts (e.g., a corporation engages in consumer fraud to solve a pressing financial problem). Similar arguments can be made for the characteristics of *public condemnation* and *state sanction*.

It should be noted that certain explanations may apply to acts that possess *any* of the core characteristics of crime. For example, individuals who are low in self-control may be unaware of or unconcerned about the harm they cause, the condemnation of others, *and* the risk of sanction. Individuals who belong to criminal peer groups may learn justifications and excuses for the harm they cause, may be insulated from the condemnation of others, and may discount the certainty and severity of punishment. Other explanations may be more relevant to certain types of crime. For example, the possession of power may be associated with the commission of many "unrecognized blameworthy harms" and "repressive state crimes," but may be less relevant to the explanation of "core crimes" (see Box, 1983; Reiman and Leighton, 2010; Sutherland, 1940).

The identification of core characteristics can also guide efforts to control crime. Again, consider the characteristics of harm and blameworthiness. Among other things, we might reduce crime by making individuals more aware of the harm caused by certain acts, increasing their empathy for the victims of harm, challenging the justifications they employ for inflicting harm, increasing their sense of responsibility, and reducing their pressure or incentive to engage in harmful behavior. The major efforts to control crime in the United States fail to employ these strategies, although certain other crime-control efforts make use of several of them. This is the case with the restorative justice approach, which explicitly focuses on the harm caused by crime (Braithwaite, 2002). A central component of this approach is a conference in which the offender meets with the crime victim(s). There is much discussion of the harm caused by the crime, and the excuses and justifications offered by the offender are often challenged. As a consequence, offenders frequently develop a greater awareness of the harm caused by their behavior, more empathy for their victims, and a greater sense of responsibility for their behavior.

2. It Provides a Reasonable Level of Precision. The issue of precision has been the Achilles heel of most efforts to develop alternatives to the legal definition, particularly efforts to define crime in terms of blameworthy harm. The integrated definition focuses on a core group of harms involving death, physical injury, and the theft and destruction of property. In addition, it draws on the international human rights law to provide a reasonably precise definition of blameworthiness and additional harms. As a result, it allows for the identification of a range of blameworthy harms, many of which are not defined as crimes by particular nations. Further, defining blameworthy harm in this manner links criminology to the rapidly expanding field of human rights law, which is producing additional refinements in the definitions of harm (rights violations) and blameworthiness.

3. It Captures Key Insights from Different Perspectives. The integrated definition draws on mainstream, essentialist, and constructionist approaches to defining crime, since each has something critical to offer to the study of crime. The mainstream approach directs attention to the advantages of the legal definition and to a range of acts that cause great harm, are common, and elicit much concern. The essentialist approach helps ensure that criminologists do not overlook blameworthy harms that—for political or other reasons—are not condemned or sanctioned. The constructionist approach directs attention to how the state and public view and react to behavior, the factors affecting such views and reactions, and the consequences of such views and reactions. As indicated, these consequences have major implications for the causes and control of crime.

4. It Is Parsimonious. At the same time, the integrated definition is parsimonious, focusing on just three core characteristics of crime (although each characteristic has two or more dimensions). These characteristics—when considered together—allow researchers to capture most of the key insights of the pyramid of crime, prism of crime, and other approaches. Consider, for example, the idea that crimes differ in terms of the visibility of the harm they cause, a key part of the prism of crime. This idea is reflected in the fact that some blameworthy harms are condemned by the public (e.g., "core crimes"), while others are not (e.g., "unrecognized blameworthy harms").

5. It Suggests a Range of New Research Questions for Criminology, Many with Major Policy Implications. Most notably, the integrated definition encourages open discussion and research on each of the core characteristics of crime. Criminologists, in particular, are encouraged to refine the descriptions of each characteristic and apply these characteristics to general types and specific instances of behavior.[22] As a result, criminologists will actively participate in the definition of their subject matter, rather than passively accepting the legal definition.

The integrated definition also encourages criminologists to investigate the relationship between the different characteristics of crime. Most notably, to what extent are blameworthy harms condemned and sanctioned by the public and the state? And, related to this, how can we explain the fact that certain blameworthy harms are not condemned and sanctioned? Work in this area is of enormous policy relevance, providing criminologists with a major mission, that of making the public and state aware of unrecognized blameworthy harms (see Schwendinger and Schwendinger, 2001). Further, defining blameworthy harms in terms of the international human rights law raises the issue of how to best respond to such violations. Certain mechanisms of response are already in place, such as the International Criminal Court, but there is much discussion about the merits of a range of responses-from criminal sanctions to truth and reconciliation commissions (see Hagan and Levi, 2007).

Finally, the major categories of crime identified by the integrated definition can stimulate much research. Certain of these categories include behaviors that have not received much attention from criminologists. In fact, only one of the seven categories has received significant attention, that involving "core crimes." The integrated approach therefore directs attention to a range of crimes hitherto neglected by criminologists. These include state and corporate crimes; and they include acts of omission as well as commission, *particularly* the failure of states to protect and work toward the achievement of human rights. This focus in not without some controversy. For example, the failure of states to make sufficient efforts to eradicate hunger and sexism are defined as crimes. Many will likely argue that this reflects a leftist political agenda. But, as critical criminologists point out, there is no such thing as a value-free criminology; criminologists explicitly or implicitly make certain value judgments when defining crime. The integrated definition has the advantage of drawing on the most widely accepted definitions of harm and blameworthiness, those embodied in the international human rights law, and of encouraging open discussion and debate in this area.

In sum, the integrated definition of crime helps provide a foundation for a unified criminology, one that considers a broader range of crime than current approaches, provides more guidance to criminologists seeking to explain and control such crimes, opens new avenues of research, and is of increased policy relevance.

3

Determinism versus Agency

Is Crime the Result of Forces beyond the
Individual's Control or Free Choice?

The law sees people essentially as rational actors, capable of form-
ing intentions, weighing the consequences of their actions and
controlling their behavior. . . . The law is clear: Those who break
the rules we have collectively agreed upon make a choice, and
those poor choices should be punished. . . . [On the other hand] a
core tenet of the new neuroscience is that there is no single place
in the brain where free will is exercised and a kernel of "self"
resides. Instead, the science suggests, the mental states we experience are like a mirage, arising from highly complex interactions
of myriad brain systems involving electrical signals that are gov-
erned by the laws of physics. It is a highly mechanistic model that
many believe ultimately denies that free will is truly free. . . . If all
our mental states can ultimately be reduced to neuro-psycholog-
ical brain states, and there is really no such thing as free will, how
can people be held accountable for criminal behavior?
                              —Haederle, "Trouble in Mind," 72

Once criminologists have described the nature of crime, they are
in a better position to examine its causes and make recommendations for
its control. In particular, what causes individuals and groups to intentionally harm others without legitimate justification or excuse, to risk public condemnation, and/or to risk state sanction? Related to this, what actions can be
taken to reduce such behavior? The answers given to these questions depend
on the assumptions that criminologists make about the nature of individuals and society. This chapter focuses on the assumptions that criminologists
make regarding the ultimate origin of crime: do individuals freely choose to
engage in crime or is crime the result of forces beyond their control?

Most mainstream criminologists explicitly or implicitly assume that crime is determined by forces beyond the individual's control, including forces of a biological, psychological, and social nature. And, related to this, they assume that the best way to control crime is to alter these forces through the use of rehabilitation and prevention programs. This view is sometimes referred to as "determinism," and it is part of the "positivistic" approach which dominates mainstream criminology. Some mainstream and critical criminologists, however, question the assumption of determinism. They argue that individuals exercise some independent control or *agency* over their behavior.[1] And according to certain of these criminologists, some individuals *choose* to engage in crime because they believe it will minimize their pain and maximize their pleasure. Therefore, the best way to control crime is to increase its costs and reduce its benefits (e.g., increase the likelihood and severity of punishment).

The exercise of agency has two components (Agnew, 1995a; Kane, 2002). First, individuals are able to intentionally make choices that are not fully determined by forces beyond their control. This means that, given the same set of conditions, they could have made a different choice. Second, individuals are able to act on their choices. That is, they are not prevented from doing what they choose to do by forces beyond their control. Some researchers use the term "free will" rather than agency, but I prefer the term "agency" since behavior is never fully free. As argued below, while our actions may not be fully determined by forces beyond our control, they are strongly *influenced* by such forces.

The first section of this chapter describes the assumption of determinism and its implications for research on the causes and control of crime. The second section describes the assumption of agency and its implications. The third section presents an integrated assumption, which states that behavior ranges from fully determined to agentic. Further, some individuals are more likely than others to possess resources and be in environments that are conducive to agency. The final section discusses the implications of this integrated assumption for efforts to explain, predict, and control crime. In brief, behavior is more unpredictable and crime is somewhat more likely when conditions favor agency, but it is possible to guide the exercise of agency in a positive direction.

The Assumption That Behavior Is Fully Determined

Most mainstream criminologists have embraced the "positivistic" approach since the late 1800s.[2] Positivism explicitly rejects the idea of free will or agency, and instead assumes that crime is caused by forces beyond the individual's control. The rejection of free will is well expressed in the following quote by Enrico Ferri, one of the founders of positivistic criminology (quoted in Goldkamp, 1987:128):

> The admission of free will is out of the question. . . . Free will would imply that the human will, confronted by the choice of making voluntarily a certain determination, has the last decisive word under the pressure of circumstances contending for and against this decision; that it is free to decide for or against a certain course independently of internal and external circumstances, which play upon it, according to the laws of cause and effect.

Having rejected free will, positivists focus on the identification of those forces that cause crime. And they make use of the scientific method in doing so. That is, positivists systematically test their ideas about the causes of crime against observations of the "real world."

The positivistic school developed in reaction to the classical school of criminology, which dominated the discipline during much of the 1800s. According to the most accounts, classical criminologists assume that individuals freely choose to engage in crime in an effort to maximize their pleasure and minimize their pain.[3] Individuals, in particular, are assumed to be self-interested and rational. They therefore evaluate their behavioral options, with the goal of choosing that option which maximizes their net pleasure. A close reading of classical criminologists indicates that they do not believe that individuals are *fully* free. Classical criminologists recognize that individuals are influenced by certain factors when deciding whether to engage in crime, with much emphasis being placed on the threat of punishment (Beirne, 1993; Gottfredson and Hirschi, 1987; Vold et al., 2002). Nevertheless, the ultimate decision to engage in crime is seen as influenced but *not* fully determined by forces beyond the individual's control. Humans, unlike other animals, are assumed to be capable of rational deliberation; as such, they are not simply slaves to their environment and inner urges.

The work of Darwin and others put an end to the classical school. Darwin argued that humans are not qualitatively different from other animals. And, like other animals, the behavior of humans is determined by forces beyond their control. Initially, such forces were said to be biological in nature, with psychological and social forces receiving increased emphasis as the twentieth century progressed. The large share of work in contemporary criminology, especially mainstream criminology, now reflects the positivistic approach. Criminologists list what they believe are the leading causes of crime. They then examine the extent to which these causes explain crime. Most commonly, they try to explain why some individuals have higher rates of offending than others. Criminologists are moderately good at explaining differences in offending, although they are still unable to explain *most* of the variation in offending (Weisburd and Piquero, 2008). The unexplained variation in crime, however, is usually not attributed to the exercise of agency. Rather, it is attributed to such things as the failure to examine certain causes, the poor measurement of causes and of crime, and limitations in the way data are collected and analyzed.

Implications of Determinism for Crime Control

The assumption of determinism has major implications for the control of crime. It raises questions about the morality and effectiveness of punishment. If crime is due to forces beyond the individual's control, we cannot hold offenders "responsible" for crime, and punishing them is therefore unjust (although see Kane, 2002; Pinker, 2002:174–94). Rather than focusing on punishment, efforts to control crime should instead focus on addressing its many causes. In particular, programs should be developed both to prevent individuals from becoming criminals and to rehabilitate existing offenders (Agnew, 2009; Lipsey and Cullen, 2007). As an example, Farrington and Welsh (2007) have written an excellent text on preventing delinquency. They first review the best research on the causes of delinquency, with the aim of identifying its key causes. These causes include individual factors (e.g., low intelligence, impulsiveness); family factors (e.g., antisocial parents, poor parental supervision); socioeconomic deprivation; peer influences (e.g., associating with delinquent peers); and residence in deprived, disorganized communities. They then review the best research on efforts to prevent delinquency, with the aim of identifying those programs that are most effective at addressing these causes. Such programs include high-quality preschool enrichment programs, such as Head Start; child-training programs that teach such things as social skills and self-control; parental-education programs, that teach a range of parenting skills and provide support to parents; and certain community-based programs, such as high-quality mentoring programs.

In sum, the dominant perspective in criminology states that crime is fully determined by forces beyond the individual's control. A number of such forces have been identified, although most of the variation in crime remains unexplained. Further, the best way to reduce crime is through prevention and rehabilitation programs that alter these forces.

The Assumption That Individuals Exercise Agency

The assumption of determinism has been criticized by some mainstream and, especially, critical criminologists. Matza (1969:92–93) was one of the first critical criminologists to argue that individuals exercise agency:

> Capable of creating and assigning meaning, able to contemplate his surroundings and even his own condition, given to anticipation, planning and projecting, man-the-subject stands in a different and more complex relation to circumstance . . . . A subject actively addresses or encounters his circumstance, his distinctive capacity is to reshape, strive toward creating, and actively *transcend* experience.

Taylor et al. (1973:50–51) quote Matza with approval in their classic text, *A New Criminology*, and state that:

> Man is both the product and producer of society. At times he accepts, at times he reinterprets, at times he transcends and resists existing values . . . reason is not merely a set of deterministic reflexes-rather it is a consciousness of the world, an ability of the individual to give meaning to his universe, both to interpret and to creatively change the existing moral order.

Many feminist criminologists have also come to emphasize agency. Much of the early work on female offenders portrayed them as passive victims of their environment, engaging in acts such as prostitution and theft because they had no choice. More recent work, however, frequently claims that "women offenders are active, innovative, rational *agents* making choices in relation to their criminality" (Ajzenstadt, 2009:202).

Critical criminologists are not the only advocates of agency. Some mainstream criminologists have also come to suggest that individuals are capable of exercising agency.[4] Not surprisingly, agency plays an important role in rational choice theory, the contemporary reincarnation of classical theory (Clarke and Cornish, 1985; Goldkamp, 1987; Nagin, 2007). Rational choice theory does not deny that a range of factors influence crime, including both the general decision to become involved in crime and the decision to commit particular crimes. In fact, rational choice theory draws heavily on positivistic criminology when listing those factors that predispose individuals to crime. But rational choice theorists do not state that such factors fully determine crime. Rather, individuals more or less rationally take these factors into account when *deciding* whether crime is in their interest. Goldkamp (1987:131) nicely describes the position of rational choice theory in this area when he states that "predisposition is not predestination."

More recently, issues of agency have come to play a central role in life-course criminology. Here, however, the focus is not on how agency may lead to crime, but rather on how agency may contribute to desistence from crime.[5] A central theme in this literature is that offenders are able to desist from crime because they develop new, pro-social identities (e.g., parent, provider) and come to view crime and the criminal lifestyle in a negative light. These changes are said to be influenced by changes in their environment, including terms in jail or prison and the development of pro-social ties (e.g., marriage, a job). But many individuals experiencing these environmental changes do not desist from crime. Whether individuals desist is also said to depend on "agentic" factors, such as an openness to change and the belief that one has the ability to change (see especially Giordano et al., 2002; Maruna, 2001). LeBel et al. (2008) found some support for this position in a longitudinal study of 130 male, property offenders. Those offenders with a belief in their ability to "go straight" were more likely to desist from crime, even after environmental factors were taken into account.

The assumption of agency has had some effect on crime research. Most notably, researchers have devoted increased attention to the decision-making process of offenders (e.g., Ajzenstadt, 2009; Clarke and Cornish, 1985; Giordano et al., 2002; Wikstrom, 2005). For example, they have examined the factors that offenders take into account when deciding whether to offend or desist from crime. Also, a few researchers have begun to look at certain of the factors that influence the exercise of agency, such as self-efficacy or the belief that one has the ability to change. Even so, the large share of research in criminology remains deterministic in nature, examining the impact of various factors on crime, explicitly or implicitly assuming that crime is fully determined by these factors.

Implications of Agency for Crime Control.

The assumption of agency has been used to justify both progressive and repressive crime-control strategies. Critical criminologists point out that agentic individuals have the ability to rise *above* their circumstances. They can seek a better life for themselves and, in some cases, may seek to change the larger community in positive ways. Certain life-course criminologists make a similar point: agentic individuals are sometimes able to desist from crime, despite the pressures to keep offending. And there has been some discussion of how agentic individuals might be assisted in this process. For example, Giordano et al. (2002) argue that this might be accomplished through the provision of "positive hooks for change," with such hooks including participation in treatment programs and the formation of close ties to pro-social others. Based on their research, they conclude that the most effective hooks appear to be those that encourage offenders to think about their future in positive terms; to develop a positive identity that is incompatible with crime (e.g., parent, employee); to view crime in a negative light; to create a clear plan for desisting from crime; and to connect with new, pro-social environments that support positive change (also see Laub and Sampson, 2001; LeBel et al., 2008; Maruna, 2001).

More commonly, however, the proponents of agency argue that the best way to control crime is to increase its costs and reduce its benefits. Potential offenders, being rational and possessing agency, should respond by reducing their level of crime. Perhaps the best example of this approach is situational crime prevention, which is rooted in rational choice theory (e.g., Clarke, 1995; Clarke and Eck, 2005; Felson, 2002). Practitioners of situational crime prevention look for ways to increase the costs of crime. For example, the likelihood that crimes will be detected by community residents might be increased by improving street lighting. Or the guilt that potential offenders feel might be increased by emphasizing the harm caused by acts such as shoplifting and employee theft. Also, practitioners look for ways to reduce the benefits of crime. For example, the amount of cash that store clerks have on hand might be reduced (thereby reducing the benefits of robbery). Such practices have shown some success in reducing crime.

The major crime-control initiative to emerge out of the agentic perspective, however, involves increasing the certainty and severity of punishment by the criminal justice system. That is, punishing more offenders and punishing them more severely. It is said that this will deter both potential and active criminals from committing crime. This initiative has been advocated by certain criminologists (e.g., Bennett et al., 1996; Wilson, 1975), but has been pushed most strongly by the general public and politicians. Most people in the United States agree with the assumption of agency. One of the best studies in this area found that close to 80 percent of the public believe that "crime is the product of a person's free will" (Sims, 2003).[6] And, not surprisingly, those who believe that individuals exercise some choice over whether to engage in crime are more likely to favor punitive crime-control policies (Sims, 2003). Likewise, many politicians claim that criminals freely choose to engage in crime in an effort to benefit themselves. Further, certain of these politicians also state that social factors—particularly factors such as poverty and racism—do *not* cause crime (see Cullen and Agnew, 2011). These views are reflected in the following quote from President Ronald Reagan:

> Choosing a career in crime is not the result of poverty or an unhappy childhood or of a misunderstood adolescence; it is the result of a conscious, willful choice made by some who consider themselves above the law, who seek to exploit the hard work and, sometimes, the very lives of their fellow citizens. . . . The crime epidemic threat is [not] some inevitable sociological phenomenon. . . . It is, instead, a cumulative result of too much emphasis on the protection of the rights of the accused and too little concern for our government's responsibility to protect the lives, homes, and rights of our law-abiding citizens. . . . [T]he criminal element now calculates that crime really does pay. (Quoted in Beckett and Sasson, 2000:61–62)

This assumption of agency allowed politicians to argue that an increased emphasis on punishment would be both just and effective. If offenders choose to engage in crime in an effort to benefit themselves, increased punishments should cause them to reconsider that choice. Also, this assumption raised questions about the utility of rehabilitation and prevention programs, particularly given the assertion that crime was *not* the result of such things as poverty or "an unhappy childhood." And, for the past several decades, the agentic view of crime has prevailed in policy circles. Since the early 1970s, the major strategy for controlling crime in the United States has been to increase the certainty and severity of punishment. To illustrate, the rate of imprisonment in the United States increased fivefold from 1970 to 2009 to the point that one out of every one hundred adults is now behind bars. At the same time, the emphasis on rehabilitation and prevention declined significantly (see Useem and Piehl, 2008).

Further, most criminal justice systems are based on the assumption of agency. With certain exceptions, such as the insane, criminal justice systems treat criminals as individuals who freely chose to engage in crime. As such, punishment is seen as a just response to crime. It is also felt that punishment will reduce crime if it is sufficiently certain and severe. In particular, deterrence is one of the primary rationales for the infliction of punishment. If individuals choose to engage in crime to maximize their pleasure, it makes much sense to believe that sufficiently certain and severe punishments will deter them.

Related to this, the legal definition of crime, as well as the definition presented in chapter 2, assumes that individuals exercise some agency. As indicated, behaviors are defined as crimes in part because they are *blameworthy* or seen as blameworthy. Blameworthy behaviors are voluntary, intentional, and committed without legitimate justification or excuse. Blameworthy behaviors, then, are by definition not fully determined by forces beyond the individual's control. Such behaviors reflect some agency on the part of individuals; that is, the individuals *could have acted otherwise*. We therefore feel it is appropriate to at least partly *blame them* for their acts.

An Integrated Theory of Bounded Agency

This section presents an integrated theory of "bounded agency." This theory draws on the deterministic and agentic perspectives just described; my own prior work on agency (Agnew, 1989, 1990, 1995); and recent work in philosophy, biology (neuroscience), psychology, anthropology, and sociology.[7] I discuss the nature of agency, with a core argument being that behaviors range from fully determined to agentic. I then describe those individual and environmental factors that influence the extent to which individuals exercise agency. I conclude by discussing the implications of the integrated theory for the prediction, explanation, and control of crime. Before presenting the theory, however, I briefly address a critical question that cannot be given a definitive answer.

Does Agency Exist?

A lead article in the Science Section of the *New York Times* was titled "Free Will: Now You Have It, Now You Don't" (Overbye, 2007). This article described the very active debate over whether free will exists, with the debate fueled in part by a series of experiments carried out by Benjamin Libet and associates (1999). In these experiments, subjects are asked to perform a voluntary act, such as flicking their wrist, within a certain time period. The experimenters measure (a) when the act occurs, (b) when the subject becomes conscious of the intention to act, and (c) when the brain prepares to act, as indicated by an electrical charge in the brain indicating "readiness potential." These experiments indicate that subjects become aware of the intention to act *after* the charge indicating readiness potential occurs. As Libet (1999:51) states, "the initiation of the freely voluntary act appears to begin in the brain unconsciously, well before the person consciously knows he wants to act!" Free choice is therefore said to be an illusion when it comes to the initiation of voluntary acts.[8] Further, experiments such as this are just one part of a growing body of evidence suggesting that our thoughts and behavior are frequently determined by factors beyond our conscious awareness, including both internal dispositions and external stimuli (see Dijksterhuis, 2010 for an overview; also see the discussion of rationality in chap. 4).

A number of researchers, however, have questioned this attack on free will (e.g., Bertelsen, 2005; Prinz, 2003). They question the experiments of Libet, claiming that it is not possible to precisely measure when a subject decides to act and wondering whether these findings would apply to more complex acts. Libet (1999) himself has stated that while his work suggests that people do not freely decide to initiate acts, some evidence suggests that they can exercise "conscious volitional veto power" (also see Goschke, 2003). That is, people can elect to inhibit an act that has already been initiated. This point is especially relevant to crime, suggesting that while people may not be able to freely control the impulse to engage in crime, they can control whether they act on this impulse. More generally, these researchers point to data which allegedly demonstrates the existence of agency in a range of areas, including the initiation of acts.

Many psychologists and sociologists have pointed to the ability of people to develop novel solutions to the problems they face, to evaluate the likely consequences of these solutions, and to implement these solutions-modifying their actions based on the feedback they receive. These abilities, in fact, are said to be essential if people are to function effectively in a complex social world. Further, these abilities are the source of major innovations in human society.[9] As Bandura (2001:3–5) states: "To make their way successfully through a complex world full of challenges and hazards, people have to make good judgments about their capabilities, anticipate the probable effects of different events and courses of action, size up socio-structural opportunities and constraints, and regulate their behavior accordingly." Bandura emphasizes the role that agency plays in these processes:

> Forethoughtful, generative, and reflective capabilities are, therefore, vital for survival and human progress. . . . People can designedly conceive unique events and different novel courses of action and choose to executive them. Under the indefinite prompt to concoct something new, for example, one can deliberately construct a whimsically novel scenario of a graceful hippopotamus attired in a chartreuse tuxedo hang gliding over lunar craters, while singing the mad scene from the opera *Lucia di Lammermoor.*

In sum, there is a very active debate over whether agency exists. It is not possible to adequately describe the debate in this short chapter (although see the references cited in nn7–9). And some think that it may never be possible to resolve this debate (see Libet, 1999). As Matza (1964:21) has argued, determinism and agency are faiths and "a faith is not capable of empirical test." Nevertheless, I *assume* that agency exists. I make this assumption because I believe that it is a useful one, allowing criminologists to better predict, explain, and control crime. Further, while the belief in agency may be a faith, a faith "may be tentatively assessed according to its consequences" (Matza, 1964:21). I shortly describe the consequences of agency for the prediction, explanation, and control of crime. These consequences can be empirically examined, providing a tentative assessment of my faith.

The Nature of Agency

There have been numerous discussions about the nature of agency, with the following points often emerging:[10]

- Agency involves conscious deliberation, an internal conversation with oneself.
- The exercise of agency typically involves the following: Individuals evaluate their circumstances, usually in response to a problem or novel situation. This evaluation involves the exercise of agency, as individuals make choices about such things as what information is relevant and how to evaluate it. Individuals then consider their options for dealing with the problem or novel situation. In particular, they consider the goals they want to achieve and the possible means for achieving them. Again, agency is exercised. Individuals imagine the outcomes associated with various goals and means. This process of imaging alternative futures is critical, allowing individuals to transcend the immediate situation. The goals and/or means selected may sometimes be quite novel, from the perspective of the individual and occasionally the larger social group. More commonly, however, individuals adapt familiar goals and means to better fit their situation. Individuals then implement their plan, often resisting the constraints they encounter and reshaping themselves and their environment in the process. This plan may involve physical action on the individual's part (e.g., engaging in crime). The plan, however, may also involve changing internal aspects of the self, such as identities, values, and beliefs. Individuals monitor their progress and, when necessary, modify their goals and means.

- Behaviors can be arranged on a continuum according to the degree of agency they reflect. At one end of the continuum are innate reflexes, which are triggered in a fixed manner by stimuli (e.g., removing one's hand from a hot stove). No agency is involved here. Close by on the continuum are relatively specific learned habits or schemas (scripts) for action. While the habit/schema in question is learned, it is frequently performed with little or no conscious deliberation (e.g., driving, brushing teeth). In certain cases, the stimuli eliciting the behavior may not even be consciously perceived (Bargh and Chartrand, 1999; Bargh and Ferguson, 2000; Prinz, 2003). Farther along the continuum are more general learned habits or schema for action, again elicited by stimuli. Examples include studying for exams and engaging in conversation when friends are encountered. While individuals have a general sense of what to do in such situations, the specific actions they take depend on the particulars of the situation (e.g., the nature of the exam). As a result, individuals may need to engage in some conscious deliberation (e.g., what materials should I review, what is an appropriate topic of conversation). And there may be some exercise of agency, with individuals making choices and engaging in behaviors not fully determined by forces beyond their control. The degree of agency exercised in such situations, however, is typically small. That is, the amount of conscious deliberation is brief and the focus is on a narrow range of choices (e.g., which of a small number of topics do I discuss with my friends).[11] Toward the other end of the continuum are behaviors that reflect a significant degree of agency.
- The exercise of significant agency is usually initiated in response to novel or problematic circumstances, that is, circumstances that do not produce the outcome the individual expects or desires. These circumstances may be confined to particular situations, such as a specific interaction with another person. And they may involve larger issues that transcend particular situations, such as coping with unemployment, marital problems, or ongoing peer harassment. Individuals are under some pressure to engage in agentic behavior, since established modes of thought and action are not suited to the circumstances at hand.
- While agency involves some freedom of choice and action, choices and actions are *not* fully free, random, or entirely unpredictable (although they are *somewhat* unpredictable, as described later). The exercise of agency is guided by certain principles and factors. It is partly rational in nature—with the aim of selecting the most appropriate adaptation to novel circumstances or solution to one's problem. It is not fully rational, however, since the deliberative process is sometimes hurried and imperfect (see Clarke and Cornish, 1985, chap. 4). Also, the exercise of agency is influenced by the indi-

vidual's dispositions, with these being a function of such things as innate and learned habits, emotional states, psychological traits (e.g., low constraint, negative emotionality), identities (e.g., criminal, parent), values, and moral beliefs. Further, the exercise of agency is influenced by the individual's resources, such as intelligence, knowledge, creativity, self-efficacy, power, and social supports. Likewise, it is influenced by numerous features of the environment, including social norms, reinforcement contingencies, and the opportunities for various types of action. Given these influences, it is easy to understand why some scholars recommend the use of the term "*bounded agency*."[12] I use this term to describe my integrated theory, since it emphasizes the link between the deterministic and agentic perspectives.

- While the exercise of agency is influenced by a range of factors, agentic individuals may at the same time alter certain of these factors. For example, the identities that individuals hold will likely influence the goals and means they consider when attempting to adapt to problematic circumstances. But, in the process of adapting to these circumstances, individuals may alter their identities. Individuals with criminal identities, for example, may be struggling with the negative consequences of crime–such as rejection by conventional others and imprisonment. One outcome of this struggle may be a change in identity, with such individuals rejecting their criminal identities and adopting new, pro-social identities such as parent or "born again" Christian (see Giordano et al., 2002). To give another example, the opportunities available to agentic individuals will likely influence the choices they make (e.g., individuals who lack access to drugs will be less likely to consider selling drugs when in need of money). Individuals who exercise agency, however, may create new opportunities for themselves (e.g., seek out others who can provide drugs) (see Agnew, 1990; LeBel et al., 2008). So many of the factors that influence the exercise of agency are *not* beyond the control of agentic individuals. This makes it difficult to predict the behavior of agentic individuals, since the factors that we employ to make our predictions may well change during the exercise of agency.
- The mental activities involved in the exercise of agency may occur in several regions of the brain (see Goschke, 2003). However, the individual or "self" who exercises agency is an *emergent* phenomena with a unique set of properties. These properties include the ability to engage in internal conversation, imagine alternative futures, and speculate about the likely consequences of various actions. That is, the self is more than the simple sum of the physical entities in brain and the relations between them. Bandura (2001:4) uses water as an analogy, pointing to its unique emergent properties, such

as fluidity, viscosity, and transparency. These properties are not simply the aggregate properties of its micro-components of oxygen and hydrogen (also see Elder-Vass, 2007). Further, the self is said to be capable of exercising *downward control*, that is, the self can exercise influence over the physical entities in the brain and the relations between them (Bandura, 2001, 2006; Bertelsen, 2005). The process of setting goals, for example, changes the connections between certain neurons in the brain. This is not to deny, however, the existence of *upward control*—with the structure and functioning of the brain influencing the exercise of agency in important ways.

This description of the nature of agency can undoubtedly be refined and extended, but it gives a rough sense of what is involved in the exercise of agency, as well as the many ways in which individuals may partly transcend the constraints they face when making choices and acting on them.

Certain Individuals Exercise Greater Agency Than Others

Despite the above description, it is again important to emphasize that the existence of agency is an assumption and that agency cannot be directly measured.[13] But all is not lost. While we cannot directly measure the exercise of agency, I believe that we can make a convincing case that individuals with certain characteristics and in certain types of environments exercise greater agency than others. That is, they exhibit more freedom of choice and action. And by taking account of those individual and environmental characteristics that affect agency, I believe that we can improve our ability to predict, explain, and control crime—an idea that we can empirically test. I next list those factors that increase the likelihood of agentic behavior.

Agency Is More Likely When Individuals Are Strongly Motivated to Change Their Behavior. Individuals are motivated to engage in agentic behavior when they confront novel or problematic circumstances.[14] Strain theories of crime are of some use in identifying those circumstances likely to motivate agency. Such theories essentially describe the nature of problematic circumstances, with my general strain theory (GST) providing the most comprehensive description (Agnew, 1992, 2006a,b). Strain is said to occur when individuals are in circumstances where (a) they are not able to achieve their valued goals (e.g., monetary or status goals), (b) they lose or are threatened with the loss of those things they value (e.g., money, romantic partners), and (c) others present or threaten to present them with negative stimuli (e.g., verbal or physical abuse). This strain makes people feel bad, thereby creating pressure for corrective action, possibly involving agentic behavior. It is important to note that strain, as used here, does not create pressure to engage in crime, but rather creates pressure to engage in corrective action of either a criminal or pro-social nature. That said, GST does state that *certain* types of strain are more conducive to crime than others; a point I return to below.

Agency Is More Likely When Individuals Believe They Have the Ability to Produce Desired Change. Individuals who confront a novel or problematic situation are motivated to search for a solution to their difficulties, but many do not. They may believe that there is little they can do to alter their circumstances for the better. As a result, they simply live with their difficulties, making little effort to engage in agentic behavior. A key factor affecting the exercise of agency, then, is the belief that one has the ability to produce desired change. Several individual traits are said to index this ability, with the most well known being "self-efficacy" (Bandura, 2001, 2006; also see Hitlin and Long, 2009; LeBel et al., 2008; Maruna, 2001). People high in self-efficacy believe that they can produce desired change, are strongly motivated to work for change, and persevere even in the face of setbacks. It is important to note, however, that self-efficacy is often domain specific. For example, an adolescent may report much self-efficacy with respect to peers, but little with respect to parents and teachers.

Agency Is More Likely When Individuals Have the Resources to Make Independent Choices and Implement Them. While one's perceived ability to bring about desired change is critical for the exercise of agency, so too is one's *actual* ability. A range of resources increase the ability to make and implement independent choices. Key among them is creativity, which refers to the ability to engage in novel and adaptive behavior (Agnew, 1989). Much evidence suggests that some individuals are substantially better than others at generating novel and adaptive solutions to problems and devising ways to implement them. A variety of measures of creative ability have been developed, with divergent-thinking tests being one of the more common (see Agnew, 1989; Kaufman et al., 2008). Such tests ask respondents to generate solutions to problems or puzzles, with the solutions being scored on several criteria, including novelty and effectiveness.

Creative individuals benefit from material to work with, since the novel ideas they generate usually represent new applications, revisions, or combinations of existing ideas. Agency is therefore more likely when individuals have a broad knowledge base (sometimes referred to as "cultural capital"). This includes knowledge of the schemas for action employed in different areas (Sewell, 1992). The importance of this knowledge base is one reason why some argue that agency is more likely among individuals who occupy multiple roles; such individuals are more knowledgeable about a range of schemas (Emirbayer and Mische, 1998; Thoits, 2006).

Also important for the exercise of agency are autonomy and power (Agnew, 1990; Loyal and Barnes, 2001; Sewell, 1992). Autonomy involves the ability to resist the influence of others and exercise self-direction. Power involves the ability to "produce intended and foreseen effects on others" (Wrong, 1979:2). Individuals with autonomy and power should, by definition, be better able to make and implement independent choices. A variety of factors contribute to autonomy and power, including financial resources, status, authority, ties to others (social capital), physical size and strength, and intelligence.[15]

Agency Is More Likely When Individuals Are in Environments That Contain Low or Countervailing Constraints, Provide a Range of Behavioral Options, and Encourage the Exercise of Agency. Individuals are more likely to exercise agency when they are in environments that do not constrain them to make certain choices and act in a particular manner. These environments may involve low social control (Agnew, 2009; Cullen and Agnew, 2010; Cullen et al., 2008). Here, individuals have weak ties to other people, including family, friends, teachers, and neighbors. They have a low investment in institutions such as school and work. For example, they have low grades, are unemployed, or work in the secondary labor market. They are poorly supervised, such that there is little risk of sanction if they deviate. And they are not strongly committed to a particular code of conduct, either pro– or anti-social. Rather, they are amoral in orientation. As a result of such low control, they are freer to consider a range of behavioral options, and they are less concerned about jeopardizing their ties to others or investments if they behave in a certain manner.

These environments may also involve countervailing constraints. Since this book deals with crime, I focus on the constraints to engage in conventional versus criminal behavior. Individuals face countervailing constraints when some of their associates differentially reinforce conventional behavior, while others reinforce criminal behavior; they have close ties to both conventional and criminal others; they have investments in both conventional and criminal activities (e.g., they derive income from both legal and illegal work); and they have been taught both conventional and criminal beliefs. Due to such countervailing constraints, they do not face a preponderance of pressure to think and act in one particular way versus another. This too increases their freedom to think and act as they choose. It also increases their ability to exercise agency since they have been exposed to a range of thoughts and actions, expanding their breath of knowledge. Further, it increases their motivation to exercise agency; having one foot in the criminal world and one in the conventional, they are more likely to find themselves in problematic or novel situations.

Rational choice and routine activities theories point to another type of constraint, one affecting the ability of individuals to act on the choices they make. As Felson (1986:120) points out with respect to criminal choices, "although people may have lots of desires and inclinations, they cannot always carry them out. The opportunity structure of society places a limit on human ability to act, including acting on inclinations to commit crimes." To give an example, imagine a young man with a criminal record living in a deprived, inner-city community. When this young man faces financial problems, he may consider a range of options for obtaining money. Unfortunately, many of these options may be unavailable or very difficult to utilize; such as obtaining legitimate work that pays a decent wage or securing a bank loan. The actions this young man may take to deal with his financial difficulties are therefore severely constrained. So the exercise of agency is more likely in environments that provide a range of behavioral options, both criminal and pro-social.

Weak constraints, countervailing constraints, and varied opportunities for behavior *allow* for the exercise of agency. Certain environments may also *encourage* the exercise of agency. This encouragement occurs in environments that present beliefs encouraging the exercise of agency, provide direct instruction in the exercise of agency, contain agentic models, and reinforce the exercise of agency. Some societies, for example, have cultural beliefs that encourage originality, at least in certain domains, while others have beliefs stressing conformity and obedience to authority (Hitlin and Elder, 2007). Also, environments may encourage the exercise of agency by exposing individuals to a broad range of behaviors and cultural models, providing the material upon which the exercise of agency is based.

Summary

Individuals will exercise greater agency when they (a) are motivated to alter their behavior, (b) believe they can produce desired change, (c) have the resources to exercise agency (e.g., creativity, broad knowledge, autonomy, power), and (d) are in environments that have weak or countervailing constraints, provide numerous opportunities for agency, and encourage agency. Individuals can be ranked on a continuum, according to the extent to which they possess these characteristics. The middle portion of this continuum will contain individuals who possess these characteristics to a moderate degree and those who possess certain of these characteristics, but not others. Of special note are those individuals who are motivated to change their behavior and are in environment that provide some freedom to change, but who lack the ability to exercise agency (e.g., self-efficacy, creativity, power). Lower-class individuals and adolescents may be more likely to fall into this category.[16] As Matza (1964) states, such individuals are in a state of "drift." While they are motivated to change and have the freedom to change, they are often incapable of self-direction. As a result, their behavior is especially subject to the influence of minor events and temptations. I make special note of such individuals below.

Bounded Agency and Efforts to Explain, Predict, and Control Crime

The argument that some individuals exercise greater agency than others has important implications for the explanation, prediction, and control of crime. In particular, the behavior of these agentic individuals should be (a) more unpredictable than those constrained to crime or conformity, (b) more criminal than those constrained to conformity, and (c) more amenable to change in a pro-social direction.

The Behavior of Agentic Individuals is More Unpredictable

Rational choice theorists and conservative criminologists state that the exercise of agency often results in crime. Life-course criminologists state that agency often results in the desistance from crime. Critical criminologists state that agency allows individuals to rise above their circumstances: resisting oppression and striving for a better life and perhaps world. Agency, then, has been implicated in crime, conformity, and positive accomplishment. These varied outcomes have been noted by others (see Agnew, 1989). One of the founders of sociology, for example, stated that the social forces that promote agency may result in both great accomplishment and crime. In the words of Durkheim (1938:71), "in order that the originality of the idealist whose dreams transcend his century may find expression, it is necessary that the originality of the criminal, who is below the level of his time, shall also be possible."

It is important to remember that the exercise of agency is a process, one that involves making choices, developing plans for action, and implementing these plans. And this process may result in a variety of outcomes, including crime, conformity, and positive accomplishment. At the same time, I believe that the exercise of agency does have some predictable outcomes. Generally speaking, the major effect of agency is to make behavior more unpredictable. As defined, agency involves making choices and engaging in behaviors that are not fully determined by forces beyond the individual's control. To say that choice and behavior are not fully determined is to say that they are not fully predictable. That is, whatever choices individuals make and behaviors they perform, they *could have chosen and acted differently.* This being the case, we can predict that behavior will be more unpredictable when individual and environmental factors favor the exercise of agency.

We would also expect more unpredictability when conditions favor drift. As noted, individuals in a state of drift are easily influenced by minor events and temptations. And, as Matza (1964:29) states, such events and temptations are "so numerous as to defy codification." So the behavior of those in drift will often *appear* unpredictable. It is difficult to predict whose behavior will effectively be more unpredictable: agentic individuals or drifters. However, we might expect less in the way of positive accomplishment from drifters given their limited capacity for self-direction.

The ability to predict unpredictability is quite important. Consider predictions regarding crime. The major causes of crime include low self-control, weak ties to conventional others and institutions, association with criminal peers, certain strains, beliefs favorable to crime, and exposure to situations where the costs of crime are low and the benefits are high (see Agnew, 2009). Individuals subject to these causes are predicted to have a high mean level of crime. Individuals not subject to these causes (e.g., those who associate with conventional peers) are predicted to have a low mean level of crime. Criminologists implicitly assume that while these two groups of individuals differ from one another in their mean level of crime, they do not differ in the amount of variation around this mean.[17] A simplified version of this model is shown in figure 3.1.

If one assumes the existence of agency, however, there is good reason to expect that some groups of individuals will exhibit more variation around their mean level of crime than others. As discussed earlier, a range of factors increase the likelihood that individuals will exercise agency, particularly when these factors work in combination with one another. Agency should be most likely when individuals (a) experience strains or stressors; (b) are high in self-efficacy; (c) are high in creativity, breath of knowledge, autonomy, and power; and (d) are in environments that have weak or countervailing constraints to crime and conformity, provide opportunities to engage in a range of behaviors, and encourage agency. Individuals who possess all or most of these factors should be somewhat high in crime (more below) *and* should exhibit more variation around their mean level of crime.

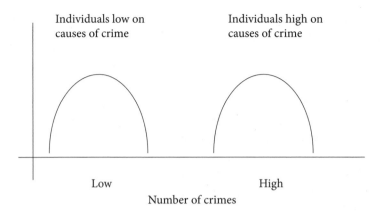

Figure 3.1. The traditional model of crime.

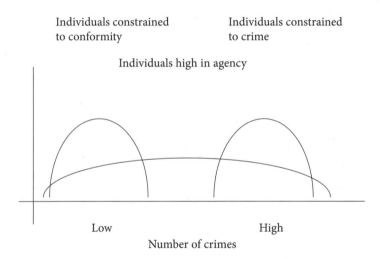

Figure 3.2. The alternative model of crime assuming agency.

They should exhibit more variation partly because they desire change. Also, they are not strongly constrained to crime or conformity, giving them more freedom to choose either. Further, they have the perceived and actual ability to exercise this freedom; among other things, they can imagine a range of behavioral options, believe they can produce desired change, have the ability to act on their choices, and are in environments that permit them to act. The result is more variability or unpredictability in behavior. A simplified version of this prediction is shown in figure 3.2.

I found some support for this prediction using data from two national samples of adolescents (Agnew, 1995a). It was not possible to measure all of the factors predicted to increase agency, but it was possible to measure whether the adolescents were high in strain, high in flexibility (a trait related to creativity), and faced weak or countervailing constraints to crime and conformity (e.g., were low in social control or had both delinquent and conventional friends). The data indicated that when these factors were present, there was *more variation in the level of crime.* For example, those adolescents who were flexible, high in strain, and low in control (weak constraints) showed the greatest amount of variation in their level of crime, with some engaging in little or no crime, some in moderate levels of crime, and some in high levels.

The model of crime shown in figure 3.2 does not replace the deterministic model. Rather, it supplements this model by arguing that individuals differ not only in their level of crime but also in the amount of variation around this level. This represents a more complete model of crime, and the use of this model will allow researchers to more fully understand and control crime. Most notably, this model helps us determine when our efforts to explain and predict crime will be most and least accurate. When conditions favor the exercise of agency, our efforts to explain and predict will be less accurate.

The model of crime shown in figure 3.2 may also shed light on such enduring problems in criminology as the "false positive" problem in prediction research (Loeber et al., 1991; White et al., 1990), the problem of "resilient youth" or "good kids in bad areas" (Rutter, 1985), and what might be called the problem of "bad kids in good areas" (Agnew, 2009). Data indicate that many of the people predicted to be offenders turn out to be non-offenders ("false positives"), that many children in aversive environments are not delinquent, and that many children in advantaged environments are delinquent. It is commonly assumed that the reason for this is that researchers have not taken account of all of the determinants of crime and that eventually accurate prediction will be possible. The inaccuracy of our predictions, however, may also stem from the existence of agency. Research, for example, may reveal that "false positives," "good kids in bad areas," and "bad kids in good areas" possess at least some of the factors conducive to the exercise of agency, thereby allowing them to transcend their circumstances. A study by Wright et al. (1999) provides some support for this argument; they found that the delinquency of middle-class adolescents was partly explained by their possession of "social power," or their ability to avoid detection and resist the efforts of others to punish them (also see Chambliss, 1973). The research on desistance also supports this argument, suggesting that agentic individuals are more likely to end their criminal careers than others in similar circumstances.

Agency Contributes to Somewhat Higher Levels of Crime

As indicated, some researchers state that agency increases crime, while others state that it increases conformity. It is possible to make a good case for both positions. Agency contributes to conformity by allowing individuals to better adapt to the particular circumstances they encounter.[18] And, related to this, agency increases the ability of people to cope with stressors in a pro-social manner. There is limited support for this view; for example, individuals high in self-efficacy—a factor contributing to agency—are less likely to respond to stressors with negative outcomes such as depression (Bandura, 2006: Thoits, 2006).

Nevertheless, I believe that agentic individuals will be moderately higher in crime than most others. As indicated, agentic individuals are willing and able to think and act "on their own," that is, to think and act in ways not fully determined by forces beyond their control. Such forces typically favor conformity, so agentic individuals should therefore be more likely to engage in deviance of both a positive and negative nature, including crime. Agentic individuals, however, should *not* be more likely to engage in crime than the small percentage of individuals who are strongly constrained to crime (more below).[19] It is unclear whether agentic individuals will be more criminal than those in a state of drift.

There is some support for the argument that agency is associated with somewhat higher levels of crime. *Certain* of the factors that encourage agency also increase the likelihood of crime. In particular, crime is more likely among those who experience *certain* strains (Agnew, 2001, 2006a). And crime is more likely among those who experience weak or countervailing constraints to crime and conformity (Agnew, 1995a, 2009; Conger, 1976). For example, crime is *somewhat* more likely among those with weak ties to both criminal and conventional others, and among those with both criminal and conventional friends. The relationship between crime and those traits that increase the ability to think and act independently is mixed. Some studies suggest that self-efficacy is associated with lower levels of crime, although the self-efficacy measures employed in such studies usually have a pro-social bias (see the overview in Ludwig and Pittman, 1999).

For example, individuals are asked about their ability to resist pressure to engage in negative behavior. A study employing a more neutral measure of self-efficacy found that it was associated with higher delinquency, with this measure focusing on whether individuals feel strong, brave, and powerful (Ludwig and Pittman, 1999). The relationship between creativity and crime is unclear, but popular and scholarly discussions have long linked creativity with both negative and positive deviance (see Agnew, 1989; Cropley et al., 2008). Also, limited data suggest that creative individuals are somewhat more likely to engage in certain types of negative deviance (see Agnew, 1989; Cropley et al., 2008).

Further, I found that crime is higher among individuals possessing several factors conducive to agency (Agnew, 1995a). My study on agency and unpredictability also examined levels of crime, and found that crime was highest among those individuals who were high in strain, high in flexibility, and low in the constraints to crime and conformity. It was not possible to compare the crime rates of these agentic individuals with those of individuals constrained to crime. Such individuals are uncommon and not inclined to participate in surveys. Nevertheless, there is good reason to believe that such individuals would have reported higher levels of crime than the agentic individuals I examined. Other research suggests that individuals constrained to crime engage in an extraordinarily large amount of crime, including much serious crime (e.g., Conger, 1976; Mullis et al., 2005; Topalli, 2005).

Agency Is More Likely to Lead to Crime in Certain Conditions and to Conformity in Other Conditions

While agentic individuals may have somewhat higher levels of crime in general, there is reason to believe that agency increases conformity in some circumstances and crime in other circumstances. As indicated, a range of factors influence the exercise of agency, including strain, self-efficacy, creativity, breadth of knowledge, autonomy, power, constraints to crime and conformity, opportunities for behavior, and the encouragement of agency. The particular nature of these factors may influence whether agency has positive or negative outcomes.

Consider the strain that prompts the exercise of agency. As general strain theory states, certain strains are more likely than others to lead to crime (Agnew, 2001, 2006a). Those strains most conducive to crime are high in magnitude, are seen as unjust, are associated with low social control, and are easily resolved through criminal coping. For example, a strain such as financial difficulties is easily resolved through crimes such as theft and drug selling. By contrast, the strain experienced by a parent caring for a sick child or a scientist seeking a cure for cancer is not easily resolved through crime. Such strains, however, may well inspire pro-social coping.

A second factor influencing whether agency results in pro-social or criminal behavior is the nature of self-efficacy. Some individuals may be high in what I call "pro-social self-efficacy," that is, they believe that they have the ability to achieve their desires through pro-social behavior. And this belief may motivate them to exercise their agency in a pro-social manner (see Ludwig and Pittman, 1999, for studies suggesting that this is the case). Other individuals may be low in pro-social self-efficacy but high in what I call "criminal self-efficacy"; such individuals believe that they have much ability to achieve their desires through criminal behavior (see Agnew, 2006a:97–98). For example, they believe that they are skilled fighters, excellent thieves, and able to avoid detection by the police. We would of course expect this type of self-efficacy to be associated with higher levels of crime.

Similar arguments can be made regarding the other factors that facilitate the exercise of agency. Certain types of autonomy and power may be more conducive than others to the criminal exercise of agency. For example, those high in coercive power (e.g., physical strength, fighting ability) may be more inclined to crime than those high in legitimate power. The nature of the behavioral opportunities available to individuals may also affect the exercise of agency. Some individuals may have a large number of pro-social opportunities available. If confronted with financial problems, for example, they may be able to work extra hours, obtain a second job, borrow from friends or family, secure a bank loan, or negotiate more favorable arrangements with creditors. Other individuals, however, may have none of these options. They may, however, have numerous opportunities for crime-such as selling drugs or fencing stolen items. Not surprisingly, research suggests that crime is more likely when the opportunities for crime are seen as high (Agnew, 2009; Felson, 2002).

Finally, the nature of the constraints to crime and conformity may also influence how agency is exercised. While agency is fostered by weak or countervailing constraints, agency is sometimes exercised by individuals who are predominately constrained to crime or conformity. If individuals are predominantly constrained to crime, they should of course be more likely to exercise agency in a criminal manner. In support of this view, I found that certain of the factors associated with agency, such as flexibility, are more likely to increase crime when individuals are disposed to crime (Agnew, 1990).

Agency Is Subject to Guidance

The above arguments suggest that it may be possible to manipulate certain of the factors that influence the exercise of agency, thereby increasing the likelihood that agency will be used for pro-social purposes. In fact, agentic individuals may be a prime target for policy interventions since they are motivated to change, engaged in conscious deliberation about the direction of change, and better able than others to act on the choices they make. It should be kept in mind, however, that agentic individuals are not always in this state. They are most strongly motivated to change and deliberation when dealing with novel or problematic situations; suggesting that interventions may be more effective if implemented during these times. It may be possible to identify these "teachable periods" through interviews with individuals and an examination of their circumstances (e.g., are they currently experiencing severe strains). And it may be possible to induce teachable periods by making individuals more aware of the negative repercussions of their criminal behavior. This is sometimes done in restorative justice conferences, for example, when victims, community representatives, friends, and family members talk about the negative consequences of the offender's crime (Braithwaite, 2002).

Any of the factors that increase the pro-social use of agency can be targeted for intervention. For example, we might reduce the individual's exposure to those strains that increase crime, increase their "pro-social self-efficacy," increase their disposition for conformity, and increase their opportunities for pro-social behavior. A range of prevention and rehabilitation programs have shown some success in these areas (Agnew, 2009, Farrington and Welsh, 2007). Of special note are programs that teach social- and problem-solving skills; these programs essentially teach individuals to exercise agency in a pro-social manner. In particular, these programs encourage individuals to carefully consider both the negative and positive consequences of the choices they are considering. And they equip individuals with the knowledge and skills to respond to problems in a pro-social manner (Agnew, 2009). The research on the desistance from crime also suggests strategies for guiding the exercise of agency, as discussed earlier. The same is true of the creativity literature (Agnew, 1989). For example, it has been suggested that creative adolescents are more likely to use their talents in positive ways when they (a) are gifted in some way, (b) are guided by an interested adult, and (c) encounter a limited amount of coercion in school and from authority figures.

Agency and the Criminal Justice System

Finally, the image of the agentic actor presented in the integrated theory has much relevance to the criminal justice system. As indicated, the criminal justice system is based on the assumption that crime is generally the result of free choice; therefore, punishment is just and will have a deterrent effect. The bounded agency that I describe does not view behavior as *fully* free, but does argue that behavior is sometimes *partly* the result of free choice and action. This is especially true of crime. The nature of crime, as described in chapter 2, encourages the exercise of bounded agency. Crime involves the unjust and inexcusable harm of others, behavior that is condemned by others, and/or behavior that is sanctioned by the state. These characteristics make the commission of crime problematic; crime threatens to disrupt the life of potential offenders and frequently raises moral issues for them. As such, individuals are encouraged to pause and reflect, however briefly, before engaging in crime. Further, they have some freedom of choice and action when considering crime, for the nature of crime is such that non-crime is typically an option. The idea of bounded agency, then, provides a *moral* foundation for the criminal justice system.

At the same time, the idea of *bounded* agency directs greater attention to those factors that influence the exercise of agency than does the idea of "free will." Even the most agentic behavior is strongly influenced by a range of individual and social factors. As such, there is also much justification for the use of rehabilitation and prevention programs. Further, it is sometimes the case criminal behavior is fully determined by forces beyond the individual's control. The discussion of those factors influencing the exercise of agency may allow criminal justice officials to better determine when this is the case and to consider reductions in or alternatives to punishment.

The notion of bounded agency also provides a *pragmatic* foundation for the criminal justice system, suggesting that punishment may reduce crime. Punishment helps prompt the exercise of agency when people experience the impulse to engage in crime, since punishment makes crime problematic. (So, in an interesting twist, punishment encourages the sort of agentic behavior that justifies its existence.) Also, the threat of punishment may result in the decision to refrain from crime, since agency involves some deliberation about the costs and benefits of possible actions. The deliberation prompted by the threat of punishment may also generate other reasons for not engaging in crime. Research supports this idea, suggesting that the threat of punishment is effective in part because it increases concern about other of the negative consequences of crime, such as guilt and jeopardizing ones ties to others (see Nagin, 1998, for an overview). Related to this, *some* research suggests that punishment may be *especially* likely to deter agentic individuals, since these individuals are inclined toward deliberation, are not strongly constrained to crime or conformity, and have more control over their behavior.[20]

Having said this, it is important to note that punishment does not have a large deterrent effect; many other factors influence the decision to engage in crime. Also, the effect of punishment depends on its characteristics, including its certainty and the manner in which it is administered.[21] Further, I again emphasize that the idea of *bounded* agency is also quite compatible with an emphasis on prevention and rehabilitation.

Conclusion

The integrated theory of bounded agency presented in this chapter states that behavior ranges from fully determined to agentic, and lists those individual and environmental factors that influence the extent to which individuals exercise agency. Agency is more likely when individuals (a) are motivated to alter their behavior, (b) believe they can produce desired change, (c) have the resources necessary to exercise agency (e.g., creativity, broad knowledge, autonomy, power), and (d) are in environments that have weak or countervailing constraints, provide numerous opportunities for agency, and encourage agency.

While this theory focuses on agentic behavior, it is compatible with the major elements of the deterministic approach. Criminologists are still encouraged to identify the causes of crime and estimate their effect on the level of crime. This theory, however, substantially broadens the deterministic approach. It allows criminologists to predict not only the level of crime but also the amount of variation around that level. This makes it possible for criminologists to predict the accuracy of their predictions. It also sheds light on such difficult issues as the decision to desist from crime, the "false positive" problem in prediction research, the existence of "good kids in bad areas," and the presence of "bad kids in good areas."

The integrated theory also sheds additional light on the causes of crime. In particular, those factors that foster agency may also result in somewhat higher levels of crime. Certain of these factors—such as strain, weak constraints, and countervailing constraints—partly overlap with the causes of crime. But other of these factors—such as self-efficacy, creativity, autonomy, and power—are rarely considered in crime research. Further, it is possible to (imperfectly) predict when the exercise of agency will result in crime and when it will result in conformity. Doing so also calls attention to factors that are rarely considered in crime research, such as pro-social and criminal self-efficacy. It also involves the examination of interaction effects that have not been considered in criminology, such as the interactions between creativity and those factors that predispose individuals to crime.

Finally, the agentic perspective has important implications for the control of crime. It provides some justification for punishing offenders, since offenders often bear some responsibility for their behavior. This perspective also helps identify those individuals who may be most amenable to control attempts, including punishment, rehabilitation, and prevention. Finally, the agentic perspective suggests strategies for guiding the exercise of agency in a pro-social direction.

These implications of the integrated theory are subject to empirical examination. Indeed, several quantitative and qualitative studies have already investigated certain of these implications (e.g., Agnew, 1990, 1995; LeBel et al., 2008; Giordano et al., 2002; Maruna, 2001; Pogarsky, 2002). Such research is generally supportive of the agentic perspective, although more research is needed. If such research is also supportive, it will demonstrate that, although the belief in bounded agency is a faith, it is a useful faith for criminology to embrace.

4

The Nature of Human Nature

*Are People Self-Interested, Socially
Concerned, or Blank Slates?*

Not long ago, a team of researchers watched a one-year-old boy
take justice into his own hands. The boy had just seen a puppet
show in which one puppet played with a ball while interacting
with two other puppets. The center puppet would slide the ball
to the puppet on the right, who would pass it back. And the
center puppet would slide the ball to the puppet on the left . . .
who would run away with it. Then the two puppets on the ends
were brought down from the stage and set before the toddler.
Each was placed next to a pile of treats. At this point, the toddler was asked to take a treat away from one puppet. Like most
children in this situation, the boy took it from the pile of the
"naughty" one. But this punishment wasn't enough: he then
leaned over and smacked the puppet in the head.

—Bloom, "The Moral Life of Babies," 46

Given that crime is at least partly caused by forces beyond the individual's control, it is critical to ask about the nature of these forces. In particular, what individual and environmental forces increase the likelihood
of crime? There are literally thousands of characteristics that *might* impact
crime. These characteristics include aspects of the individual's biology (e.g.,
physical size and strength, level of lead in the body, heart rate). They also
include psychological factors (e.g., cognitive abilities, emotions, personality
traits, beliefs and values, goals, identities). They include the many components of the social environment (e.g., family, school, work, peer, religious,
neighborhood, and societal characteristics). And they include elements of
the larger physical world (e.g., climate, geography).

Clearly, it would be difficult to examine all of the individual and environmental characteristics that might affect crime. As a result, criminologists are selective in their focus, considering certain potential causes but ignoring others. The causes they consider are based partly on the definition of crime employed, as indicated in chapter 2. They are also based on the academic disciplines in which criminologists were trained. Criminology has been dominated by sociologists for the last several decades, and so the search for causes has focused on the social environment. Until recently, biological and psychological factors received little attention (see Andrews and Wormith, 1989; Raine, 1993). But perhaps most important of all, the causes considered are based on the assumptions that criminologists make about human nature and the social environment.

This chapter focuses on the nature of human nature. By human nature I refer to individual characteristics (including ways of thinking, feeling, and acting) that are universal or nearly universal, and that are biologically based to a substantial degree. I argue that criminologists make three distinct sets of assumptions about human nature. Some view people as self-interested and rational, seeking to maximize their pleasure and minimize their pain. According to this view, people are naturally inclined to crime since it is often the easiest way to maximize their pleasure (e.g., to obtain money). Others view people as socially concerned; caring about others, desiring close ties to them, and eager to conform. According to this view, people must be pressured to engage in crime. And still others view people as blank slates; having no natural disposition to crime or conformity. Rather, people learn to conform or engage in crime from others. Each of these views has had a fundamental impact on the causes of crime that are examined and the strategies for controlling crime that are recommended.

The chapter opens by describing the three sets of assumptions that criminologists make about human nature and their implications for the causes and control of crime. I next discuss recent research on human nature, much of it carried out by biologists, psychologists, and anthropologists. Such research provides some basis for determining the extent to which people are self-interested, socially concerned, or blank slates. Perhaps not surprisingly, this research suggests that each view of human nature has captured a part of the truth. I conclude by presenting a new, integrated view of human nature and discussing its implications for the causes and control of crime.

Criminologists' Assumptions about Human Nature
The Self-Interested/Rational Actor

Many criminologists view individuals as *self-interested and rational*. This assumption is at the heart of classical theory, the first of the contemporary theories of crime; it is at core of several leading crime theories today, and it provides the primary justification for our major crime-control strategies. This assumption also plays a central role in the other social sciences, particularly economics. And it has a long history in philosophy. Hobbes, in particular, argued that people focus on the pursuit of their interests and that, unless restrained by the state, they would soon clash with one another in a "war of all against all" (see Bernard, 1983; Pinker, 2002, for overviews). In particular, this view of human nature assumes that people are self-interested, out to maximize their pleasure and minimize their pain. By self-interested, we mean that "people think of and act first for themselves, that they are not naturally inclined to subordinate their interests to the interests of others" (Gottfredson and Hirschi, 1990:5). Further, people display some level of rationality in the pursuit of their interests. That is, they evaluate the actions they might take in terms of their possible benefits and costs (or pleasures and pains), and engage in those acts believed to provide the greatest net benefit.[1]

Criminologists do not assume that people are perfectly rational. That is, they do not assume that individuals have complete and accurate information about all of the behaviors in which they might engage; including the probability that these behaviors will result in particular costs and benefits. They do not assume that individuals carefully compare the costs and benefits of possible actions, weighted by their probability of occurrence. And they do not assume that individuals consider only costs and benefits when deciding how to act. Rather, criminologists more often embrace a notion of "bounded" or limited rationality.[2] They recognize that individuals often have incomplete and inaccurate information regarding costs and benefits, that this information is often evaluated in a hurried manner, and that the choices individuals make are also influenced by factors beyond costs and benefits. Such factors include social norms and the individual's emotional state. Cornish and Clarke (1986:1) describe bounded rationality as follows:

> Offenders seek to benefit themselves by their criminal behavior; that this involves the making of decisions and of choices, however rudimentary on occasion these processes might be; and that these processes exhibit a mea-

sure of rationality, albeit constrained by limits of time and ability and the availability of relevant information.

The Self-Interested Actor and the Causes of Crime. The assumption of a self-interested actor is at the heart of several leading crime theories, including social and self-control theories, deterrence theory, and rational choice theory.[3] The assumption also plays an important role in several other theories, including social learning theory (Akers, 1990). And this assumption has had a fundamental impact on the causes of crime identified by these theories. If individuals are self-interested, seeking to maximize their benefits and minimize their costs, they should be most likely to offend when the benefits of crime are seen as high and the costs as low. And the above theories focus on the costs and/or benefits of crime when explaining why individuals offend. I begin with deterrence and control theories, which focus on the costs of crime.

Deterrence theory focuses on perhaps the most obvious cost of crime, punishment by the criminal justice system (Ward et al., 2006). Deterrence theory states that individuals are less likely to offend when they believe that the certainty and severity of such punishment are high. *Social control* theories, by contrast, focus on the "informal" costs of crime.[4] Social control theorists state that individuals are less likely to offend when others–such as family members and neighbors—set clear rules that prohibit offending, monitor their behavior, and consistently sanction offending in a meaningful way. Offending is also less likely when individuals have strong bonds to conventional others, such as family members and teachers. Offending might jeopardize these bonds and hurt people that one cares about. In addition, offending is less likely when individuals have a large "investment in conventional society," such as good jobs and good grades at school. Such investments might also be jeopardized by crime. Finally, offending is less likely when individuals have been taught that crime is wrong, since offending will lead to feelings of guilt and shame (sometimes referred to as the "moral costs" of crime).

Self-control theory (Gottfredson and Hirschi, 1990) points to yet another major factor affecting crime, the individual's *responsiveness* to the costs of crime. Individuals high in self-control are very concerned about the costs of crime. In particular, they tend to hesitate when tempted to engage in crime. They consider the possible costs of crime, including the long-term as well as the short-term costs, and the costs to others as well as to themselves. They take such costs seriously, and so often restrain themselves from engaging in crime. Individuals low in self-control give little thought to the costs of crime, both to others and themselves. This is especially true of the long-term costs, such as diminished job prospects. In fact, they are attracted by the risks and excitement associated with crime. And so they exercise little restraint when tempted to engage in crime.

In sum, deterrence and control theories focus on the costs of crime or, in the case of self-control theory, responsiveness to the costs of crime. Individuals are said to engage in crime because the costs are low for them. For example, imagine an individual who is unmarried, unemployed, believes that crime is sometimes justified, is low in self-control, and lives in a neighborhood where people tend to "mind their own business." The costs of crime are quite low for this person; it is unlikely that others will sanction the person for crime, she has little to lose if sanctioned, she will not feel guilty for engaging in crime, and she cannot restrain herself when tempted to engage in crime.

Deterrence and control theories do *not* focus on variation in the benefits of crime. They assume that the benefits of crime are high and roughly comparable across individuals. This is said to be the case because *all* individuals have *unfulfilled* needs and desires, such as those for money and sex. And crime is usually the most expedient way to fulfill these needs and desires. As Gottfredson and Hirschi (1990:12) state, "the use of force or fraud is often easier, simpler, faster, more exciting, and more certain than other means of securing one's ends." More concretely, crimes "provide money without work, sex without courtship, [and] revenge without court delays." As such, everyone is strongly motivated to engage in crime.[5] Hirschi (1977:329) nicely summarizes the position of control theory in this area:

> Control theories assume that the potential for asocial conduct is present in everyone, that we would all commit delinquent acts were we not somehow prevented from doing so. The important differences between delinquents and nondelinquents are not differences in motivation; they are, rather, differences in the extent to which natural motives are controlled.

Other theories of crime also assume that individuals are self-interested and rational. And, like control and deterrence theories, they argue that individuals are more likely to offend when the costs of crime are low. These other theories, however, differ from deterrence and control theories in a fundamental way. They do *not* assume that everyone is equally motivated to engage in crime. Some individuals are said to be more strongly motivated than others because the benefits of crime are higher for them. These theories therefore focus on both the costs *and* benefits of crime (see Agnew, 1993, 1995b, 2009). *Social learning theory*, in particular, argues that the benefits of crime are higher for some individuals because they are in environments where crime is more likely to be reinforced. Some individuals, for example, associate with criminal peers who reward crime with approval and status (Akers, 1990, 1998). *Rational choice theory* likewise focuses on both the costs and benefits of crime (Clarke and Cornish, 1985; Cornish and Clarke, 1986; Ward et al., 2006).

Studies testing social learning and rational choice theories typically examine such costs and benefits of crime as the perceived certainty and severity of official punishment, the legal income of the individual (which might be jeopardized by crime), school grades, the belief that crime will result in much money, the perceived excitement and "coolness" of crime, the anticipated reaction of parents and friends to crime, the belief that crime is physically dangerous, and the anticipated guilt and shame that will result from crime.[6] Such studies routinely find that there is significant variation in both the costs and benefits of crime, and that *both* costs and benefits explain offending (also see Agnew, 1993; Greenberg, 2008). In sum, the assumption that people are self-interested and rational has had a fundamental impact on the causes of crime that are examined. Most of the causes that are considered by criminologists, in fact, deal with the costs and benefits of crime.

The Self-Interested/Rational Actor and Efforts to Control Crime. If actors are self-interested, taking account of the costs and benefits of crime, than crime is best controlled by increasing its costs and reducing its benefits. (A similar point was made in chap. 3, when discussing free will and *rationality*). Most efforts to control crime have focused on increasing its costs, particularly the costs associated with official sanction. This has been especially true in recent decades (Useem and Piehl, 2008). A range of initiatives have attempted to increase the certainty and, especially, the severity of punishment. Such initiatives include mandatory prison terms for convicted drug offenders, life sentences for offenders upon their third conviction for a serious crime ("three strikes and you're out"), the abolition or limitation of parole, and making it easier to try juveniles as adults (see Agnew, 2009; Cullen and Agnew, 2011:616–29). These initiatives have had a modest effect on crime rates, but they have been less successful than originally envisioned. Among other things, this stems from the fact that we do not punish in an effective manner. We focus on increasing the severity of punishment, when the certainty of punishment has a larger effect on offending. We punish in ways that backfire; for example, official punishments often make it difficult for ex-offenders to find legal work. Further, we largely neglect the other costs and benefits of crime.

Several initiatives, however, have attempted to increase the *certainty* of official sanction and to punish in ways that do not backfire. New methods of policing increase the likelihood that crimes will be detected (Agnew, 2009; Sherman et al., 2002). And the restorative justice approach minimizes the negative effects of sanctions (Braithwaite, 2002; Sherman and Strang, 2007). A variety of prevention and rehabilitation programs have attempted to address the other costs and benefits of crime. For example, such programs attempt to strengthen ties to conventional others, improve school performance, foster the belief that crime is wrong, increase self-control, and reduce association with criminal peers (Farrington and Welsh, 2007; Greenwood, 2006). In addition, a range of "situational crime prevention" programs attempt to increase the costs and reduce the benefits of particular crimes by altering the situations conducive to these crimes (Clarke, 1995; Felson, 2002; Hayward, 2007). For example, lock-proof change boxes reduce the benefits of robbing bus drivers. Evidence suggests that many of these programs are effective (see the sources listed earlier).

The Socially Concerned Actor

The assumption of the self-interested actor who turns to crime unless controlled has been challenged by other criminologists, particularly certain *strain theorists*. Merton (1938), in fact, began his classic article on "Social Structure and Anomie" with an attack on this position. He stated that deviance was commonly blamed on the failure of society to control people's drives or impulses. He then challenged the idea that crime was the result of "an untamed bundle of impulses," and instead argued that social circumstances pressured individuals to engage in crime. The other classic strain theorists made the same point. Cohen and Short (1961:106), for example, criticized control theories for assuming that that "the impulse to delinquency is an inherent characteristic of young people and does not itself need to be explained; it is something that 'erupts when the lid . . . is off.'"[7]

Instead of assuming that individuals are naturally self-interested, classic strain theorists assume that they are socially concerned. The socially concerned actor cares about others, and so is inclined to help others in distress and to avoid harming them. This actor also desires close ties to certain others, including emotional and instrumental ties. Further, the socially concerned actor has a strong inclination to conform to the norms of others, partly out of a desire to avoid jeopardizing ties with them. Cohen (1955) provides the best description of the socially concerned actor, focusing on the desire for close ties to certain others and the inclination to conform. Cohen (1955) states that contrary to the assertions of control theory, people are under great "pressure to conform." In particular, "every one of us wants to be a member in good standing of some groups. . . . We all want to be recognized and respected" (Cohen, 1955:56–57). Given this desire for close ties, we are quite reluctant to engage in behaviors that might jeopardize our relations with these others. Rather, Cohen states that a "first requirement" of any behavior in which we engage is that it be "acceptable to those on whose cooperation and good will we are dependent" (1955:56; also see Cloward and Ohlin, 1960; Wilson, 1993; the discussion in Kornhauser, 1978).

More recently, Randall Collins (2008, 2009) has developed a theory of violence that also assumes that people are socially concerned. Collins argues that people have a natural aversion to personal violence, reflected in the "confrontational tension and fear" they experience when in violent situations, such as combat and fights. This aversion is said to be universal and to stem from the fact that violence runs counter to "the tendency within ones own nervous and endocrinological systems to become entrained in the rhythms and emotions of the other person" (Collins, 2009:569). It is not entirely clear what Collins means here, but he seems to be referring to the fact that we are inclined to empathize with others and feel some solidarity with them.

So while control theorists assume that people are self-interested and naturally motivated to crime, other criminologists assume that people are socially concerned and naturally motivated to conformity. This rather different assumption regarding human nature also has a long history (see Bernard, 1983; Pinker, 2002, 2006). Philosophically, it is most closely associated with Rosseau, who vigorously challenged the idea that people are "naturally cruel" and instead described human nature as "gentle" (as exemplified by the "noble savage"). In the social sciences, this assumption was championed by sociologists who challenged the economic assumption that people are self-interested, conforming only because they fear the costs of crime. These sociologists instead claimed that people conform largely out of desire. In one version of this argument, they conform because they have internalized norms that define conformity as good and deviance as bad. In another version, they conform because they desire acceptance and respect from others. The two versions, however, are related in that the internalization of social norms is said to be motivated by a desire for acceptance from others. As Cohen (1955:57–58) states, the recognition and respect we receive from others is "contingent upon the agreement of the beliefs we profess and the norms we observe with their norms and beliefs."[8]

The Socially Concerned Actor and the Causes of Crime. The assumption of a socially concerned actor also has had a fundamental effect on the causes of crime that are examined. If people care about others and are inclined to conform, one cannot argue that crime results when social control is weak or "the lid is off." As Hirschi (1969:5) states: "Clearly, if men desire to conform, they must be under great pressure before they will resort to deviance." And when strain theorists describe the causes of crime, they do in fact focus on those factors that pressure individuals into crime. (Indeed, my book on strain theory is titled *Pressured into Crime* [Agnew, 2006a].)

The classic strain theorists focus on a particular type of pressure or strain, one reflecting the origins of classic strain theory in the Great Depression. Namely, strain is said to result from the inability of individuals to achieve the goal of monetary success. In particular, individuals are encouraged to pursue this goal by the cultural system, but those in the lower rungs of the stratification system are frequently prevented from achieving monetary success through legitimate channels. This goal-blockage is said to create much frustration or pressure, and crime is one possible response. Individuals, for example, may try to obtain the money they so desperately desire through theft, drug selling, or prostitution. It is important to note that this goal-blockage is socially produced; it does not originate in the individual. As Merton (1968:186) stated, his primary aim was "to discover how some *social structures exert a definite pressure upon certain persons in the society to engage in nonconforming rather than conforming conduct*" (emphasis in original).

Later versions of strain theory expand the list of strains that might pressure individuals into crime, with my general strain theory (GST) providing the most comprehensive list (Agnew, 2001; 2006a). Again, such strains tend to be socially produced, with GST focusing on three major categories of strain: (1) others prevent the individual from achieving valued goals, (2) others take things that the individual values, and (3) others treat the individual in a negative manner. GST states that these strains are most likely to result in crime when they are high in magnitude, seen as unjust, associated with low social control, and create some pressure or incentive for criminal coping. Examples of strains that meet these criteria include parental rejection; harsh or abusive discipline; negative school experiences, such as low grades and ridicule by teachers; peer abuse, including verbal and physical abuse; chronic unemployment or work in "bad" jobs; criminal victimization; discrimination; homelessness; and the failure to achieve monetary and certain other goals. Collins (2008, 2009) also lists several factors that allow individuals to overcome their "confrontational tension/fear," with some of these factors related to the pressures described by strain theorists. In sum, certain criminologists assume that individuals are socially concerned and, as a consequence, engage in crime only when under much pressure to so.[9]

The Socially Concerned Actor and the Control of Crime. The image of the socially concerned actor also influences recommendations for controlling crime. Strain theorists do *not* place great stress on increasing the costs of crime. Rather, they focus on reducing those strains that pressure individuals into crime. The classic strain theorists, in particular, argued that the best way to control crime is to make it easier for people to achieve the goal of monetary success through legitimate channels. And several programs were created to do just that. Among the best know are Project Head Start, a preschool enrichment program designed to improve the school performance of children in poor areas; and Job Corps, a jobs training program focusing on those with limited educational prospects. Both programs have been found to reduce crime (Agnew, 2009).

GST focuses on a much broader array of strains, but the prime crime-control recommendation from GST also involves reducing the exposure of individuals to those strains that cause crime. Family training programs, for example, attempt to reduce such strains as parental rejection and the use of harsh discipline. School-based programs attempt to improve school performance and relations with teachers, as well as reduce peer abuse or bullying. In addition, some programs attempt to reduce the likelihood that individuals will respond to strains with crime. This is the case with programs that teach problem-solving and anger-management skills. (For overviews of these and other crime-control recommendations from general strain theory, see Agnew, 2006a; 2010a.)

The Blank Slate

A third assumption regarding human nature states that individuals are "blank slates," inclined to neither crime nor conformity. Rather, their inclinations are shaped by the social environment (see Einstader and Henry, 2006; Kornhauser, 1978). Philosophically, this assumption derives from Locke, who described the mind as a "white paper devoid of all characters, without any ideas," and who stressed the central role of experience in shaping ideas and inclinations. In the social sciences, the idea of the blank slate is at the core of several sociological, anthropological, and psychological approaches, including cultural determinism and behaviorism (for overviews, see Pinker, 2002, 2004, 2006).

The view of individuals as blank slates is most closely associated with differential association and social learning theories in criminology. Sutherland's differential association theory states that both crime and conformity are learned from others, and that individuals become criminal because they have been exposed to "an excess of definitions favorable to violation of law over definitions unfavorable to violation of law" (Sutherland et al., 1992:89). These "definitions" include "motives, drives, rationalizations, and attitudes" favorable to crime or conformity. Individuals are most likely to learn those definitions that are "presented more frequently, for a longer time of exposure, earlier in life, and from either a more prestigious source or a more intense relationship" (Matsueda, 1988:281).

Sutherland critiques strain theories. He acknowledges that crime is sometimes committed out of a desire to obtain money or social status, but he states that such desires also motivate lawful behavior. Therefore, they are not adequate explanations of crime. Individuals engage in crime only if they have learned to define it as an appropriate response to their needs or desires (see Agnew, 1993; Akers, 1998:28). As Sutherland states:

> Thieves generally steal in order to secure money, but likewise honest laborers work to secure money. The attempts by many scholars to explain criminal behavior by general drives and values, such as the happiness principle, striving for social status, the money motive, or frustration, have been and must continue to be futile since they explain lawful behavior as completely as they explain criminal behavior. (Sutherland et al., 1992:90)

Sutherland also questions control theory, which argues that freedom from control allows individuals to satisfy their needs and desires in the most expedient manner possible, which is often crime. Sutherland states that few individuals are free of control; rather individuals are members of groups that are organized for criminal behavior, against criminal behavior, or some combination of the two. And individuals engage in crime only if they are exposed to an excess of definitions favorable to crime.

Social learning theory builds on differential association theory by better describing the mechanisms by which individuals learn to engage in crime (and conformity). In particular, individuals learn to engage in those behaviors that are differentially reinforced, approved of or justified by others, and modeled by others, particularly admired others (Akers, 1998). Social learning theory therefore views individuals as blank slates as well. As noted above, however, social learning theory is also compatible with the view of actors as self-interested. People are predisposed to learn those behaviors that result in the satisfaction (reinforcement) of their wants and desires (Akers, 1990). Thus, self-interest shapes the nature of learning process. Nevertheless, it is the *content of what is learned* that determines whether individuals engage in crime or conformity. Individuals engage in crime if it is differentially reinforced and they engage in conformity if it is differentially reinforced. There is no *natural* inclination to crime or conformity (also see Kornhauser, 1978:35).[10]

The Blank Slate and the Causes of Crime. Not surprisingly, the assumption that people are blank slates has had a strong impact on the causes of crime that are considered. If individuals are blank slates, criminologists should focus on how they learn to engage in crime (or conformity). And this is precisely what differential association, social learning, and related theories do. Individuals are said to learn to engage in crime from others, particularly close others such as family members and friends. They learn through the mechanisms just described: differential reinforcement, imitation, and exposure to the beliefs favorable to crime. These beliefs typically approve of, justify, or excuse crime in certain circumstances (Agnew, 2009; Anderson, 1999; Sykes and Matza, 1957).

The Blank Slate and the Control of Crime. Finally, the image of the actor as a blank slate has had a large effect on recommendations for controlling crime (see Agnew, 2009: Akers, 2010). Programs have been developed to help parents teach their children to conform and avoid crime. Among other things, such programs teach parents how to reinforce conformity and punish misbehavior. Other programs have been developed to reduce the likelihood that juveniles will associate with delinquent peers or join gangs. Programs have also been developed to alter delinquent peer groups and gangs, although efforts have been less successful here. Still other programs try to teach juveniles that crime or particular types of crime (e.g., drug use) are bad. These programs tend to focus on juveniles partly because most forms of crime peak during the adolescent years, but also because juveniles are believed to be more susceptible to influence. Beyond that, any program that reinforces or otherwise encourages conformity, or that punishes or otherwise condemns crime, is compatible with learning theories.

Summary

Three sets of assumptions regarding human nature dominate criminology: people are seen as self-interested and rational, socially concerned, or blank slates. These assumptions are seldom discussed in detail by criminologists; in fact, most criminologists do little more than assert that the particular assumption they favor is correct. This is the case even though these assumptions have a fundamental impact on the causes of crime that are examined and the recommendations for controlling crime that are made. It is therefore critical that they be more fully evaluated, and so I next discuss the accuracy of these assumptions.

Evidence Regarding Human Nature

Even though the three sets of assumptions regarding human nature are at odds with one another, it is easy to understand how each emerged. Depending on where one looks, there is abundant evidence of self-interest, social concern, or human malleability. Consider first the assumption that people are self-interested. The mass media regularly report cases where individuals pursue their self-interest in a rational manner, often causing great harm to others. When I was writing this section of the book, I came across a *New York Times* article titled "Kenya's Criminals Tap a Growth Industry: Kidnapping" (Gettleman, 2009). The article reported that many Kenyan criminals have started kidnapping people in the Kenyan capital, having discovered it was a good way to make money. The article began:

> Little Emmanuel Aguer was one of the most recent victims. A month ago he was snatched on the way to his grandmother's house. Four days later, after his middle-class family received calls asking for $70 or else . . . his uncle found his corpse stuffed in a sugar sack. His head had been bludgeoned and his eyes were gouged out. Emmanuel was six years old.

While the violence inflicted on this boy may seem senseless, it is calculated to frighten the relatives of kidnap victims so that they are more likely to pay ransoms.

Horrific violence of this sort is unfortunately quite common. A few days after the above article appeared, the *New York Times* reviewed *Worse than War* by Daniel Jonah Goldhagen (2009). The book focuses on genocides in the twentieth century, such as those in Nazi Germany, Stalin's Russia, Mao's China, the Sudan, Rwanda, Cambodia, and Yugoslavia. It is estimated that such genocides have claimed 150 million lives, about twice as many as the various wars during this period. The central point of the book is that while genocides are often viewed as beyond rational explanation, they are in fact self-interested, rational acts, intended "to achieve political outcomes." Given such violence, it seems quite reasonable to conclude that people are self-interested, with little concern for others.

But at the same time, it is easy to find instances where people have shown much social concern, often at great personal cost to themselves. My local TV news station, in response to complaints that it covers only negative events, now ends each broadcast with a profile of someone who has sacrificed much to help others. And such acts of social concern are not uncommon. Data from the National Philanthropic Trust indicate that 89 percent of adults in the United States make charitable contributions each year, the contributions averaging $1,620 per year and going to over one million charities. Further, 55 percent of adults participate in volunteer activities each year. Beyond that, people routinely engage in selfless acts that do not show up in statistical compilations. The concern shown by parents for their children is but one example. So while there is certainly much self-interest and violence in the world, there is also much sacrifice and generosity, suggesting that individuals are socially concerned.

Finally, there is much evidence for the assumption that people are blank slates. There is little doubt that human infants must undergo a long process of learning before they can function effectively on their own. The great diversity among societies suggests that people are quite plastic, able to be shaped and molded in a variety of ways (see Wilson, 1993:4–5). Bandura (2001:21) uses aggression as an example, noting that "wide intercultural diversity challenges the view that people are inherently aggressive. There are fighting cultures that breed aggression by modeling it pervasively, attaching prestige to it and according it functional value for gaining social status, material benefits, and social control. There are also pacific cultures in which interpersonal aggression is a rarity because it is devalued, rarely modeled, and has no functional value." Further, he states that there are cases where warring societies have rapidly transformed into peaceful ones, the Swiss being an example. Given this, he concludes that "the human species has been selected for learnability and plasticity of behavior adaptive to remarkably diverse habitats."

So on the face of it, a good case can be made for each view of human nature. Individuals who make the case for one view, such as the self-interested actor, are aware of the above sorts of evidence for alternative views. They challenge such evidence, however. For example, they claim that social concern is the exception rather than the rule. Further, they state that much of the behavior that seemingly reflects social concern, such as helping others, is in fact motivated by self-interest. Take, for example, Mother Teresa, perhaps the prime example of a socially concerned person. A recent book, built on the assumption that people are self-interested, suggests that Mother Teresa's sacrifice was "tied to her faith in an external reward" and that "it makes sense to pay the price of sacrifice for the short, finite time of a life span if the consequence is a reward that goes on for infinity in heaven" (de Mesquita, 2009). Those who believe that people are socially concerned make similar arguments for their position, claiming that "bloodletting and savagery" are the exception rather than the rule (Wilson, 1993:2). Stephen Jay Gould, the renowned evolutionary theorist, claimed that "good and kind people outnumber all others by thousands to one," and that "we perform 10,000 acts of small and unrecorded kindness for each surpassingly rare, but sadly balancing, moment of cruelty" (quoted in Pinker, 2002:125). Those who view people as blank slates argue that people can be both cruel and kind, evidence for their plasticity and the importance of social influences.

How, then, do we adjudicate between the different views of human nature? Until recently, it was quite difficult. But research in several areas is now shedding important light on the nature of human nature. This research better measures traits such as self-interest and social concern, better estimates how common such traits are, and better determines whether such traits have some biological basis. This research does suffer from certain problems, but taken as a whole it makes a compelling case for a new view of human nature. Perhaps not surprisingly, this research suggests that each of the above views has some merit.

How Do Researchers Determine the Nature of Human Nature?

The new research on human nature is of several types:

Experiments. Experiments involve doing something to a group of people and then observing the consequences. For example, individuals in one set of experiments participate in games that provide the opportunity to act in a self-interested manner (e.g., reward oneself and not give anything to others) or a socially concerned manner (e.g., share rewards with others). While these games create artificial situations, they do replicate the types of choices that people make in the real world. They also allow researchers to better measure self-interest and social concern (see Fehr and Gintis, 2007). For example, suppose people share their rewards with others. As suggested in the example involving Mother Theresa, this does not necessarily mean that they are socially concerned. They may be sharing in order to establish a good reputation, for example. Researchers, however, can take account of this possibility by making the participants anonymous, so that sharing cannot enhance their reputation. These games are easily administered to large groups of people, including people from a range of backgrounds and societies throughout the world. Thus, they allow us to better estimate how common traits such as self-interest and social concern are.

Surveys. Surveys involve asking people questions. Most notably, people have been asked how they would respond to certain moral dilemmas. For example, would they push one person into the path of an oncoming train if this would save the lives of five people? Dilemmas of this type allow researchers to examine whether there are certain moral principles that are widely shared. People are also asked about the reasons for their responses to these dilemmas. This allows researchers to examine whether moral decision-making is the result of rational deliberation. As described below, the results here are quite interesting, suggesting that the moral choices we make are not always the result of a conscious consideration of costs and benefits.

Observations. In addition, people have been observed in a broad range of societies, with some scholars drawing on these observations in an effort to determine whether certain traits and behaviors are universal. Anthropologists have conducted most of the studies in this area, particularly in nonindustrial societies. The research here is limited, however. These studies were conducted by different people over a period of many decades, so they do not systematically measure traits/behaviors in a uniform way. Further, statements about the universality of a trait/behavior are always based on a sample—albeit a broad one—of all societies. So any assertion that a trait/behavior is universal must be viewed with caution. At the same time, it should be noted that anthropologists have focused on describing differences across societies, with similarities often being ignored or taken for granted. This focus stems from the dominance of the "blank slate" perspective in anthropology for many decades; a perspective that led anthropologists to focus on how the social environment shapes people in different ways (see Brown, 1991; Wilson, 1993).

Nevertheless, studies indicate that there are certain widely shared traits and behaviors across societies. The origin of these traits/behaviors is another matter, however. As Brown (1991, 2004) points out, widely shared traits/

behaviors are not necessarily biological in origin. They may be widely shared because all societies face similar adaptive problems, with the traits/behaviors being an effective solution to these problems. The traits/behaviors may have developed independently or they may have diffused across societies. For example, the behaviors of fire-making and cooking likely diffused across societies. Certain types of research, however, allow us to explore whether widely shared traits/behaviors are biologically based to a substantial degree.

Examining Infants and Very Young Children. One type of research examines those traits and behaviors that emerge early in life, among infants and very young children. I began this chapter with an example of such research. It is assumed that there may be some biological basis for such traits/behaviors, since there has not been much opportunity for learning. For example, if infants show signs of concern for others, particularly before there has been an effort to teach such concern, the implication is that social concern is biologically based to a substantial degree. Studies in this area, however, must be interpreted with caution, since learning can occur quite early in life—perhaps even in the womb.

Examining Nonhuman Primates. Another line of research examines the traits and behaviors exhibited by nonhuman primates, particularly the great apes with whom we are most closely related. Learning plays a much less important role among the great apes than among humans, such that ape behavior/traits are biologically based to a large degree. Since humans share a common ancestor with apes and sometimes confronted similar environments after their divergence from apes, there is some reason to believe that the behaviors/traits we share have some biological basis. At the same time, it should be noted that learning does occur among nonhuman primates. Also, different nonhuman primates sometimes exhibit different traits/behaviors. Chimpanzees, for example, can be quite aggressive toward other chimpanzees, whereas bonobos are known for their gentle nature (Wrangham and Peterson, 1996). Caution should therefore be exercised before concluding that a shared trait/behavior is biologically based.

Evolutionary Psychology. The rapidly growing field of evolutionary psychology also sheds light on the biological basis of traits and behaviors. Evolutionary psychologists employ a variety of methods to determine whether particular traits/behaviors have adaptive value, such that individuals with the traits/behaviors have a greater chance of reproducing and passing their genes on to others. Such methods include computer modeling, behavioral experiments, and examinations of foraging societies in which humans spent most of their evolutionary history (see Schmitt, 2008, for an overview). If the traits/behaviors have adaptive value, there is reason to believe they may have been selected for in the evolutionary process and so have a biological basis.

Biological Studies. Finally, researchers have examined whether certain traits and behaviors are reflected in the biological structure and functioning of individuals. Certain of this research examines whether there is a genetic basis for traits/behaviors, with genetic factors playing a role in the existence of or variation in the strength of the trait/behavior. Other research examines whether certain parts of the brain are associated with the expression of particular traits/behaviors. For example, researchers have noted that certain traits are absent in individuals with particular types of brain injuries (see Tancredi, 2005, for an overview).

Taken as a whole, these types of research provide some basis for drawing conclusions about human nature, particularly when the different research strategies reach similar conclusions. However, these conclusions should be viewed as tentative, given that this research is at an early stage and often problematic for the reasons just indicated. I briefly describe this research below, focusing on the assumptions of self-interest and rationality, social concern, and the blank slate.

Experiments That Shed Light on Human Nature

Games Examining the Assumptions of Self-Interest and Social Concern. Individuals have been asked to play games that provide the opportunity to act in a self-interested or socially concerned manner.[11] The best known of these games are Ultimatum and the Public Goods game. Ultimatum involves two players, the proposer and the responder. The proposer starts off with a certain amount of money, say $10, and has the option of giving the responder some portion of the money or none at all. The responder has the option of accepting or rejecting the proposer's monetary offer. If the responder accepts, she keeps the amount that was offered and the proposer keeps what is left. If the responder rejects the offer, neither the responder nor the proposer get any money. The game is played for one round and the proposer and responder do not know one another's identities. If individuals are strictly self-interested, the proposer should keep most of the money, say $9, and offer a small portion to the responder, say $1. The responder should accept this offer since the alternative is no money. This usually does not occur, however.

Typically, the proposer offers a substantial amount to the responder, 50 percent of the total being the modal amount. The responder typically rejects offers below 30 percent of the total, even though rejection means that no one gets any money. However, a significant fraction of proposers (about one-quarter) do offer the minimum amount. One might attribute the apparent generosity of most proposers to the fact that the responders can reject offers. There is some support for this. Offers are less generous in the Dictator game, where responders must accept whatever is offered. But even here, most pro-posers offer more than the minimum amount. The results for the Ultimatum game generally hold in cross-cultural studies involving diverse societies. The characteristics of the society, however, have some influence on how individuals play the game. Proposers are more likely to offer substantial amounts, and responders are more likely to reject minimal amounts, in societies where people are involved in cooperative arrangements (they regularly exchange goods and services with one another).

The Public Goods game is played by several players and lasts multiple rounds. In each round, the subject is grouped with several other anonymous players and given twenty points, redeemable at the end of the experiment for money. Each subject then places certain of her points in a "private account" and certain in a "common account." The experimenter tells the subjects how many points were contributed to the common account, then doubles that amount and divides it among all the players, regardless of whether they contributed to the common account. The game is set up in such a way that all will benefit if everyone contributes to the common account, but individual players have the option of placing all their points in their private account and benefiting from the generosity of others. That is, players can engage in what is known as "free riding." There is some incentive to free ride, since players will only get back a fraction of what they personally contribute to the common account (their contribution is doubled, but then split among several players). Given this fact, we would expect the players to place all of their points in their private accounts if they were strictly self-interested.

Instead, most subjects begin the game by contributing half their points on average to the common account. But their contribution to the common account declines with each new round, so that most players are contributing nothing to the common account by the tenth round. Subjects report that they became angry with those who contributed less than they did, and they sought to retaliate against these free riders in the only way they could; contributing nothing to the common account. In another version of this game, subjects are given the opportunity to directly punish one another after their contribution in each round is revealed. In particular, each player can assign "punishment points" to the other players, with these points significantly reducing the other players' payoffs. The use of punishment points, however, also reduces the payoff of the *punisher* by a moderate amount. Despite this personal cost, most players do punish the free riders. This punishment dramatically reduces the level of free riding, such that the free riders are soon contributing all or most of their points to the common account.

Taken as a whole, these and other experiments suggest that most individuals are not strictly self-interested. That is, most do not act in ways that maximize their immediate payoffs in the games. Rather, most individuals have an inclination to share with others, to participate in cooperative arrangements, and to punish free riders–even at some personal cost. At the same time, it is important to note that a minority of individuals do act in a strictly self-interested manner; they do not share and they free ride off the contributions of others. In addition, the sharing and cooperative behavior exhibited by most players is influenced by costs and benefits. Individuals are *more likely* to share when they are subject to sanction if they do not, as is the case in the Ultimatum game. Individuals will continue cooperating only if others reciprocate in an equitable manner. And individuals will not punish free riders if the cost of doing so is very high. Further, while the inclination to share/ cooperate is common across a broad range of societies, it is most common in societies that stress cooperation, suggesting a role for social learning.

Experiments Suggesting a Desire to Help Others in Distress. There are other aspects to social concern, one of which is a willingness to help others in distress (part of caring for others). A number of experiments indicate that people are inclined to help others in distress, particularly when they personally encounter these others, the others are not to blame for their distress, and the costs of helping are not too high (for overviews, see Batson, 1990; Krebs, 2008; Wilson, 1993:34–40). To illustrate, experimenters have exposed individuals to others who seem to be in need of assistance; for example, others who have seemingly received a severe electric shock. People usually provide assistance in such situations, even when there is some cost and little benefit to doing so. So once again, we find that the notion of a strictly self-interested actor is challenged; people have an inclination to help others, even at some personal cost, although helping behavior certainly declines when the cost becomes very high.

Experiments Suggesting an Inclination to Conform. Another aspect of social concern involves the inclination to conform. A range of experiments indicate that individuals have a strong inclination to conform, even when there may be some cost to doing so.[12] The classic experiment in this area was conducted by Solomon Asch, who placed a subject in a room with seven other people, all of whom were collaborators in the experiment. The people in the room were shown a line. They were then shown a second line, which was obviously much longer than the first. They were next asked if one of the lines was longer than the other. The collaborators each said that the two lines were of equal length, after which the most of the subjects in the experiment agreed, reflecting their inclination to conform. Other experiments have produced similar results. For example, most individuals will ignore smoke spewing out of a duct—a potentially life-threatening situation—when others in the room do the same. Again, these results do not mean that self-interest is irrelevant. People conform partly because they wish to avoid the costs associated with nonconformity, such as ridicule and rejection by others. Reflecting this fact, individuals are generally more likely to conform when they express their opinions in public rather than private, although the conformity bias is still evident for privately expressed opinions.

Experiments Demonstrating an In-Group Bias. The concern that people show for others is not unlimited. Not only is it influenced by costs and benefits but also by the nature of the others in question. A series of experiments indicate that people are inclined to divide others into in-groups and out-groups ("us" and "them"), and to favor members of their in-group. For example, they are more likely to share rewards with in-group members and to act aggressively toward out-group members (see Baumeister and Leary, 1995; Brewer, 1999; Harris, 1998 for overviews). The classic study in this area is known as the Robbers Cave experiment. Twenty-two boys, selected to be as similar to one another as possible, were divided into two groups at a summer camp. The boys in the two groups quickly developed hostile attitudes toward one another, even before they were involved in competitive games. And it did not take long before they were engaging in name-calling and aggressive acts against one another. It appears, then, that our social concern is focused on those closest to us (see Pinker, 2002, for further discussion).

Experiments Challenging the Assumption of Rationality. Self-interested actors are assumed to be rational. A range of experiments, however, indicate that the rationality exhibited by people is often quite limited and that behavior is influenced by factors other than costs and benefits.[13] Experiments indicate that individuals usually exhibit several types of bias when processing and acting on information, such that it is quite unlikely that they will consider all of their behavioral options, accurately determine the probability that these options will result in particular costs and benefits, and select the option that maximizes their cost-benefit ratio. Among other things, individuals exhibit a consistency bias; they are more likely to attend to information that supports their existing views, as well as reshape information so that it is consistent with their views. Individuals tend to rely on anecdotal evidence, including personal experiences, when estimating probabilities and costs/benefits. Individuals often select the first behavioral option that seems to produce some benefit, rather than carefully weighing the costs and benefits of all behavioral options. And, due to their limited willpower, individuals often engage in acts that they know are not in their interests, or at least their long-term interests. For example, many individuals smoke even though they would prefer not to. (See the references in note 13 for still other biases.)

The behavior of individuals is also strongly influenced by factors other than costs and benefits. One such factor has already been mentioned: individuals tend to conform to those around them, even when it is not in their self-interest to do so. Related to this, individuals tend to follow social norms, with certain of these norms requiring behavior that runs counter to individual self-interest (e.g., returning found items). Indeed, the emphasis on social norms is a defining feature of sociology and has its origins in an effort to distinguish sociology from economics, which assumes that people are self-interested and rational (see Boudon, 2003; Fehr and Gintis, 2007). Further, individual action is strongly influenced by emotions, many of which interfere with rational deliberation and lead to actions that run counter to self-interest. Anger, for example, may lead individuals to ignore or discount the negative consequences of anticipated acts, to overlook possible courses of actions, and to seek revenge against others, even if doing so carries a high risk of sanction (Agnew, 2006a; Carmichael and Piquero, 2004).

A range of experiments, then, challenge the image of the rational actor. These experiments do not deny that actors give at least some consideration to costs and benefits; but they do indicate that individuals are not fully rational and that factors other than costs/benefits affect behavior as well. These sorts of limitations are acknowledged by most criminologists, although many may not be aware of how pervasive they are. A final set of experiments, however, questions even this notion of limited rationality. Bargh and Chartrand (1999:462) state that these experiments suggest that "most of a person's everyday life is determined not by their conscious intentions and deliberate choices but by mental processes that are put into motion by features of the environment that operate outside of conscious awareness and guidance."

In particular, these experiments suggest that environmental stimuli often unconsciously activate emotions, evaluations, preferences, goals, and behavioral inclinations. These, in turn, affect behavior (see Bargh and Chartrand, 1999; Dijksterhuis, 2010; Greene and Haidt, 2002 for overviews). To give an example, individuals in one study were told that they were participating in a language experiment. They were divided into three groups: one group was exposed to words related to rudeness (e.g., impolite, obnoxious), another to words related to politeness (e.g., respect, considerate), and a third to neither rudeness nor politeness words (the control group). The individuals were then given a chance to interrupt a conversation. Those primed with the rudeness words were much more likely to do so than those primed with the politeness words, with the control group in the middle. The work of Berkowitz (1994) relatedly suggests that such unconscious priming may be relevant to crime as well. Berkowitz found that the mere presence of a gun in a setting helps trigger an aggressive response in some individuals.

These experiments do not mean crime is entirely or even largely the result of unconscious processes. As argued in chapter 3, the decision to engage in crime is a special one, likely to involve some conscious deliberation. And much research suggests that individuals do give at least some limited consideration to costs and benefits when contemplating crime. This research involves interviews with offenders, experiments that manipulate the costs and benefits of acts such as cheating, and surveys that ask about the costs and benefits of crime.[14] Nevertheless, the data suggest that rationality is limited, that factors other than the consideration of costs and benefits influence crime, and that some of these factors may be beyond the conscious awareness of individuals.

The Response to Moral Dilemmas

Researchers have also conducted surveys relevant to human nature. Most notably, they have asked individuals how they would respond to various moral dilemmas.[15] I focus on the responses to three of these dilemmas. The first involves a runaway trolley that will kill five people unless a switch is pressed; with the switch diverting the trolley onto an alternative track where it will kill one person instead of five. Individuals are asked whether they should divert the trolley. Most say yes, that saving five people justifies the death of one. Individuals are then presented with a similar moral dilemma. A trolley threatens to kill five people. They can prevent it from doing so by pushing a stranger off a bridge and onto the track. Should they push the stranger? Most people immediately say no. When pressed, most people have trouble explaining why they say they would press the switch but not push the stranger; in each case one person is sacrificed to save five.

Some researchers explain the difference in response by arguing that individuals have an innate predisposition to avoid causing *direct* harm to innocent people (e.g., Gazzaniga, 2005, 2008; Hauser, 2006; Mikhail, 2007). This predisposition is said to be evolutionarily based. Much of our history involved face-to-face interaction with others, and harming innocents would have severely disrupted such interaction. Thus, when confronted with the prospect of pushing an innocent individual off a bridge, people immediately experience a negative emotional reaction. This argument has some support; that part of the brain associated with emotion is activated when individuals respond to this moral dilemma. However, the small social groups in which we evolved did not provide much opportunity for causing *indirect* or impersonal harm. So individuals do not experience a strong negative emotional reaction when confronted with the decision to flick a switch that diverts the trolley to another track. Rather, individuals make this decision strictly on the basis of reason. And, in fact, that part of the brain associated with abstract reasoning and problem solving is activated when individuals confront this decision, while that part associated with emotion is not.

In the second moral dilemma, individuals are told to imagine that they are driving in their new car and see a badly injured man on the side of the road. They can stop and take him to the hospital, saving his life, but doing so will get blood all over their car. Individuals are asked whether it is OK to leave the man on the side of the road. Most immediately say no, even though assisting the man imposes a cost. Next, individuals are told that they receive a request in the mail asking for $100, which will save the lives of ten starving children. They are asked whether it is OK to ignore the request. Many say yes. This is the case even though they can save ten children at relatively low cost. Once more, individuals have trouble explaining their decisions. The first situation, however, involves a *personal* experience with an individual in need of help; while the second situation involves an *impersonal* experience. Similar to the first moral dilemma, it may be the case that individuals have a disposition to help others in need only when they personally encounter them.

In the third moral dilemma, individuals are told that a brother and sister, on vacation from college, are traveling together. They decide to have sex one night. She is on birth control and he uses a condom. They enjoy the experience, but decide not to do it again and to keep it a secret. Individuals are asked if they approve, and almost all immediately say no. Again, however, they struggle to explain why. People simply have a "gut feeling" that brothers and sisters should not have sex. As above, some researchers argue that this gut feeling is evolutionarily based. Offspring produced by incest have higher rates of mortality and disability and so are less likely to reproduce (see Brown, 1991). Therefore, those who have an aversion to incest are more likely to produce offspring who survive and spread throughout the population, carrying the aversion to incest with them.

Based on the responses to these and other moral dilemmas, it is said that humans possess certain underlying moral principles: principles that are biologically based and that partly transcend considerations of self-interest. These principles are said to have a biological basis because they are widely shared; people immediately act on them, with little conscious deliberation; and that part of the brain associated with emotion is activated when people act on them. In addition, the principles seem to have some adaptive value when one considers the evolutionary history of humans (see the discussion of evolutionary psychology that follows). Hauser (2006) refers to these principles as "moral instincts," Haidt (2001) as "moral intuitions," and Mikhail (2007) says they are part of a "universal moral grammar."

In the above cases, the principles include not causing *personal* harm to innocent others, helping innocent others in distress when they are *personally* encountered, and avoiding incest with close relatives. Still other moral principles have been suggested (see below). Researchers stress that these principles are quite general, and that they are specified, modified, and elaborated in social groups. Among other things, groups help define who is worthy of moral consideration (e.g., certain groups are sometimes dehumanized and so not viewed as worthy of moral consideration); the specific behaviors that are considered harmful (e.g., secondhand smoke has recently been defined as harmful); and the justifications and excuses for causing harm that are acceptable.[16] As an example, Waters (2007) provides an overview of the crime of murder, noting that the justifications and excuses accepted for killing another person vary a moderate amount over time and across societies. So once again, we find that there is some room for social learning.

These data are important not only because they suggest that there may be innate moral principles that guide behavior but also because they too challenge the notion that people are rational actors. In fact, some have argued that "conscious moral reasoning often plays no role in our moral judgments." Rather, our "innate moral sense" allows us to make such judgments "rapidly, involuntarily, and without recourse to well-defined principles." The reasons we might later offer for these judgments are said to be "post-hoc justifications or rationalizations" (Hauser, 2006:21, 24, 25; also see Greene and Haidt, 2002; Haidt, 2001, 2007). As Haidt (2001:830) states in his article, "The Emotional Dog and Its Rational Tail," "moral emotions and intuitions drive moral reasoning, just as surely as a dog wags its tail." This is not to say, however, that all moral decisions are based on this innate moral sense (see Haidt, 2001, 2007).

As suggested, decisions involving harming and helping others in *impersonal* circumstances often involve moral reasoning. Moral reasoning is also likely when we move against our moral intuitions; for example, when we think about personally harming another. In addition, moral reasoning is likely when others raise arguments about our behavior that trigger new moral emotions in us (e.g., others point out that our actions do cause personal harm). Likewise, taking the role of others may trigger new moral emotions, again prompting moral reasoning (e.g., an offender takes the role of her victim). These circumstances suggest that moral reasoning may play a significant role in deciding whether to engage in crime, including both crimes that cause personal harm (which violate our moral intuitions) and impersonal harm (provided that individuals are aware of the harm). This suggestion reinforces one of the central points of chapter 3: the nature of crime is such that it prompts conscious deliberation and the exercise of bounded agency.

Human Universals

In addition to conducting experiments and surveys, researchers have drawn on the observations of others to describe those social and individual characteristics that appear to be universal or nearly universal (Brown, 1991, 2004; Pinker, 2002). Brown's (1991) book, *Human Universals*, represents the most ambitious effort in this area. At the social level, he lists such universals as material inequality, differences in prestige, age grading, kinship systems, ethnocentrism or in-group bias, exchange, cooperation and reciprocity, aggression, and laws proscribing violence and rape. At the individual level, universals include language; emotions such as anger, disgust, and contempt; empathy; notions of intention and responsibility for one's actions; the strong attachment of children to their caregivers; socialization of the young by senior kin; and the tendency to favor close over distant kin.

More recently, several researchers have argued that certain moral inclinations are universal or nearly universal.[17] Their claims regarding universality are based on examinations of anthropological and historic data, as well as the surveys and experiments just described. These examinations are often unsystematic, so the claims should be regarded with caution; nevertheless, there is much overlap in the moral inclinations listed across researchers. These inclinations include:

- The tendency to feel distress at the suffering of others, particularly kin and members of one's in-group
- An inclination to help innocent others in distress and avoid causing harm to them, especially members of one's in-group
- A desire for close ties with and the approval of certain others (see especially Baumeister and Leary, 1995)
- A tendency to distinguish in-groups from out-groups and to favor in-groups (see Brewer, 1999)
- A tendency to cooperate with others in instrumental endeavors
- A commitment to fairness, which includes repaying favors, engaging in equitable exchanges, and punishing free riders
- An inclination to follow social norms
- Concern with notions of purity, manifested, for example, in the regulation of eating and sexuality (e.g., incest norms)

Researchers again stress that these inclinations are general; they are specified, elaborated, and stressed to varying degrees in social groups. Also, individuals differ in the extent to which they possess these inclinations, although they still "shape the judgments and behavior of almost all people" (Wilson, 1993). Further, researchers readily acknowledge that these inclinations are often violated. For example, data suggest that infanticide was common in certain countries at certain points in time (Wilson, 1993). Given this fact, one may wonder how researchers can claim that inclinations, such as not harming innocent others, are "universal." Moral inclinations, however, are distinct from behavior. As Wilson (1993:25–26) states, behavior is a "product of our [inclinations] interacting with our circumstances." In particular, individuals sometimes violate their moral inclinations in extreme circumstances. Wilson (1993) states that this is the case with infanticide: parents kills their children when there is insufficient food for them, they are so deformed or sickly that survival is unlikely, or their paternity is uncertain. And infanticide usually occurs before parents have formed strong bonds with their children. This argument, of course, is similar to that made by strain theorists, who contend that individuals must be pressured into crime.

Traits/Behaviors That Appear Very Early in Life

The fact that certain traits or behaviors are widely shared does not necessarily mean that they are biologically based. Researchers have tried to determine whether certain traits/behaviors have a biological basis in several ways, including examining the traits and behaviors of infants and very young children. Recent research indicates that infants and very young children exhibit a range of traits, many relevant to the views of human nature described earlier.[18] Infants are inclined to develop strong attachments to their caregivers. They engage in a range of behaviors that help cultivate such attachments, such as smiling and cooing. Attachments are easily formed. And distress is experienced when attachments are threatened. Infants also show evidence of empathy. Newborns display signs of a rudimentary empathy, crying in response to the crying of others. Newborns, however, do not cry in response to loud noises or a tape recording of their own crying. This empathy becomes more developed during the second year of life. Reflexive crying stops, and there is some evidence that infants distinguish themselves from others, imagine the emotions that these others are experiencing, and sometimes feel distress when others are suffering. Older infants frequently try to help others in distress, particularly their caregivers, but sometimes strangers as well. This help may take the form of comforting others or sharing things with them. Tomasello (2009) and others present evidence suggesting that this helping behavior is not learned. For example, the inclination of young children to help others is maintained regardless of whether it is rewarded or ignored.

Infants also have something of a moral sense. They understand the difference between intentional and unintentional acts. And, as the example used to open this chapter suggests, they make a distinction between good and bad ("naughty") behaviors. Based on his experiments with infants, Bloom (2010:46) goes so far as to state that "some sense of good and evil seems to be bred in the bone." At two-and-a-half years, children can distinguish between social conventions (e.g., rules about how to dress) and moral principles that prohibit real physical or psychological harm to others. In particular, they understand that behaviors like hitting and stealing cause real harm, while behaviors like dressing inappropriately do not. Young children show a tendency to follow social norms, feel guilt when they do not, and enforce social norms when interacting with others (see especially Tomasello, 2009). This tendency seems to stem partly from a desire to be liked and respected by others.

These findings provide some support for the assumption that individuals are socially concerned. At the same time, it is important to note that infants and young children divide others into in-groups and out-groups, with in-group members eliciting more social concern. Further, as any parent will testify, infants and young children also have an unpleasant side. They get angry, particularly when they cannot get what they want. And when they are physically able, they sometimes respond to their anger and frustration by attacking others and taking things from them. Criminologists commonly claim that rates of violence and theft peak during the adolescent and young adult years (see Agnew, 2009). New research, however, suggests that rates may actually peak in late infancy. Tremblay (2006) reports that physical attacks on others (assaults) increase from nine to thirty months, by which time about half of all children hit others. Forcibly taking things from others (robbery) shows a similar pattern, with virtually all children having done this by thirty months. Then assault and robbery start to decline. Similar patterns have been found for stealing, vandalism, and lying. And these patterns have been found in a range of countries. Tremblay (2006:6) states:

> We [are] trying to answer the wrong question when we [ask]: How do humans learn to aggress? Humans do not appear to need to learn to use physical aggression. As soon as they are in sufficient control of their muscles they use physical aggression to express their anger and obtain what they desire.

Thus the social concern of infants exists alongside a strong streak of self-interest, with this self-interest often resulting in behaviors that we classify as "crimes" when committed by older individuals (also see Wright et al., 2008). It is important to note, however, that the aggression of infants typically occurs in response to strains or stressors.

Research also suggests that infants and very young children differ in the extent to which they possess traits related to social concern and self-interest. In particular, infants differ in temperament, with temperament being defined as "individual differences that appear from birth onward, remain relatively stable across the lifespan, and presumably have a strong genetic or neurobiological basis" (De Pauw et al., 2009:309).[19] Infants differ in the extent to which they form close attachments to others, show concern for and help others in distress, and are irritable (e.g., throw temper tantrums when they do not get what they want). Differences in these traits influence the likelihood of problem behavior, including aggression and theft in childhood and beyond (De Pauw et al., 2009; Lahey et al., 2008).

In sum, data on infants and very young children provide evidence for both social concern and self-interest. There is also some support for the blank slate assumption. While infants possess certain traits related to social concern and self-interest, they obviously have much to learn. And evidence suggests that they in fact come into this world quite disposed to learn from others. For example, infants readily imitate other people, but not inanimate objects. Even newborns imitate the facial expressions of others. And imitation quickly becomes more sophisticated, such that one-year-olds can often discern the goals of an act and use that information to guide their imitative behavior. Further, the general tendencies toward social concern and self-interest are specified and modified as children age. For example, children are taught that some categories of people are more deserving of social concern than others (see the references in n18).

Primate Behavior

One can also gain insight into human nature by examining the great apes with whom humans are most closely related. Richard Wrangham and Dale Peterson performed such an examination in their classic book *Demonic Males: Apes and the Origins of Human Violence* (1996; also see Wrangham, 2004). Much of the book focuses on chimpanzees, our closest relatives. Chimpanzees, like humans, commit much violence against members of their own species. They deliberately seek out and intentionally kill males in other groups of chimpanzees. In particular, chimpanzee males will enter the territory of a neighboring group and kill the males they encounter, especially lone males. Chimpanzee males also fight with other males in their own group, particularly over the issue of rank or dominance. And chimpanzee males regularly batter females in their group. Chimpanzees stand in contrast to bonobos, a "gentle ape" that engages in little violence. Gorillas and orangutans, the remaining great apes, have high levels of certain types of violence–but do not engage in the inter-group violence that characterizes chimpanzees.

Wrangham and Peterson argue that the violence exhibited by certain apes is rooted in the evolutionary process. That is, such violence increases the chances that the perpetrators will survive and reproduce, passing their genes onto others. The inclination to violence thus becomes a part of the ape's "nature." This is not to say that the violence is consciously committed to increase the odds of survival or reproduction, but rather that the disposition for certain types of violence has this effect and so is selected for in the evolutionary process. Wrangham and Peterson further argue that the evolutionary forces that favored particular types of violence in chimpanzees are operative to some extent among humans.

Take the case of inter-group aggression. Chimpanzees are said to engage in such aggression because the costs are low and the benefits are high, thus conferring an adaptive advantage. Chimpanzees travel in groups of varying size looking for food. As a consequence, a larger group of chimpanzees sometimes encounters a smaller group or a lone chimpanzee from a neighboring territory. In such cases, there is little cost to attacking. There is also much benefit; the attacking chimpanzees may expand the territory where they regularly forage for food, obtain females from the other group, and weaken potential adversaries. None of the other great apes experience such circumstances. Humans, however, have experienced similar conditions for much of their evolutionary history (Wrangham, 2004). Humans regularly foraged for food, sometimes encountering smaller groups from neighboring territories. As such, there may be some "natural" inclination for inter-group aggression among people. The same may also be the case for within-group aggression. Like chimpanzees and certain other apes, human males compete with one another for status or rank. Those of higher rank are more likely to survive and reproduce, so there may also be a natural tendency among humans to aggressively vie for rank.

Wrangham and Peterson focus on the aggressive tendencies that we share with chimpanzees and certain other great apes. De Waal (2006a, b), however, argues that great apes and other primates also have a non-aggressive side, which we share as well (also see Tomasello, 2009). De Waal states that while evolutionary forces have favored aggressive traits and behavior in certain circumstances, they also favored concern for others, particularly kin and members of one's community. Such concern makes cooperative behavior possible, with such behavior increasing the ability of primates to find food and defend themselves against predators. De Waal draws on his extensive observations of primates, as well as the observations of others, to offer evidence for such social concern.

De Waal states that nonhuman primates often show concern for the pain of others, attempt to comfort injured others; try to avoid causing harm to others (even at some cost to themselves), and form alliances with others, coming to their aid in fights. These tendencies are more common with close others, although they are sometimes exhibited with strangers. To give an example, rhesus monkeys will refuse to pull a chain that delivers food if doing so shocks a companion. The monkeys, in fact, will come close to starving themselves in their effort to avoid harming their companion. In addition, certain nonhuman primates display a commitment to reciprocity. For example, they will share with others beyond their offspring, especially if these others have previously performed a service for them, such as grooming.

Based on these observations, de Waal challenges what he calls "Veneer Theory," or the idea that humans are naturally "asocial, even nasty creatures," with morality being "a cultural overlay, a thin veneer hiding an otherwise selfish and brutish nature" (2006a: 6). He instead argues that while people may have inherited certain aggressive tendencies, they have also inherited inclinations for empathy, sympathy, fairness, and reciprocity; traits that allow for the maintenance of close ties to and cooperation with others. So, once again, the evidence suggests that human nature is somewhat complicated, reflecting both social concern and self-interest.

Evolutionary Psychology

Those characteristics that comprise human nature are said to emerge out of the evolutionary process. Gazzaniga (2008:84) provides an overview of this process:

> According to the laws of natural selection, *for any characteristic to be selected in a competitive environment, it has to provide a survival advantage to the individual.* That advantage must manifest itself in a greater number of surviving offspring. The characteristic may allow the individual to be more successful at finding food (so s/he is stronger and healthier and hence can reproduce more and longer), at mating (so s/he will reproduce more), or at fighting off predators (s/he will live longer and be able to reproduce more). These characteristics are coded for in the individual's genes and are passed on to the next generation. Thus, *genes that code for any behavior that increases reproductive success will become more prevalent in the population.* (Emphasis in original)

Researchers have focused on the evolution of physical characteristics, but evolutionary psychologists argue that psychological characteristics may also provide a survival advantage and so be selected for.[20] For many years, it was widely felt that evolution selected for selfishness, since selfish individuals should be more likely to survive and reproduce than those who help others.[21] As Johnson et al. (2008:332) state: "Since genetic information is passed directly only from parents to offspring, any strategy [behavioral inclination] so foolish as to sacrifice itself for unrelated others will die a quick death." But at the same time, it is clear that people and other animals do not always act in a selfish manner; in fact, they sometimes help others—even non-kin—at a substantial cost to themselves. Darwin and others struggled to explain such behavior in terms of evolutionary theory.

Much progress has been made in this area in recent years. In particular, research suggests that socially concerned behaviors such as cooperation and helping others do provide a survival advantage in certain circumstances. Evolutionary psychologists explain the evolution of cooperation and helping behavior in several ways. One such way is through "kin selection." Because we share our genes with closely related kin, efforts to help our kin will contribute to the spread of our genes since these efforts help our kin survive and reproduce. Parents thus sacrifice for their children, with whom they share 50 percent of their DNA. But we also cooperate with and help non-kin.

Cooperating with non-kin provides a survival advantage if people are pursuing a common goal that they all achieve at the same time (e.g., hunting large game, defending against raiders). Also, cooperating with and helping non-kin provides a survival advantage if these others reciprocate at a later time. Cooperative endeavors are more efficient than individual efforts at addressing a range of adaptive problems. And there is a survival advantage in being able to turn to others for assistance during times of need.[22] Cooperation and helping behavior, however, provide a survival advantage only if the others do in fact reciprocate in an equitable manner. And it is said that several traits have evolved to ensure that this occurs. In particular, individuals have strong inclinations for equity/fairness, for the identification and punishment of free-riders, and—according to certain accounts—for the internalization and enforcement of social norms that promote cooperation (see especially Bowles and Gintis, 2003). Further, it is argued that the inclination to help non-kin, even at some personal cost, has evolved because it is a particularly effective way to establish a reputation for trustworthiness and generosity, thereby increasing the likelihood that others will cooperate with and assist us.

So evolutionary forces may have favored cooperative and helping behavior in certain circumstances, particularly with respect to kin and members of ones' in-group. But at the same time, evolutionary forces have favored self-interested and aggressive behavior in other circumstances, particularly with respect to out-groups and the competition between males for rank (see Schaller and Neuberg, 2008). Further, evolutionary forces are such that we can expect some variation in cooperative/helping behavior across individuals. Such variation is partly due to random genetic mutations. In addition, when cooperators dominate a population, a minority of cheaters can survive and reproduce, taking advantage of the benefits produced by the cooperators. The cooperators will of course try to detect and punish these free-riders, but the free-riders will take steps to avoid detection and punishment. The result is an arms race, with the cooperators and free-riders continually trying to outmaneuver one another.

Finally, it should be noted that evolutionary psychology also provides some support for the assumption that people are blank slates. Humans live in a complex and variable environment, and so characteristics that favor learning and the ability to adapt have much survival value. Humans, compared to other animals, have an enormous ability to learn and adapt, as reflected in our large brains, long period of dependence on caregivers, and traits that favor learning and adaptation, such as the inclination and ability to imitate others and to engage in rational deliberation when problematic circumstances arise (see Bandura, 2001). The research on evolutionary psychology is important because it helps explain *why* characteristics such as the ability to learn, social concern, and self-interest may have a biological basis.

Biological Research

If the above characteristics are biologically based to a substantial degree, we would expect to find some biological foundation for them. This foundation may be genetic, such that there is evidence that the characteristics are inherited. And the foundation may be reflected in the biological structure and functioning of people, particularly brain structure and functioning. Research on the biological foundations of traits and behaviors is at an early stage, but it is progressing rapidly. There is good reason to believe that many of the traits and behaviors discussed in the previous sections have some biological basis.

Most of the genetic research has examined the extent to which variation in traits such as empathy, conformity, and self-interest is genetically based. Studies suggest that genetic inheritance plays a substantial role in explaining variation in these traits, as well as in the major dimensions of personality more generally. More recently, molecular genetic studies have begun to point to the specific genes associated with certain of these traits.[23] Researchers have also made much progress in linking many of these traits to brain structure and functioning.[24] For example, researchers have found that damage to certain sections of the brain severely reduces such aspects of social concern as empathy and self-control, with the damaged individuals often acting in a strictly self-interested manner.[25] Related to this, traits such as empathy and self-control are related to age and sex, with the relationship at least partly explained by biological factors (see Pinker, 2002; Wright et al., 2008).

It is important to note, however, that individual traits are not fully rooted in biology.[26] The latest data suggest that both genetic and environmental factors are important, frequently having both independent and interactive effects on the traits that individuals possess. Most notably, the environment often plays a role in determining whether genetic propensities are "expressed" or activated. Genes may influence how individuals respond to certain environmental stimuli. Certain genes for example, may increase the likelihood that individuals respond to abuse with aggressive behavior. Whether the genes lead to aggressive behavior, then, is influenced by whether individuals are exposed to abusive environments.[27]

Finally, much research suggests that humans are biologically equipped to learn from others and adapt to the environment. As Bandura (2001:22) states, these abilities depend upon "specialized neurophysiological structures and mechanisms that have evolved over time. These advanced neural systems are specialized for channeling attention, detecting the causal structure of the outside world, transforming that information into abstract representations, and integrating and using them for adaptive purposes" (also see Pinker, 2002).

An Integrated View of Human Nature and Its Implications for Criminology

Human nature is clearly complex. It is not the case that people are simply self-interested and rational, or socially concerned, or blank slates. There is substantial evidence for all three views. This complexity is reflected in the statements of those who have closely examined human nature:

> We're full of contradictions. We know competition as well as co-operation, selfishness as well as sociability, strife as well as harmony. Human nature is inherently multidimensional. (de Waal, 2006b:10)
>
> Together with all their nasty and brutish motives, all peoples display a host of kinder, gentler ones; a sense of morality, justice, and community, an ability to anticipate consequences when choosing how to act, and a love of children, spouses, and friends. (Pinker, 2002:58)
>
> We have a moral sense . . . [but it] must compete with other senses that are natural to humans—the desire to survive, acquire possessions, indulge in sex, or accumulate power—in short, with self-interest narrowly defined. (Wilson, 1993:12)
>
> Are humans by nature kind or mean-spirited? As always in these types of all-encompassing questions, the answer is a bit of both. (Tomasello, 2009:44)

Complicating matters even more is that there is some variation across individuals and perhaps groups (e.g., males and females) in social concern and self-interest, with this variation having some biological basis. Given this complexity, one wonders whether there is such a thing as human nature, defined in terms of universal or near universal traits.

Drawing on the above research, I believe that there are certain statements we can make about the nature of the vast majority of people. With respect to the assumption of *social concern*, these statements include:

- People care about others, particularly those in their in-group. They empathize with others, are inclined to help innocent others in distress, and are inclined to avoid causing personal harm to innocent others, even at some personal cost to themselves.
- People desire close emotional ties to others, particularly kin and members of their in-group.
- People care about their rank or status with others, particularly in-group members.
- People are inclined to cooperate with others, so long as these others reciprocate in an equitable manner. People are inclined to punish free riders or those who do not reciprocate, reflecting their strong sense of fairness.
- People are able to distinguish intentional from unintentional acts, as well as acts that cause physical/psychological harm from those that simply violate social conventions. Related to this, people are inclined to sanction those who intentionally cause harm and, to a lesser extent, those who violate social conventions.
- People are concerned with notions of purity, particularly in the areas of eating and sex.
- People are inclined to conform to those around them and to social norms more generally.
- Some individuals and perhaps groups are more socially concerned than others, with this variation in social concern being in part biologically based. But the large share of individuals have at least some limited social concern. As Bouchard (2005:70) states, "humans are all alike . . . [but] they vary in their likeness." The very small percentage of individuals who are completely lacking in one or more aspects of social concern are viewed as "abnormal"; examples include extreme psychopaths and severely autistic individuals.

Thus, there is some evidence for social concern, although this concern is largely directly toward in-group members. In fact, another major characteristic of human nature is the tendency to divide others into in-groups and out-groups, and to favor in-group members. The factors used to distinguish in-groups from out-groups can sometimes be quite trivial, and they often vary over time and across societies. However, kin and those in our immediate community are usually part of our in-group.

While humans show much social concern, particularly for those in their in-group, they also exhibit much *self-interest*. In particular:

- The mentioned inclinations for social concern are often qualified by considerations of self-interest. For example, people are less likely to help others, conform to social norms, and sanction free-riders if the personal costs of doing so are high.
- Considerations of self-interest are particularly important in certain circumstances, such as competitions for rank and scarce resources, and interactions with those in out-groups.
- While much human behavior is motivated by forces of which we are not consciously aware and is habitual in nature, individuals are inclined to engage in conscious deliberation when considering crime. Such deliberation is rational to a *limited* degree, with the costs and benefits of crime receiving *some* consideration. The decision to engage in crime, however, is also affected by factors other than costs and benefits, particularly those having to do with social concern (e.g., our reluctance to harm innocent others, desire to conform to socials norms).
- Some individuals and perhaps groups are more self-interested than others, with the variation in self-interest being in part biologically based.

Finally, people also exhibit a strong ability and inclination to learn from others, providing some support for the "blank slate" assumption. In particular:

- People learn much from others. The evolutionary process, in fact, has equipped people with an extraordinary ability and inclination to learn and consciously adapt to their environment.
- Related to this, the inclinations for social concern and self-interest are specified, modified, and stressed to varying degrees in social groups. For example, characteristics such as the extent of cooperation in a society affect the degree of social concern and self-interest shown by individuals.

These statements about human nature should of course be viewed as tentative, given the limitations in the research noted earlier. It is quite likely that they will be revised and extended as more research is completed. Criminologists need to keep abreast of this research, since the nature of human nature has important implications for the discipline. I conclude with a brief discussion of certain of these implications.

Implications: The Definition of Crime

Crimes have been defined as acts that cause blameworthy harm, are condemned by the public, and/or are subject to state sanction. And it was noted that acts are frequently, but not always, condemned and sanctioned because they are seen as blameworthy harms. The research on human nature suggests that people are naturally inclined to view some acts as blameworthy harms, particularly those that intentionally cause direct harm to innocent others. Further, people are inclined to condemn and sanction those acts. Thus there is some basis in human nature for the definition of crime presented in chapter 2. It is important, however, to distinguish between the different types of crime described in that chapter. Of the several types, people have the strongest natural inclination to view "core crimes" as blameworthy harms. Core crimes include murder, rape, and theft. All involve direct harm and are readily perceived as intentional. It is therefore no surprise that such crimes are condemned in most or all societies. Other types of crime include "unrecognized blameworthy harms" (blameworthy harms that are not condemned or sanctioned) and "constructed crimes" (acts that cause little blameworthy harm but are condemned and sanctioned). A full understanding of the origins of these types of crime requires that we consider the nature of society (see chap. 5). But the research on human nature also provides some insight here.

Consider blameworthy harms that are not publicly condemned or sanctioned. Many of the crimes in this category involve indirect or impersonal harms, which do not provoke the strong emotional reaction that personal harm does. Corporate crimes frequently fall into this category. Also, many of these crimes are committed against categories of people that elicit little social concern, such as the members of out-groups and those viewed as free riders. Examples include blameworthy harms committed against other race/ethnic groups, wartime adversaries, and members of the lower class. As argued in chapter 2, criminologists need to convince the public and policymakers that these blameworthy harms should be condemned and sanctioned; but criminologists should draw on the research on human nature in doing so (see Singer, 2000, for a discussion of human nature and social policy). For example, they should use personal examples when arguing that corporate crime causes harm. And they should attempt to convince others that certain categories of people are worthy of full moral consideration.

The research on human nature also sheds light on those relatively harmless acts that are condemned by the public and/or sanctioned by the state. In some cases, these acts violate social conventions. As indicated, people are naturally inclined to conform to social norms; an inclination that helps explain the criminalization of certain relatively harmless acts. At the same time, people are usually able to distinguish acts that violate social conventions from those that cause real harm. So we would expect acts that violate social conventions to be less severely condemned and sanctioned, which is typically the case. In other cases, the condemnation and sanction of relatively harmless acts may be justified by appealing to notions of purity. As we have seen, humans have some natural concern over purity, particularly involving food and sex. There is an evolutionary basis for this, since the consumption of tainted food and incest with close relatives reduces adaptive success. Others sometimes tap into this concern by condemning harmless acts as impure or filthy (e.g., gay marriage). In still other cases, the condemnation of relatively harmless is justified by linking them to out-groups or free-riders. The criminalization of certain drugs in the United States, for example, was facilitated by linking them to out-groups such as Mexican immigrants and portraying drug users as free-riders (Auerhahn, 1999).

Implications: Agency versus Determinism

The research on human nature is also relevant to the debate over whether crime involves the exercise of agency. Chapter 3 stated that individuals on the verge of crime are motivated to engage in the conscious deliberation at the core of agency. One reason for this is that crime often raises moral issues for them, causing them to stop and think. The research on human nature provides some support for this. Many crimes are at odds with our natural inclination to avoid causing direct harm to innocent others. Many crimes are also at odds with the moral inclinations of others, including close others; which further prompts conscious deliberation. And even crimes that cause indirect harm may prompt conscious deliberation, provided that individuals are aware of the harm.

It is important, however, to make a subtle but critical point: while engaging in crime typically involves the exercise of agency, *not* engaging in *core* crimes is likely an intuitive response for most people, involving little or no agency. Agentic behavior occurs only when individuals reach the point of seriously considering crime, but many never reach this point because they have a natural inclination against committing acts that cause direct harm to innocent others (mostly "core crimes"). This argument runs counter to a key assertion of certain control theorists, namely that all individuals are motivated to engage in crime.

Implications: Causes and Control of Crime

All Crime Theories Are Relevant. As discussed, each conception of human nature has some merit. Individuals are socially concerned; among other things, they are reluctant to directly harm innocent others and to violate social norms. We must therefore explain why some individuals act against this concern by engaging in crime, particularly crimes that cause direct harm or are strongly condemned/sanctioned. We cannot assume that crime simply occurs when social controls are weak or the "lid is off." Strain, social learning, and rational choice theories have much to say about the motivation for crime.[28] Strain theories state that individuals are pressured into crime by the strains or stressors they face.[29] These strains create negative emotions, which in turn create pressure for corrective action. Individuals feel bad and want to do something about it, and crime is one possible response. Crime may be used to reduce or escape from strains, seek revenge against the source of strain, or alleviate negative emotions (i.e., through illicit drug use). Social learning and rational choice theories state that individuals are enticed into crime by the expectation of reinforcement or pleasure. In particular, some individuals are in circumstances that lead them to expect that crime will provide significant benefits, including such things as money, status, and excitement.

Individuals also pursue their self-interests, although they do so against a backdrop of social concern. Considerations of self-interest are particularly important when dealing with those belonging to out-groups, for whom we have less concern; when competing with others for rank or scarce resources; and when considering whether to commit those crimes classified as "unrecognized blameworthy harms" (see chap. 2). As such, it is also important to examine those factors that constrain individuals from pursuing their interests in a criminal manner. Deterrence, self – and social control, social learning, and rational choice theories are relevant here; each describes certain of the individual and social controls that restrain the criminal pursuit of self-interest. A breakdown in these controls is usually not the sole cause of crime, given the social concern just described. But weak controls certainly facilitate the commission of crime. That is to say, individuals motivated to act against their social concern still give some consideration to the costs of crime.

Finally, individuals have much to learn, along with a strong desire and ability to learn from others. Among other things, the general inclinations for social concern and self-interest are specified and modified through social learning. This learning may influence the stress placed on social concern and self-interest, the categories of people seen as worthy of social concern, what acts are viewed as harmful, and what justifications and excuses are accepted for harm. This is not to say that individuals are completely malleable. As noted earlier, for example, people have a strong natural inclination to view acts that cause direct harm to innocent others as wrong. But there is nevertheless much room for social influence; thus, criminologists must also examine the ways in which social learning promotes crime and conformity. This is of course the central concern of social learning and differential association theories.

In brief, all major theories of crime are relevant. And a complete explanation of crime must therefore integrate these theories, describing the relationship between them and how they work together to affect crime. My book *Why Do Criminals Offend?* (Agnew, 2005) begins this task. Most notably, I argue there that crime is most likely when individuals experience strain, are low in control, *and* have learned to engage in crime. I further argue that the leading causes of crime impact each of these mechanisms: they create strain, weaken controls, and involve the social learning of crime, which is the reason that they are the leading causes of crime. For example, harsh parental discipline creates much strain, weakens ties to parents, and models aggressive behavior. This integrated theory, however, is incomplete in many ways. For example, it focuses on the explanation of street crimes (see chap. 2) and says little about the role of agency in explaining crime (see chap. 3).

Criminologists Must Take Account of Individual Variation in Social Concern and Self-Interest. While the vast majority of individuals are both socially concerned and self-interested, levels of concern and self-interest do vary across individuals. This variation is partly a function of biological factors, although it·is also influenced by social factors. And this variation challenges the leading crime theories, which tend to assume a uniform human nature. All individuals are said to be self-interested, socially concerned, *or* blank slates to roughly the same degree. This assumption is partly responsible for the neglect of bio-psychological factors in criminology. If human nature does not vary, it is not necessary to consider it when explaining crime. But self-interest and social concern do vary, and such variation is quite relevant to the explanation of crime. We would generally expect self-interested individuals to be more likely to engage in crime and socially concerned individuals less likely. Bio-psychological factors therefore need to be a central part of any integrated theory of crime.

Consider social concern. Social concern has several components: a desire for close emotional ties to and the respect of certain others, an inclination to cooperate with others, empathy, a willingness to help innocent others in distress, a reluctance to cause direct harm to innocent others, and a strong tendency to conform. We would expect each of these components to reduce the likelihood of crime, particularly among those who associate with conventional others. These components may have a direct effect on crime, and they may have an indirect effect through factors such as attachment to conventional others, commitment to school and work, the belief that crime is wrong, and self-control. For example, individuals with a strong desire for close ties to others are more likely to form attachments to parents and teachers. Those with strong desires for conformity, cooperation, and respect are more likely to develop strong commitments to school and work. And all of the above traits directly or indirectly contribute to the development of self-control. Criminologists, however, seldom consider these components of social concern in their research; although certain of these components have been examined by psychologists (e.g., Schaffer et al., 2009; Jolliffe and Farrington, 2007).

Likewise, we would expect variation in self-interest to impact crime. This reflects the fact that the components of self-interest are generally the converse of those that characterize social concern. For example, those high in self-interest have little empathy for others.[30] Many of the studies cited earlier provide suggestions about how to measure self-interest and social concern, through the use of both surveys and experiments. And measures of these concepts should be routinely included in crime research. In this area, it is important to note that while the concept of self-interest overlaps somewhat with Gottfredson and Hirschi's (1990) concept of self-control; there is a critical distinction between the two. Self-control focuses on traits that allow for the restraint of self-interest; traits such as the ability to delay gratification and to pause and consider the possible consequences of planned acts. But it is assumed that the underlying level of self-interest is high; in fact, a basic tenet of self-control theory is that all individuals are strongly self-interested. That is, self-interest is considered a constant rather than a variable.

Criminologists Must Also Take Account of Circumstantial Variation in Social Concern and Self-Interest. The levels of social concern and self-interest also vary across circumstances. As noted earlier, self-interest is greater (and social concern is lower) when individuals are interacting with the members of out-groups, when males are competing over rank, when individuals are competing over scarce resources, and when the behavior being considered does not involve direct harm to innocent others and is not strongly condemned/sanctioned (e.g., "unrecognized blameworthy harms"). We would therefore expect crime to be more common in such circumstances, since the pursuit of self-interest is generally more conducive to crime than is social concern (with an exception to be noted shortly). The quantitative studies that dominate mainstream criminology, however, rarely ask individuals about the in-group/out-group distinctions they make or their competition with others for rank and resources. Further, such studies typically focus on core crimes, which cause direct harm and are strongly condemned and sanctioned.

The qualitative research in criminology, however, suggests that the circumstances mentioned are quite relevant to the explanation of crime. A central theme in this research is that crime often emerges out of the competition between males for rank or status. This is especially true in environments where legitimate opportunities for status are limited (e.g., Anderson, 1999; Messerschmidt, 1993; Short and Strodtbeck, 1965). Also, the distinction between in-groups and out-groups looms large in such research, particularly the research on gangs. Gang members make a sharp distinction between in-groups and out-groups, and they show little social concern (but much hostility) to those belonging to out-groups or other gangs (e.g., Decker and Van Winkle, 1996; Miller, 2001). Certain research also suggests that individuals routinely engage in a range of "unrecognized blameworthy harms" that serve their immediate interests, such as the consumption of meat raised on factory farms (Agnew, 1998) and a range of activities that contribute to climate change (e.g., Freund and Martin, 2008). Quantitative researchers would do well to devote more attention to those circumstances that influence variation in self-interest and social concern.

While social concern generally inhibits crime, there is one major circumstance where it may promote crime: situations where socially concerned individuals are encouraged by close others to engage in crime.[31] Social concern does involve an inclination to avoid harming innocent others, but it also involves a desire for close ties to and respect from others as well as a strong inclination to conform. These later features of social concern may lead individuals to engage in crime when they associate with others who model crime, encourage crime, and reinforce crime with acceptance and status. The classic experiment on "Obedience to Authority" cited by Milgram (1983) illustrates this point; many individuals delivered what they thought were painful, even life-threatening shocks to another person. While they often hesitated and expressed misgivings when doing so, their desire to conform to the instructions of an authority figure were sufficient to overcome their reluctance to cause harm. So we would expect certain elements of social concern to be positively associated with crime among individuals in criminal groups. Differentiation association and social-learning theories focus on such groups, but they have not devoted much attention to how the components of social concern influence the effect of these groups on crime.

In sum, research examining the individual and circumstantial variation in social concern and self-interest should dramatically improve efforts to explain crime, since it will focus on a range of factors that are either ignored in quantitative criminology or erroneously assumed to be similar across individuals.

Policy Implications. As Singer (2000) argues, the effectiveness of social policies can be enhanced by taking account of human nature. For example, the research on rationality indicates that individuals usually do not carefully estimate the probability that behaviors will produce various outcomes. Rather, they often roughly estimate probabilities based on anecdotal information. This suggests that a carefully chosen and well-publicized example of a social sanction may do much to deter crime—even if the actual certainty of punishment remains unchanged. Perhaps the major policy implication to emerge from the research on human nature is the suggestion that social concern and self-interest are subject to influence. In particular, they are *general* traits and are specified, modified, and stressed to varying degrees in social groups. Given this, we might take steps to increase social concern and reduce self-interest.

The research on human nature suggests that we can influence the strength of both these traits. As indicated in the discussion of the Ultimatum game (see pages 89-91), the desire to cooperate and share is stronger in societies that are based on and stress cooperative endeavors. Conversely, self-interest is greater in societies that are based on and stress competitive individualism.

Certain critical criminologists make a similar point, stating that the intense competition associated with capitalism promotes self-interest, sometimes to the point of suppressing the natural concern that individuals have for one another (e.g., Bonger, 1969; Currie, 1997, 1998). Similarly, Messner and Rosenfeld's (2007) institutional anomie theory states that both the "American Dream" and the highly competitive economic system in the United States encourage the pursuit of personal interests, particularly material interests, with little concern for others. It is difficult to alter the cultural values and economic organization of total societies. But social concern might be cultivated in smaller programs, for example, those conducted in schools, religious institutions, business organizations, and prisons. Drawing on social learning theory, such programs might reinforce and model social concern, as well as present beliefs fostering social concern. The effectiveness of such programs will of course be limited by the nature of the larger society, but these programs might nevertheless moderate the intense self-interest that characterizes many societies.

We might also broaden the scope of social concern. This can be done by altering views about what constitutes harmful behavior (see Pinker, 2002). While a core group of acts are seen as harmful in most places, there is much variation around this core, as we read in chapter 2. Criminologists and others can help broaden the definition of harm by calling attention to those "unrecognized blameworthy harms" described in that chapter. In addition, an effort can be made to challenge certain of the justifications and excuses that individuals accept for the infliction of harm.[32] As an example, several programs have had some success in challenging "rape myths" or the justifications and excuses that some males accept for rape (Anderson and Whiston, 2005).

The scope of social concern may also be broadened by influencing who is seen as worthy of concern (see Pinker, 2002; Singer, 1981). Certain categories of people are often defined as members of out-groups or, in extreme cases, as less than human (Bandura, 1990; Brewer, 1998). As such, they are seen as less worthy of social concern. Expanding the range of people seen as worthy of social concern may do much to reduce crime (e.g., Laham, 2008; Pinker, 2002, Singer, 1981). In fact, it has been suggested that the major factor accounting for the large reduction in violence in recent centuries is the tendency to view an ever-widening circle of people—including people in different race/ethnic, class, and gender groups—as worthy of social concern (Pinker, 2002; Singer, 1981; Wilson, 1993). Several factors are said to account for this "expanding moral circle," including increased knowledge about and cooperation with the members of different groups. The literatures on prejudice/discrimination and in-group biases contain many recommendations for further increasing the size of the moral circle (e.g., Aberson and Haag, 2007; Dovidio and Gaertner, 2010; Pettigrew and Tropp, 2006).

In sum, we may be able to do much to shape human nature by fostering social concern and reducing self-interest. Doing so would build significantly on current policy initiatives, most of which focus on restraining the criminal expression of self-interest through the threat of punishment.

Conclusion

The assumptions that criminologists make about human nature are critical; they have a large effect on both the causes of crime that are considered and the control strategies that are recommended. As was the case in previous chapters, we find that the assumptions made by criminologists are overly simplistic. Human nature is complex. It is not the case that people are simply self-interested, or socially concerned, or blank slates. At the most basic level, people tend to show some social concern, largely but not entirely with respect to members of their in-group; but people also pursue their interests against this backdrop of social concern. The inclinations for social concern and self-interest, however, are general and there is much room for social learning. This more complex view of human nature also helps pave the way for a unified criminology. It suggests that all of the major theories have some role to play in the explanation of crime-as well as suggesting several new directions for research and policy.

5

The Nature of Society

Is Society Characterized by Consensus or Conflict?

For the better part of three decades, the car plant [in Lordstown, Ohio] was a seemingly endless source of trouble for General Motors. In the 1970s, the factory's 7,000 workers were so bitter toward management that thousands of Chevrolet Vega's rolled off the assembly line with slit upholstery and other damage. The hostility eventually led to a 22-day strike in 1972 that cost G.M. $150 million . . . today [the plant] is preparing to build a new compact car, the Chevrolet Cruze, that is integral to G.M.'s hopes of becoming a successful company again. United Automobile Workers' leaders in Lordstown, Detroit and other cities where clashes with management were once common have since decided that their only chance to survive in a global economy is to work with, not against, their employers . . . a new tone of cooperation has emerged at Lordstown.
—Bunkley, "Laboring to Survive"

Criminologists not only make assumptions about the nature of people but about the nature of society as well. Some assume that society is characterized by *consensus*. People hold similar values, have compatible interests or goals, and generally get along. Others assume that society is characterized by *conflict*. People in different groups hold different values, have incompatible interests, and often harm one another as they promote their values and pursue their interests.[1] Not surprisingly, these assumptions also have a large effect on the causes of crime that are considered and on the crime control policies that are recommended.

To elaborate, criminologists who adopt the *consensus perspective* state that the people in a society agree on core values; most notably, everyone agrees what behaviors should be defined as crimes and punished. People also have compatible interests; they pursue the same or interdependent goals, such that the pursuits of some people satisfy the needs of other people (e.g., farmers produce the food consumed by factory workers, who in turn produce the products used by farmers). And when people do compete with one another, they agree on the rules of competition. Those adopting the consensus perspective argue that crime stems from the fact that some people are unable or unwilling to abide by this consensus regarding values and interests. This usually occurs because those people are low in self– and social control. They are unable to restrain themselves when tempted to engage in crime, and they believe that they have little to lose by engaging in crime. Therefore, the best way to reduce crime is to instill self-control and increase social control.

Criminologists who adopt the *conflict perspective* state that groups within a society often disagree over core values, including what behaviors are wrong and should be defined as crimes. Further, groups often pursue conflicting interests. For example, business owners seek to increase their profits, often by reducing the size of their workforce and paying low wages. By contrast, workers seek to increase their wages. Those groups with the greatest power oppress others in the pursuit of their values and interests. According to this view, crime stems from this difference in values and the oppression of some groups by others. For example, some people commit criminal acts because they believe such acts are justified. And some engage in crime because they cannot find work or are paid very low wages. Therefore, the best way to control crime is to reduce group conflict and the negative consequences of such conflict, such as poverty.

The consensus and conflict perspectives are linked to the assumptions regarding human nature presented in chapter 4, but the links are more complex than might first be imagined (see Bernard, 1983, for an excellent discussion). For example, the assumption that people are self-interested seems quite compatible with the conflict perspective. Self-interested people are inclined to pursue their own interests, even if doing so harms others. And some researchers have in fact argued that individual self-interest causes conflict at the societal level (see Bernard, 1983). But the opposite argument has also been made. Drawing on the work of Hobbes, some argue that self-interested individuals realize that the unrestrained pursuit of their interests will result in a "war of all against all." They therefore reach a consensus that acts such as violence and theft are wrong and should be sanctioned. And they invest some authority in the state, which enforces this consensus by punishing acts of violence and theft. Enlightened self-interest at the individual level therefore leads to consensus at the societal level. So while assumptions regarding the nature of individuals and of society are certainly related, they are nevertheless distinct.

These assumptions are distinct because the nature of society depends not only on the nature of individuals but also on the nature of social arrangements. Self-interested individuals may create social arrangements that contribute to consensus. And socially concerned individuals may be subject to social arrangements that create conflict. In particular, some Marxist criminologists argue that individuals have much natural concern for one another, but that the economic organization of society puts some groups in conflict with others. Capitalism, for example, places business owners or capitalists in conflict with workers. The competition in capitalist societies is said to be so intense that it subverts human nature. That is, the underlying social concern of individuals is suppressed as they struggle to survive in a brutal environment and considerations of self-interest become dominant (see Bonger, 1969; Lanier and Henry, 2004).

This chapter begins by describing the basic assumptions of the consensus and conflict perspectives, as well as the implications of these assumptions for the causes and control of crime. Given space limitations, I present generic versions of each perspective, but I note those areas where the particular versions of the consensus or conflict perspective differ from one another. The next section discusses the evidence for each perspective, concluding that both have some support. I then present an outline for an integrated consensus/conflict theory, noting the questions that such a theory should address and the direction that researchers might take in answering these questions. The final section discusses the implications of this theory for the causes and control of crime.

The Consensus Perspective and Its Implications for Criminology

The consensus perspective has a long history; it was advanced by philosophers such as Aristotle and Hobbes as well as by such prominent social scientists as Durkheim and Parsons (see Bernard, 1983; Dillon, 2010). It is also at the core of several major crime theories, including classical and control theories (see especially Kornhauser, 1978). Further, the consensus perspective guides current efforts to control crime in the United States. This perspective makes the following assumptions about the nature of society.[2]

Value Consensus

Individuals and groups within a society agree on core values. Most importantly, they agree that certain behaviors—particularly acts of force and theft—are wrong and should be defined as crimes. While some attribute this consensus to the natural concern of people for one another (see chap. 4), it is usually said to result stem from enlightened self-interest. Most individuals realize that they can better pursue their interests if people refrain from crime and cooperate with one another. Not all individuals, however, hold this enlightened view or are able to act on it. Therefore, individuals form states, which sanction acts such as force and theft. Also, they make an effort to properly socialize and otherwise exercise social control over one another, further increasing the likelihood that everyone will accept and abide by this consensus. The vast majority of people are said to benefit from these arrangements, since they are protected from harm and able to pursue their interests.

Shared and Interdependent Interests: Agreement Regarding Competitive Rules

It is also said that individuals have compatible interests. They share certain interests, such as the protection of society from external and internal threats. And their interests are interdependent, such that the goals pursued by some contribute to goal achievement by others. For example, Kia recently opened an automobile manufacturing plant in my home state of Georgia. A range of businesses soon opened in the vicinity of the plant, including companies that supply parts to Kia and restaurants that cater to Kia workers. The people working in these different businesses depend on one another to survive. These shared values and compatible interests bind people together; making society possible.

At the same time, consensus theorists recognize that individuals and groups sometimes compete with one another. Two individuals, for example, may compete for the same job, or two groups may compete to get their candidate elected to political office. Consensus theorists, however, argue that people agree on the rules governing such competition; those rules prohibit the use of force and fraud, and specify procedures that are viewed as fair. Conceptions of fairness vary somewhat across societies but tend to have certain elements in common (see Wilson, 1993). For example, they specify that the competitive process should be impartial, such that decisions are based on the qualifications of candidates rather than factors unrelated to the position (such as race). Such rules benefit the society, since individuals are encouraged to realize their potential and positions are filled with the most qualified people. Such rules also reduce the likelihood that those who fare poorly in the competitive process will view the outcome as unjust and turn to crime.

The State as a Neutral Actor, Promoting Consensus

Consensus theorists argue that the state seeks to promote consensus in several ways, certain of which involve the criminal justice system. The state enacts and enforces laws that reflect and maintain the social consensus, including laws that define acts such as force and theft as crimes. And the state regulates the competitive process, ensuring fair competition between individuals and groups. For example, the state prohibits discrimination in areas such as hiring and the awarding of contracts. The state acts in a neutral manner when engaging in these activities, not showing favoritism toward particular individuals or groups.

Crime Results from the Failure to Participate in This Consensus

The large share of individuals are said to participate in this consensus. They share core values with one another, particularly their condemnation of violence and theft. They pursue shared and interdependent interests. And when they do compete with one another, they accept and abide by those rules ensuring that the competitive process is fair. But not all individuals participate in this consensus. Some possess traits that undermine their *ability* to participate in the consensus. Most notably, some individuals are low in self-control and so cannot restrain themselves when tempted to engage in crime. This trait may be genetically inherited from parents or result from biological harms such as head injury (Wright and Beaver, 2005; Wright et al., 2008). And this trait may stem from a breakdown in the socialization process, particularly the failure of parents and others to teach children to exercise self-control (Gottfredson and Hirschi, 1990; Pratt and Cullen, 2000; Pratt et al., 2004).

In addition, the failure to participate in this consensus may stem from a breakdown in social control (see Agnew, 2009). If individuals are to participate in the social consensus, they must be taught to condemn criminal acts. Such instruction occurs primarily in the family. Also, individuals must have a reason to participate in the consensus. In particular, they must form close ties to others, such as parents, teachers, and neighbors. And they must develop a "stake in conformity," such as a good education, a good job, and a positive reputation in the community. Such individuals are more likely to accept and follow social rules, since they care about others and have much to lose if they do not. Finally, individuals must believe that there is a reasonable chance that they will be caught and sanctioned if they violate the social consensus. Such sanctions may be informal, administered by people such as family members, neighbors, and employers. And they may be formal, administrated by the criminal justice system. Some individuals, however, were not taught to condemn crime, do not have close ties to conventional others, have little to lose if they engage in crime, and are in environments where the risk of sanction is low. These individuals have little *willingness* to participate in the social consensus.

It is important to note that consensus theorists explain crime largely in terms of individual traits and the individual's immediate environment, such as the family, school, and work environments. Less attention is paid to the larger social environment. And when consensus theorists do discuss the larger environment they argue that institutions such as the community, media, and government are not doing enough to promote and enforce the social consensus. For example, the residents in certain communities fail to exercise sufficient control over young people; the media fails to promote "wholesome" values; and the government is not tough enough on crime.

Groups Differences Are De-Emphasized

Crime does not stem from the fact that some groups approve of crime or oppress others in the pursuit of their interests. While the consensus in a society may be fragile and imperfect, it is nevertheless the case that the large share of people—regardless of group membership—condemn criminal acts, cooperate with one another, and (more or less) follow the "rules of the game" when competing. Further, the state does not favor some groups over others. For that reason, group differences are not central to the explanation of crime. Again, crime stems from low self-control and a breakdown in social control. These factors explain crime among all individuals in all groups.

Having said that, it is important to note that consensus theorists do recognize that group membership is sometimes correlated with weak self- and social control. Males, for example, are lower in self-control than females (Moffitt et al., 2001). And lower-class individuals are lower in certain types of social control; most notably, they are by definition less likely to have good educations and well-paid jobs. However, these differences are not attributed to the oppression of some groups by others. They are in part biologically based. Moffitt et al. (2001), for example, argue that males are lower in self-control partly for biological reasons. And these group differences in control stem from the shortcomings of individuals. For example, lower-class individuals lack well-paid jobs largely because they have fared poorly in the competitive process; a process that is generally open and fair. Thus, the existence of group differences in self – and social control does not challenge the consensus perspective.

The Best Way to Control Crime Is to Increase Self- and Social Control

The recommendations of consensus theorists for controlling crime are straightforward. It is necessary to make sure that individuals participate in the social consensus. This can be accomplished by strengthening self– and social control. Parents can be taught to better instill self-control in their children. Parents, school officials, and community organizations can increase social control. For example, they can establish close ties to juveniles, help juveniles do better in school and get good jobs, and teach juveniles to condemn crime. And a variety of programs have been instituted in these areas, many of which have shown some success in reducing crime (see Agnew, 2009; Farrington and Welsh, 2007; Greenwood, 2006). The state, too, can take steps to increase the certainty and severity of punishment. As indicated in chapters 3 and 4, the state has done much in this area over the last few decades. Certain of these efforts have also shown some success at reducing crime, particularly those focusing on the certainty of punishment (Agnew, 2009; Cullen and Agnew, 2011).

The Conflict Perspective

The image of society presented by the consensus perspective is compelling to many criminologists. People condemn crimes such as force and theft, pursue shared and interdependent interests, cooperating with one another in the process, and generally play by the "rules of the game" when competing. In fact, some argue that society would not be possible unless these assertions were true (see especially Kornhauser, 1978). Imagine, for example, a society where a significant percentage of the population believed that force was acceptable. The result would be the "war of all against all" that Hobbes described. Nevertheless, the conflict perspective presents a very different image of society. This perspective also has deep roots. It was advanced by philosophers such as Plato and Machiavelli, as well as by social theorists such as Marx and Dahrendorf (see Bernard, 1982; Dillon, 2010). And it is embraced by a large and diverse group of critical theorists in criminology. Its major assumptions include:[3]

Value Conflict

Groups often differ in their core values. Most notably, groups hold conflicting views about what acts should and should not be defined as crimes. Certain groups approve of acts that are legally defined as crimes; for example, they approve of gambling and certain types of drug use. And certain groups condemn acts that are legal; for example, they condemn those legal but blameworthy harms committed by corporations and states, such as environmental pollution and the torture of suspected terrorists (see chap. 2). There is even some disagreement regarding core crimes. While critical theorists would likely agree that all groups condemn the unconditional use of violence, rape, and theft, they point out that some groups are more likely than others to justify or excuse core crimes in certain conditions. For example, many males believe that husbands are justified in having forced sex with or raping their wives. In fact, it is legal for husbands to do so in many societies. This was the case in the United States until recently (Morash, 2006). Also, the members of certain groups are more likely than others to view violence as an acceptable response to a range of provocations or insults (e.g., Anderson, 1999; Waters, 2007).

Further, critical theorists argue that any consensus that now exists regarding the definition of crime may mask conflict in the past (see Chambliss and Zatz, 1993). In particular, while the public may now agree that certain acts should be defined as crimes, there may have been much disagreement over the status of such acts in the past. The current consensus may reflect the efforts of powerful groups to persuade others that the acts are harmful and should be punished. To illustrate, most individuals and groups now agree that opium use should be defined as a crime. This was not always the case, however. Opium use was legal in the United States during much of the 1800s. The criminalization of opium was spearheaded by certain powerful individuals and groups, particularly labor unions. These unions viewed the large number of Chinese immigrants in the western United States as an economic threat, and the unions condemned the opium smoking of these immigrants as part of an effort to portray them as morally depraved and dangerous. Similar accounts of group conflict explain the criminalization of cocaine, marijuana, and alcohol use (during Prohibition) (Auerhahn, 1999; also see Meier and Geis, 2006). Critical theorists therefore argue that researchers should not only examine contemporary views regarding crime but also the origin of such views as well.

Conflicting Interests

Perhaps the central argument of critical theorists is that groups have conflicting interests or goals. In fact, these conflicting interests are said to explain the value conflict just described. Groups tend to value those actions that advance their interests, even if those actions harm others outside the group. For example, many whites favored the subordination of blacks because it advanced their political status and, in some cases, economic interests (Dowdall, 2005). And groups tend to condemn those acts that threaten their interests. Many corporations, for example, are quite critical of efforts to unionize workers or limit pollution (Domhoff, 2005b). According to the conflict perspective, then, the interests that groups pursue shape their values. This stands in contrast to the consensus perspective, where values act as a check on the unrestrained pursuit of interests, with harmful acts being condemned.

What are the conflicting interests between groups? At the most general level, the members of advantaged groups want to maintain or enhance their advantages. These advantages may include material possessions, particularly money and property; status or prestige; and a range of rights and privileges, such as the right to vote. The members of less advantaged groups often want to improve their position. Since resources such as money are often limited, the result is conflict between the more and less advantaged. At a more specific level, critical theorists focus on the conflicting interests between a range of groups, including groups that differ in terms of class, gender, age, race/ethnicity, religion, and sexual orientation. Most recently, critical theorists have focused on the conflict between those states, corporate actors, and other groups that comprise the "world system" (e.g., Dillon, 2010; Kramer and Michalowski, 2005; Rothe et al., 2009). The conflicting interests between these various groups are often economic in nature, but they frequently involve other interests as well.

To elaborate, Marxist theorists focus on class groups, particularly the conflict between capitalists (business owners) and workers. These groups have conflicting economic interests: capitalists want to increase their profits; workers want to increase their wages. More recent versions of Marxist theory point to a more complex class structure in modern societies. For example, some argue that there are divisions within the capitalist class, with small business owners often having different economic interests than large business owners (e.g., Chambliss and Zatz, 1993; Dillon, 2010). Feminist theorists focus on the conflict between gender groups. Men often want to exercise control over the sexuality, reproduction, and childrearing activities of females. Females often want to control their own bodies and have the freedom to pursue work outside the home (e.g., Morash, 2006). Life-course theorists focus on the conflict between age groups, particularly between adults and adolescents. Adults often want to limit the freedom and resources of adolescents, while adolescents often want the rights and privileges of adulthood, such as autonomy, respect, and money (e.g., Agnew, 2003). Race theorists of course focus on the conflict between race and ethnic groups, with this conflict often involving economic, political, status, and other interests (e.g., Bobo and Hutchings, 1996; Dillon, 2010; Gabbidon, 2010).

The Social Origins of Conflicting Interests

Certain critical theorists have explained these conflicting interests in terms of human nature. People are said to be self-interested, which leads those in advantaged groups to protect their advantages and those in disadvantaged groups to strive for more (see Bernard, 1983; Einstadter and Henry, 2006). Most critical theorists, however, are skeptical of biologically based arguments (see Taylor et al., 1973). Instead, critical theorists focus on the social causes of conflicting interests. These causes include the economic organization of societies, cultural beliefs and values, and the history of group relations. Marxist criminologists make the most developed arguments in this area. They contend that the economic organization of society is the major factor promoting conflicting interests. Capitalism pits business owners against workers, since business owners must maximize their profits if they are to survive, while workers must increase their wages. To give another example, the cultural system is said to promote conflicting interests between blacks and whites. Blacks are frequently portrayed as dangerous by the media and other sources, which fosters the desire of whites to exercise control over them, particularly through the criminal justice system. Blacks, of course, are resistant to such efforts at control.

Critical theorists argue that the importance of social causes is demonstrated by the substantial variation in the extent and nature of conflicting interests across societies and over time. The views of men and women regarding appropriate gender roles, for example, have become more similar over the last few decades in the United States. Males are now much more likely to state that they should share household responsibilities with women, that it is acceptable for women to work outside the home, and that women are suited for politics (Bolzendahl and Meyers, 2004; Carter et al., 2009). These changes are not easily explained by human nature, which is fairly constant across societies and over long periods. These changes, however, are related to changing social conditions, such as the increased participation of women in the labor force. (Men with spouses in the labor force hold more equalitarian gender role attitudes; among other things, these men are more aware of gender discrimination, and they benefit if their wives are able to secure higher wages).

Group Differences in Power Lead to Oppression

Not only do groups differ in their interests but in their power as well, with power defined in terms of the ability to produce intended effects (see Domhoff, 2005a). There are several bases of power, including physical strength, numbers, knowledge/expertise, material resources, organization, and legitimate authority (see Agnew, 1990; Domhoff, 2005a for overviews). Typically, advantaged groups have more power than less advantaged groups. Advantages such as money and status are a source of power, and power is used to secure additional advantages. Researchers, in fact, often measure the power of groups in terms of the advantages they possess (Domhoff, 2005a).

Some critical theorists state that certain groups—most notably capitalists—have a monopoly or near monopoly on power. Further, these groups are said to be cohesive and well organized, such that group members agree on their interests and carefully develop strategies to pursue them. Others state that power is more widely dispersed among groups and that groups are sometimes characterized by division and a lack of careful planning. But all critical theorists state that advantaged groups use their power to enhance their advantage and that, in doing so, they oppress the members of less advantaged groups. Oppression is said to be especially likely when members of the advantaged group view other groups as a threat (see Bobo and Hutchings, 1996; Gabbidon, 2010).

This oppression may take several forms. It may involve those sorts of acts that one typically thinks of when the term "oppression" is used. Such acts include physical violence, the seizure of property, and the segregation or expulsion of those in the disadvantaged group. Oppression, however, is often less blatant. It may involve the creation of institutional arrangements that favor those in the advantaged group. For example, the occupational system may be structured such that those in the advantaged group are given preference in hiring, particularly for better paid and more prestigious jobs; are provided with more supportive work environments; are paid more for the same work; and are more likely to be promoted, even after relevant qualifications are taken into account. To illustrate, Bobbitt-Zeher (2007) found that college-educated men in their twenties earn about $4,400 a year more on average than college-educated women in the same age group, even after a host of factors related to educational credentials are taken into account. Oppression may also involve cultural practices that serve to maintain the position of those in the advantaged group. Such practices may involve the indoctrination of those in the disadvantaged group, so they come to accept their disadvantage (e.g., females are told that it is God's will that they stay at home and obey their fathers and husbands). They may also involve efforts to devalue or dehumanize those in the disadvantaged group, such that their disadvantage and negative treatment are seen as deserved (e.g., blacks are portrayed as dangerous).

The State Is a Biased Actor, Promoting the Interests of Powerful Groups

Powerful groups attempt to control or influence the state in an effort to advance their interests. Critical theorists in criminology have focused on the manner in which powerful groups influence criminal justice policy. Such groups influence the definition of crime, working to criminalize acts that threaten their interests and maintain the legality of acts that advance their interests, even if such acts harm others (see chap. 2). Such groups also influence the administration of the criminal law. Laws are more rigorously enforced against the members of less powerful groups, particularly when such groups pose a threat. For example, laws may be more vigorously enforced against minority group members when they are large in size, are making political gains, or are suffering from high rates of unemployment.

There is some disagreement among critical theorists regarding the relationship between powerful groups and the state (see Chambliss and Zatz, 1993; Domhoff, 2005b; Lynch and Michalowski, 2006). Some critical theorists claim that the state is fully controlled by the capitalist class and always acts in the interest of this class. They claim that this is the case even when the state passes legislation that appears to challenge the capitalist class, such as laws protecting the environment or promoting the safety of workers. It is said that such laws are designed to reduce discontent among members of the working class by fostering the impression that the state is protecting their interests. But, in fact, such laws are never enforced in a vigorous manner. Other critical theorists claim that the state is partly independent of the capitalist class. The state usually acts in the interest of this class but sometimes yields to popular pressure and acts to restrain the capitalist class. While such actions usually run counter to the immediate interests of capitalists, they help ensure the long-term survival of capitalism by reducing the likelihood of working-class revolt. Still other critical theorists claim that power is more widely dispersed; no group controls or dominates the state. Rather, a range of groups compete with one another to influence the state, with these groups varying according to the issue under consideration (e.g., abortion, gun control, the environment). The more powerful groups usually win out in these struggles, but no one group has a general monopoly on power.

It Is Critical to Consider Multiple Groups When Studying Group Conflict

There is some debate over whether the conflict between certain groups is more central than that between others. Most notably, Marxist theorists argue that class conflict has a fundamental impact on all areas of life and underlies other forms of conflict, such as gender and race conflict. An increasingly common view, however, is that it is important to consider multiple groups when studying group conflict. The nature of group conflict is a not simply function of class or gender or race/ethnicity or other group characteristics, but rather it is a function of all of these.[4] For example, Bowleg et al. (2003) interviewed a group of black lesbians and found that the oppression they experienced was influenced by their race, gender, and sexual orientation. Among other things, the black lesbians reported that they were sometimes stopped by the police and followed around stores (because of their race), were subject to sexist remarks on the street and were paid less at work (because of their sex), and were disowned by family members and rejected by their church (because of their sexual orientation). Given findings such as these, critical theorists are becoming more likely to take an "intersectional" approach when studying group conflict, with multiple group memberships being considered.

Crime Results from Group Conflict

Group conflict influences the extent and nature of crime in several ways. The first is through its effect on the definition of crime. As noted in chapter 2, crimes are defined as acts that cause blameworthy harm, are condemned by the public, or are sanctioned by the state. Group conflict influences what acts are condemned and sanctioned as "crimes." This effect is extremely important. As critical theorists point out, many "blameworthy harms" are not condemned or sanctioned. This is especially the case for those harms that advance the interests of powerful groups or are disproportionately committed by the members of such groups. Thus, extraordinarily harmful acts such as environmental pollution are often not defined as crimes (see the discussion of "unrecognized blameworthy harms" in chap. 2). Those blameworthy harms disproportionately committed by the members of less powerful groups, however, are likely to be condemned and sanctioned. Thus, acts that cause little blameworthy harm are sometimes condemned and/or sanctioned, particularly when they threaten the interests or values of powerful groups (see the discussion of "constructed crimes" and "repressive state crimes" in chap. 2). China, for example, has imprisoned large numbers of people for expressing criticism of the government (Amnesty International, 2010). And the Taliban have banned women from leaving their homes unless accompanied by a close male relative (Feminist Majority Foundation, 2010).

Group conflict also influences whether people actually commit crimes (as defined in chap. 2). Consider those crimes committed by powerful groups. At the most general level, such crimes are committed as these groups try to advance their interests. Business owners, for example, may produce unsafe products in the pursuit of profit. And the state may restrict freedom of speech or engage in genocide as it tries to control those who threaten its power. To be more specific, group conflict may contribute to crimes by the powerful in several ways:

- Powerful groups try to ensure that the harmful acts they commit are not publicly condemned or sanctioned by the state. This reduces the social control to which they are subject, particularly direct control by the public and state. And when direct control is low, crime is more likely.
- Powerful groups try to evade or minimize sanctions for the criminal acts they commit. Among other things, the members of powerful groups may hire skilled lawyers, exploit their connections with state representatives, and justify the harmful acts they commit through the media. These actions also reduce direct control.
- Group conflict contributes to high levels of perceived strain among the members of powerful groups. Group members feel that their advantaged position is being threatened, and they engage in harmful acts both to defend their privileged position and to seek revenge against those who would harm them. The most extreme example being genocide (see Maier-Katkin et al., 2009).

- Group conflict contributes to cultural values and beliefs that are conducive to crime. At the most general level, such conflict promotes an emphasis on the pursuit of one's interests, with little regard for the welfare of others (Bonger, 1969; Currie, 1997, 1998; Messner and Rosenfeld, 2007). At a more specific level, powerful groups try to define those acts that advance their interests as desirable, justifiable, or at least excusable. In doing so, they sometimes promote values conducive to crime. Business owners, for example, place great value on the excessive consumption of consumer goods. This encourages people to spend beyond their means, contributing to crime. Also, capitalists promote negative stereotypes about those in less advantaged groups. Those living in poverty, for example, are portrayed as lazy individuals who want to "free ride" off the work of others. Such stereotypes make it easier to mistreat the poor. In certain cases, criminal subcultures may develop within powerful groups, such as the state or corporate world. The members of such subcultures play an especially active role in planning, justifying, and concealing the harmful acts that advance the interests of their group (e.g., Shover and Hochstetler, 2006).

Group conflict also causes those in less powerful groups to engage in crime. They may commit crimes in an effort to improve their situation, protect their limited resources, seek revenge against those who oppress them, symbolically express "resistance" to their oppression, or otherwise react to the negative consequences of their oppression. In particular:

- The oppression and deprivation experienced by group members contributes to a breakdown in social control. The members of disadvantaged groups often have negative school experiences, limited educations, and poor work histories. As such, they are weakly bonded to conventional institutions such as school and work. Further, they attach little value to those social norms promoted by school officials, employers, and the state. This low social control increases the likelihood of crime.
- Those in less powerful groups are exposed to the same cultural values stressing self-interest, with little regard for others. Also, they too develop values and beliefs that approve of, justify, or excuse crime. These values and beliefs may assume a variety of forms. For example, the less powerful may come to believe that crime is necessary to survive or overcome oppression, that crime is a legitimate method to seek revenge or symbolically express resistance, and that crime is excusable since the members of

powerful groups routinely commit harmful acts. In certain cases, group conflict may also encourage those in less powerful groups to form subcultures that actively encourage crime.

- Those in less powerful groups are subject to a broad range of strains or stressors. They are prevented from achieving a variety of goals, including goals involving monetary success, status or respect, and autonomy from others. And they are subject to much negative treatment, including victimization by others, deprivation of basic resources, discrimination, and segregation in low-income communities plagued by a host of problems. They may turn to crime to achieve their goals, reduce or escape from negative treatment, seek revenge against the source of strain or related targets, and alleviate the negative emotions associated with strain (through illicit drug use).

- Those in less powerful groups often lack the resources to cope with strains in a legal manner, increasing the likelihood of criminal coping. In particular, they are deprived of a range of resources that facilitate legal coping, including economic resources, political influence, and adequate police protection.

- The deprivations experienced by those in less powerful groups have a host of additional consequences that increase the likelihood of crime (e.g. Agnew, 2005; Colvin, 2000; Currie, 1997, 1998). For example, poverty tends to disrupt family ties, contribute to poor parenting practices, impede school performance, and erode social control at the community level.

Having made these arguments, it is important to note that *group conflict does not always increase crime*. Most notably, it generally reduces crime among females in the case of gender conflict. This is usually explained in terms of the extensive efforts to control female behavior. Among other things, females are subject to close supervision by parents and spouses, are taught beliefs that discourage crime, and are saddled with responsibilities that make crime difficult, particularly childcare and household maintenance (see Heidensohn, 1996; Morash, 2006). Some females, however, do respond to conflict with crime (Broidy and Agnew, 1997; Morash, 2006). One of the challenges for the conflict perspective is to account for the different types of oppression experienced by different groups, distinguishing those types of oppression that foster crime from those types that suppress it. Also, the conflict perspective needs to better explain differences in the reaction to oppression by group members.

Group Differences Are Critical

Group conflict is the primary cause of crime, so it is critical to consider group membership when explaining crime. The causes of crime sometimes differ across groups. Most notably, the members of advantaged groups often engage in crime to protect their advantages, while those in less advantaged groups often engage in crime because of the oppression they experience. Males, for example, sometimes abuse their female partners in an effort to maintain control over them, while females sometimes resort to violence to protect themselves from abuse (Morash, 2006). Some factors do cause crime across a range of groups, but groups differ in their exposure to these factors. Sexual abuse, for example, increases crime among both males and females; but females are more likely to experience such abuse (Morash, 2006). Further, the members of different groups may react differently to a given cause. Females, for example, are less likely to respond to peer delinquency with crime than are males-in part because females are more likely to condemn crime and are higher in self-control (Zahn, 2009).

The Best Way to Control Crime Is by Reducing Conflict and Its Negative Consequences

Consensus theorists argue that crime-control efforts should focus on increasing the individual's self– and social control. Critical theorists take a very different approach to controlling crime. Rather than focusing on the individual and the individual's immediate environment, they focus on changing the larger society. In particular, they argue that we should reduce group conflict and its negative consequences. There are several ways to do this. We might alter the interests and values of group members.[5] For example, we might alter the gender-role attitudes of men or reduce the perception among some whites that blacks are a threat. We might reduce the power differences between groups, making it more difficult for some groups to oppress others. As an example, there have been a range of suggestions for making corporations more subject to governmental and public control (Simpson and Weisburd, 2010). Related to this, we might better regulate the behavior of groups, prohibiting oppressive behavior. For example, a range of laws and procedures attempt to reduce the extent of discrimination, including discrimination by the criminal justice system (e.g., Building Blocks for Youth, 2007; Eitle and Monahan, 2009). Finally, the negative consequences of group conflict can be reduced. One such consequence is poverty. Poverty can be reduced by such measures as progressive taxation, an increase in the inheritance tax, preschool enrichment programs, job training programs, an increase in the minimum wage, and creating jobs through the public sector (e.g., Currie, 1997, 1998).

It is important to note that critical theorists do not deny that individual characteristics and the immediate environment contribute to crime. Rather, they argue that the *root* causes of crime lie in group conflict and its consequences. For example, they argue that many of the individual and family factors that cause crime stem from the extensive poverty in our society. This poverty disrupts families, contributes to poor parenting practices, and damages the psychological health of children. Crime-control efforts that focus on individuals and the immediate environment are ignoring these root causes. As such, their impact is limited. They can help repair certain of the damage caused by group conflict, but it is only by addressing group conflict that we can have a meaningful effect on crime.

Evidence on the Consensus and Conflict Perspectives

We have two rather different views of society, one assuming consensus and the other conflict. Which is correct? Given the general thrust of earlier chapters, it should not be surprising that there is evidence in support of both perspectives.[6] I next review certain of this evidence, with a focus on class, gender, and race/ethnic groups in the United States, examining the core predictions of each perspective.

Is There Consensus or Conflict Regarding the Definition of Crime?

Researchers have addressed this question primarily through surveys that ask individuals to rate the seriousness of various criminal acts (see Stylianou, 2003, for a review). These surveys find that all major groups rate core crimes as relatively serious in nature, both in the United States and other countries. Violent crimes causing bodily harm are rated as most serious, followed by property crimes involving theft or damage. However, there is somewhat less agreement if we focus on absolute rather than relative ratings. That is, two groups may agree that crime X is more serious than crime Y (the groups have the same relative rating), but one group may view crime X as highly serious while the other may view it as moderately serious (the groups have different absolute ratings). Also, there is less agreement regarding the ratings of victimless crimes and certain white-collar offenses (see Cullen et al., 1985).

Group differences here are often, but not always, in the direction predicted by critical theorists. For example, females rate rape as more serious than do males in certain studies (Stylianou, 2003; see Piquero et al., 2008; Unnever et al., 2008 for group differences in the ratings of white-collar crimes).

Critical theorists argue that researchers should not only examine current views about crime but also the origin of criminal laws. The laws may have originated out of conflict, with consensus emerging later as powerful groups convinced others to condemn the acts in question. Studies on the origin of certain criminal laws suggest that these laws did in fact emerge out of conflict (see Chambliss and Zatz, 1993, Kubrin et al., 2009 for overviews). As noted earlier, for example, there is good reason to believe that our laws regarding drug and alcohol use emerged out of group conflict. We can also see evidence of conflict today, with groups competing over the legal status of acts such as abortion and gay marriage (Dombrink and Hillyard, 2007).

Finally, researchers have examined the justifications and excuses that people accept for crimes. There is evidence for group differences here, even with respect to core crimes. In particular, males, lower-class individuals, and young people are somewhat more likely to accept certain justifications and excuses for core crimes (see Agnew, 2009; Cullen and Agnew, 2011). As an illustration, Markowitz and Felson (1998) found that males were more likely than females to agree that "violence deserves violence" and that "an eye for an eye, a tooth for a tooth is a good rule for living." Such group differences, however, are often small to moderate in size. And there do not appear to be race/ethnic differences here.

In sum, the research on views regarding crime provides support for both the consensus and conflict perspectives. There is much consensus regarding core crimes, with all groups condemning the unconditional use of personal violence, theft, and property destruction. There is somewhat less consensus regarding victimless crimes, certain white-collar crimes, and the justifications and excuses that are accepted for crime. In addition, certain criminal laws originated out of group conflict, even though there is now some consensus regarding these laws today.

Do Groups Have Shared/Interdependent or Conflicting Interests?

Again, we find evidence for both the consensus and conflict perspectives. Consider business owners and the working class. There is no doubt that these groups have conflicting economic interests. Historic accounts, in particular, make clear that business owners regularly pursued policies designed to enhance their profits, with such policies often suppressing the wages of workers. Such policies included efforts to stifle labor unions and to locate businesses in states or countries without a strong union presence (see Domhoff, 2005b). At the same time, business owners and workers do depend on one another. This interdependence occasionally comes to the fore, particularly during times when the survival of both workers and business owners is threatened (see the example at the beginning of this chapter). Business owners and workers also share many non-economic interests. For example, a high percentage of business owners and workers in the United States vote Republican because they favor such things as the adoption of school prayer, the prohibition of abortion, and the aggressive defense of the United States from terrorist attack. (Some argue that the Republican Party focuses on these issues to distract working-class voters from their true economic interests (see Wiener, 2005).)

Males and females in the United States provide another example. Research indicates that males and females once held rather different views regarding gender roles. Males, for example, were much more likely to state that women should not work outside the home, should not get involved in politics, and should assume major responsibility for household tasks and child care. The gender-role attitudes of males and females, however, have become increasingly similar in recent decades, with many males supporting gender equality at home, work, and in the political arena (Bolzendahl and Myers, 2004; Carter et al., 2009; Hunnicutt, 2009). To be sure, many males still hold traditional gender role attitudes. Also, there is a large gap between the expressed desire for gender equality and the reality. But it would be a mistake to describe the interests of males and females solely in terms of conflict. Similar conclusions apply to other groups, including race/ethnic groups (e.g., Quillian, 2006; Young; 1999). So there is again evidence for both the consensus and conflict perspectives, with the degree of consensus/conflict depending on the groups in question, the interests being examined, and the time period.

Do Some Groups Have More Power Than Others?

The idea that groups differ in power is central to the conflict perspective, although consensus theorists do not deny power differences. There is a large literature examining the distribution of power among groups, particularly at the national level. Power is difficult to directly measure, so researchers infer who has power based on "(1) *who benefits* in terms of having things that are valued in the society; (2) *who governs* (i.e., sits in the seats that are considered to be powerful); (3) *who wins* when there are arguments over issues; and (4) *who has a reputation for power"* (author's emphasis) (Domhoff, 2005a:2). There is some debate in the literature regarding the distribution of power. Certain researchers argue that a small elite possesses great power at the national level. For example, Dye (2002:1) begins his well-known book *Who's Running America* by stating that: "Great power in America is concentrated in a handful of people. A few thousand individuals . . . decide about war and peace, wages and prices, consumption and investment, employment and production, law and justice, taxes and benefits, education and learning, health and welfare, advertising and communication, life and leisure" (also see Dillon, 2010; Domhoff, 2005b, 2006). Others take a pluralistic stance, arguing that power is more widely dispersed. But there is much agreement that certain groups have more power than others, with the most powerful groups at the national level being dominated by upper-class, white males (see especially Domhoff, 2005a, 2006).

At the same time, the distribution of power does vary over time and across societies. For example, the power of women, Latinos, blacks, and Asian Americans has increased somewhat since the 1960s, as reflected in the gains of the civil rights and feminist movements (Dillon, 2010; Domhoff, 2006). As a result, women and minorities are now better represented in the upper echelons of government and the corporate world, although they still comprise only a minority of top officials. The power of the working class has also fluctuated over time, particularly with the rise and fall of labor unions (Domhoff, 2005b, 2006). While labor unions were never able to dominate national policy, there was a time when they were better able to extract concessions from policymakers. Likewise, the distribution of power varies across societies. For example, women are totally excluded from positions of national power in certain societies but well represented in other societies (Dillon, 2010). And the working class has more power in certain Western European societies, where there are strong labor unions and major political parties that better represent the interests of labor. Reflecting this fact, such societies have more equality in their income distributions, more progressive tax structures, and higher levels of welfare spending (Domhoff, 2005a).

Other literatures examine the distribution of power at lower levels of analysis, including communities, corporations, working groups within organizations, families, and peer groups (e.g., see Domhoff, 2005c for an overview of power at the community level). As an example, feminist scholars in criminology have focused on gender differences in power within the family and other contexts (e.g., Morash, 2006). Males typically have more power than females, with this greater power stemming from cultural factors (e.g., cultural beliefs that males are the "head" of the house), social factors (e.g., males tend to have larger incomes), and individual traits (e.g., males are more assertive and physically stronger). Again, however, feminists note that male power does vary over time, across societies, and across groups within societies (see Hagan, 1989). In sum, there is no doubt that groups frequently differ in power.

Do More Powerful Groups Oppress Less Powerful Groups?

The key difference between the consensus and conflict perspectives centers around oppression. While consensus theorists focus on shared and interdependent interests, they acknowledge that groups sometimes have competing interests and that certain groups have more power than others. Consensus theorists, however, argue that these competing interests are resolved in a just manner—either through fair and open competition or mediation by the state. Critical theorists, however, argue that more powerful groups oppress less powerful groups in the pursuit of their interests. In supporting their case, critical theorists focus on the *processes* of oppression, particularly the differential or discriminatory treatment of those in less powerful groups. And they focus on the *outcomes* of oppression, such as material deprivation and high levels of control.

It is necessary to consider both processes and outcomes, since those in less powerful groups may experiences negative outcomes for reasons other than oppression. Individuals in less powerful groups, for example, may earn less money because they have fared poorly in an open and fair competitive process, perhaps because they are less qualified (for reasons unrelated to discrimination). Or they may have higher rates of imprisonment because they are more likely to engage in crime (for reasons unrelated to discrimination). Before we can state that oppression exists, we must have evidence that the negative outcomes in question are the result of unjust treatment–typically discriminatory treatment. Discrimination involves differential treatment based on group characteristics or "inadequately justified factors" associated with a group, with such treatment disadvantaging the group (see Quillian, 2006). Discrimination is often motivated by prejudice, with prejudice involving negative feelings toward and beliefs about the group (see Quillian, 2006; Talaska et al., 2008). However, prejudice can also be an outcome of discrimination, as groups seek to justify or excuse their discriminatory behavior, with such behavior stemming from a desire to advance their interests (see Quillian, 2006; Rosenstein, 2008). Oppression, then, does not simply involve harm; it involves unjust or blameworthy harm.

There are large literatures dealing with race/ethnic, gender, and class discrimination in a variety of domains, including the political, occupational, educational, family, and cultural domains. It is not possible to review this literature here, but there is good evidence for the continued existence of discrimination against females, lower-class individuals, and the members of minority groups.[7] The extent of such discrimination is often lower now than in the past. Further, the extent varies across a range of factors, including the individuals/groups involved and the domain. And, in certain cases, there is now little or no evidence of discrimination. Taken as a whole, however, discrimination contributes to a range of negative outcomes among the groups just mentioned. Depending on the group, these negative outcomes include such things as more limited educations, lower earnings, poorer health, increased exposure to a range of stressors—including criminal victimization, and higher rates of imprisonment.

To illustrate, consider the earnings gap between whites and blacks. A recent study examined the extent to which white males earn more than black males, after taking account of factors such as education, hours worked, and type of occupation (Semyonov and Lewin-Epstein, 2009). The study found that blacks earned 6 percent less than whites in the year 2000. The earnings gap was larger in the private sector than the public sector. Blacks earned 8 percent less than whites in the private sector, but the earnings gap in the public sector had largely disappeared. The authors also found that the earnings gap had declined over time; blacks earned 27 percent less than whites in 1960, versus the 6 percent in 2000. So discrimination still exists in earnings, although it has declined and is not evident in all sectors. This study, however, underestimates the full extent of discrimination; it examines the earnings gap after taking account of education and type of occupation. As such, it does not consider the discrimination that blacks face in the educational sphere or when trying to obtain certain jobs (Quillian, 2006; Roscigno, 2007; also see Western, 2006). As a result, there are still substantial differences in the income and wealth of blacks and whites (Domhoff, 2010). For the year 2007, the median annual household income for whites was $50,000 versus $30,000 for blacks. The median net wealth of whites was $143,600 versus $9,300 for blacks (net wealth equals all assets, including one's house, minus debts).

So, again, we have evidence in support of both the consensus and conflict perspectives. There is widespread discrimination in the United States and, at least partly as a result, lower-class individuals, females, and the members of minority groups have suffered a range of negative outcomes. At the same time, evidence for discrimination has declined over time, and in certain areas there is little or no evidence of discrimination. The decline in discrimination partly reflects the "expanding moral circle" referred to chapter 4; with people increasingly coming to believe that the members of different groups are worthy of full moral consideration. And it reflects institutionalized efforts to reduce discrimination in various spheres of life, such as the educational and occupational spheres.

Is the State a Neutral or Biased Actor (with a Focus on the Criminal Justice System)?

Critical theorists not only argue that some groups oppress others, but that they have enlisted the state in the process, with the state serving the interests of powerful groups. Consensus theorists disagree, arguing that the state is a neutral actor. Criminologists have conducted two types of studies in this area. The first examines the argument that the criminal justice system is used to control those groups seen as a threat. Most of the research here has focused on race, particularly on blacks. The measures of threat used in various studies are both direct and indirect: they include the perception by whites that blacks are a threat, to both public safety and economic success; more general measures of negative attitudes toward blacks; the size of the black population relative to whites; whether the black population is increasing; the unemployment rate; and the occurrence of a riot in the recent past. Researchers usually examine the effect of such measures on crime-control efforts while taking account of the actual crime rate. The most recent and best studies tend to find that measures of threat increase the support for and the use of a range of punitive crime control strategies, including strategies directed at blacks. Such strategies include hiring more police, the increased use of deadly force by the police, higher arrest rates for blacks, and higher imprisonment rates for blacks.[8]

A second, related set of studies examine whether the police and court system discriminate against the members of less powerful groups, including the members of minority groups, lower-class individuals, and females. In particular, are individuals in less powerful groups more likely to be stopped and questioned by the police, arrested, sentenced, and given severe penalties including long prison terms and capital punishment? Studies in this area take account of such legally relevant factors as crime seriousness and prior record. Most research has focused on racial discrimination, particularly on the treatment of blacks and, to a lesser extent, Latinos. Studies in this area have produced mixed results, but the most recent and best studies suggest that the members of minority groups are treated more severely by the criminal justice system.[9] It should be noted, however, that the major determinants of treatment by criminal justice officials are crime seriousness and prior record. Also, the degree of discrimination is often small to moderate in size. Further, the degree of discrimination varies depending on such things as the type of crime being examined, the characteristics of the police and court system, and the area being examined. In some cases, there is little or no evidence for discrimination.

The research on class discrimination tends to parallel that on race, with lower-class individuals often being treated more severely (see Agnew, 2009; Barak et al., 2001; Reiman and Leighton, 2010). Related to this, evidence suggests that offenders who commit white-collar and corporate crimes are less likely to be sanctioned than those who commit street crimes. And, if sanctioned, they receive less severe penalties (Barak et al., 2001; Hagan, 1989; Reiman and Leighton, 2010). The research on gender discrimination is more complex. There is some evidence that males are treated more severely than females. However, females who violate gender role expectations, such as those who act tough, tend to be treated more severely. Also, girls are more likely than boys to be sanctioned for sexual activity or acts that put them at risk for such activity, such as running away from home (Agnew, 2009; Morash, 2006). Recent research has focused on the intersection between race/ethnicity, class, gender, and age; and suggests that young, black/Latino, lower-class males are the most likely to be severely sanctioned (e.g., Doerner and Demuth, 2010; Spohn and Holleran, 2000; Steffensmeier et al., 1998).

So once again, we have evidence for both the consensus and conflict perspectives. On the one hand, there is some evidence that the criminal justice system does exercise greater control over groups seen as threatening and, in the process, discriminates against the members of such groups. But the effects here are often small to moderate in size, with legally relevant factors typically having the greatest effect on processing by the justice system.

Is Crime the Result of a Failure to Participate in the Social Consensus or of Group Conflict?

The large share of research on the causes of crime has focused on core crimes, such as assault and theft. The consensus perspective attributes these crimes to the failure of individuals to participate in the social consensus. That is, some individuals are said to be less able and willing to refrain from violence and theft. These individuals are low in self-control, lacking the ability to resist temptations and provocations for crime. And they are low in social control, which reduces their willingness to participate in the consensus. In particular, they are weakly bonded to family, school, and work; have not been taught to condemn criminal acts; and are in environments where the likelihood of sanction for crime is low. There is much support for these claims. Low self-control is one of the leading causes of crime (Pratt and Cullen, 2000). And low social control is likewise an important cause of crime (Agnew, 2005, 2009).

These findings do not in and of themselves challenge the conflict perspective–which also states that low self – and social control cause crime. Where the consensus and conflict perspectives differ is in their discussion of the origins of low control. The consensus perspective focuses on biological factors, poor parenting, and the failure of those in the larger social environment to effectively sanction crime. The conflict perspective focuses on group conflict and its consequences. Individuals are low in control because of the consequences of past and present discrimination; most notably, economic deprivation disrupts family life, impedes school performance, leads to a breakdown in control at the community level, and promotes a focus on the immediate satisfaction of ones interests. There is some support for both sets of arguments. Low control is a function of biological factors, poor parenting, and the failure of larger groups to enforce the consensus (e.g., Pratt et al., 2004; Wright and Beaver, 2005). At the same time, poverty and other of the negative consequences of group conflict also contribute to low control.[10]

Beyond that, the conflict perspective focuses on a range of causes that receive little attention from consensus theorists. Such causes involve both the processes and consequences of oppression. At the level of individuals, they involve discriminatory treatment, chronic poverty, chronic unemployment, work in "bad jobs," feelings of injustice and anger, involvement in criminal subcultures, beliefs favorable to crime, and exposure to a range of stressors—such as the victimization of females by their parents and intimate partners. And at the level of communities and societies, they involve poverty and inequality, particularly when caused by discrimination; the existence of segregated communities, composed primarily of poor blacks; limited welfare assistance; and cultural beliefs that emphasize the unrestrained pursuit of money. The research on certain of these factors is limited, but taken as a whole the evidence suggests that they increase the likelihood of crime.[11]

Further, research suggests that it is important to consider group differences when explaining crime. Most notably, group membership has a large effect on the individual's exposure to causes of crime. For example, males are much lower in self-control than females, blacks more often encounter discriminatory treatment than whites, and lower-class individuals are more often exposed to poor parenting practices (Agnew, 2005, 2009; Colvin, 2000; Moffitt et al., 2001). Most of the leading causes appear to have similar effects on crime across a range of groups, but research suggests that the effects of certain causes do differ across groups. For example, association with delinquent peers is more likely to increase crime among males than females (Zahn, 2009). Further, certain causes are unique to particular groups. For example, social power is an important cause of delinquency among middle-class adolescents, but not among lower-class adolescents (Wright et al., 1999).

There is much less research on the causes of crime beyond core crimes. But limited data suggest that the arguments of critical theorists have some merit. Take, for example, corporate crimes. Data suggest that the social power possessed by corporate officials reduces the likelihood such crimes will be criminalized or subject to serious sanction, thereby contributing to their commission. Corporate crimes often result when corporate officials feel threatened; for example, they are more likely among corporations facing financial problems, including the inability to meet financial goals and the loss or threatened loss of financial resources. Also, corporate officials sometimes form subcultures that minimize, justify, or excuse the harm caused by corporate crimes (see Agnew et al., 2009; Cullen and Agnew, 2011; Lynch and Michalowski, 2006).

Summary

In sum, there is evidence for the existence of both consensus and group conflict, with the degree of consensus/conflict depending on such things as the groups in question, the issue or domain being examined, the society, and the time period. Related to this, there is some support for the explanations of crime offered by both consensus and critical theorists, although most research has focused on core crimes. These conclusions may strike many as self-evident. Even a causal examination of the world reveals evidence of both consensus and conflict, and certain criminologists have come to advocate a compromise between the consensus and conflict perspectives (see Akers and Sellers, 2008; Bernard, 1983). Nevertheless, the research highlights the need for an integrated consensus/conflict theory and begins to suggest the nature of such a theory. It is beyond the scope of this chapter to develop such a theory, but in the next section I describe the issues an integrated consensus/conflict theory should address and provide some direction about how to proceed when constructing such a theory.

Foundation for an Integrated Consensus/Conflict Theory of Crime

The core idea of the integrated theory is that group relations vary. There is a core consensus in all societies; the large majority of people condemn the *unconditional* use of personal violence and theft, and cooperate to some limited degree in the pursuit of certain shared interests-particularly protection from external and internal threats. Societies would not be possible without this consensus. Beyond that, levels of consensus and conflict vary a good deal across societies and over time. At one extreme, major groups within a society have compatible interests and values and generally "get along." At the other, major groups have incompatible interests/values, and there is much oppression. I next discuss the groups and interests/values that should be examined in an integrated theory. I then describe the major types of group relations, focusing on conflict given its central role in causing crime. And I conclude this section by listing the factors that influence the variation in group relations, with a focus on the factors promoting conflict.

Identifying Key Groups and Core Interests and Values

Which groups and values/interests should be examined in an integrated theory? Criminologists have given several answers to these questions. Subcultural deviance theorists focus on conflict between class, race/ethnic, and other groups over what behaviors are viewed as wrong (e.g., Sutherland et al., 1992; Anderson, 1999). Marxist theorists focus on conflict between class groups over economic interests (e.g., Greenberg, 1993; Lynch and Michalowski, 2006). Feminist theorists focus on conflict between males and females over gender roles and norms (e.g., Morash, 2006). Critical race theorists focus on conflict between race/ethnic groups over a range of interests and values, including economic, status, and political interests (e.g., Dillon, 2010; Gabbidon, 2010). Certain strain and related theorists focus on conflict between class, race/ethnic, gender, and age groups over issues of money, status, autonomy, and power.[12] And still others focus on conflicts between groups that differ in terms of sexual orientation, religion, country of origin, position in the world system, and other dimensions; with the conflicts revolving around a range of interests and values–including those just listed.[13] The research conducted by these theorists suggests that each of these conflicts may contribute to crime.

The integrated theory should therefore take a broad approach when identifying groups and core interests/values. The theory should not limit its focus to one type of group or set of interests/values. In particular:

- Any type of group that is associated with core interests and values should be considered. Certain groups tend to meet this criterion across a range of societies, including groups based on class, gender, race/ethnicity, age, and sexual orientation.
- A range of interests and values should be considered, particularly those that have a significant impact on behavior or are identified as important by group members. The theory, however, should attempt to identify those core interests and values which are most relevant to the explanation of crime. It is likely that some interests/values will emerge as more important than others, although it seems unlikely that one interest/value will trump all others when explaining crime. At present, there is reason to believe that those interests and values listed above will occupy a central place in the integrated theory.
- The theory should recognize that group membership is typically associated with multiple interests and values, reflecting the similar life experiences of group members and the effect of some interests/values on others (e.g., the effect of economic interests on values regarding crime). As a result, groups may exhibit consensus in some areas but conflict in others. In fact, powerful groups often emphasize or cultivate shared interests/values with those in less powerful groups, hoping to divert attention from conflicting interests (Wiener, 2005).
- The theory should recognize that individuals belong to multiple groups, with each group influencing their interests and values. The oppression that individuals experience (and inflict) reflects their various group memberships. Also, the nature and extent of conflict in a society reflects the patterning of group memberships. For example, we might expect conflict to be more severe when the members of one subordinate group are especially likely to belong to other subordinate groups. Thus it is critical to take account of the intersection between group memberships when studying crime.

The Nature and Extent of Consensus/Conflict

Once the integrated theory identifies key groups and core interests/values, the nature and extent of consensus/conflict around these interests and values can be estimated. I present a preliminary description of the types of consensus/conflict, focusing on conflict. Criminologists often speak of consensus and conflict in general terms, but it is important to distinguish between types since they may have different effects on crime. I then briefly discuss how the extent of conflict can be measured.

Types of Group Consensus. Consensus involves agreement over core interests/values and the associated ability of groups to get along—such that they do not inflict blameworthy harms on one another because of their group membership. There are, however, different types of agreement and ways to get along. The types of consensus include:

- *Consensus Based on Similarity.* Here the members of different groups share the same core values and/or jointly pursue the same interests, such as protection from external threats. This similarity in values and interests fosters strong emotional ties between the members of different groups; we tend to like those who are like us. Further, the similarity in interests fosters mutual dependence. As such, the members of different groups tend to get along well with one another.[14]
- *Consensus Based on Interdependence.* Here the members of different groups pursue distinct interests, but these interests are such that the achievements of one group foster those of another. For example, one group may focus on securing food and another on defense. This interdependence of interests also creates strong ties between the members of different groups, although these ties are based less on emotion and more on the rational calculation of interests.[15]
- *Consensus Based on Just Competition.* Here the members of different groups hold values or interests that are incompatible with one another. That is, the values of one group challenge the validity, moral standing, or emotional salience of those of another group. And the interests of one group threaten the achievement of those of another group. Further, the members of one group attempt to promote their values or advance their interests over those of another group. For example, one group may attempt to criminalize abortion, while another may try to keep it legal. Or the members of one group may attempt to secure jobs desired by those of another group.

However, the members of the different groups agree on what they believe are just rules for advancing their interests or values–rules that prohibit the infliction of blameworthy harm (see chap. 2). For example, the members of different groups may compete for jobs in a regulated environment where blameworthy harms such as discrimination are banned. And they may appeal to a neutral authority when disputes arise. This type of consensus is more conducive to crime than that based on similarity or interdependence, since some groups and individuals are harmed in the competitive process. For example, they fail to have their values reflected in the law or to get the jobs they want. But such groups and individuals are not the victims of *blameworthy* harm; they lost in a just struggle. As a consequence, crime is less likely than is the case with group conflict (more below). In addition, states sometimes attempt to reduce the harm resulting from competition through the provision of social supports, such as unemployment insurance and welfare assistance. This too reduces the extent of crime (Cullen, 1994; Savage et al., 2008).

- *Consensus Based on Toleration/Avoidance.* Here, the members of different groups have incompatible values or interests, but they agree not to advance their interests/values over one another. That is, they agree not to compete or engage in conflict. This type of consensus may assume several forms, making it difficult to generalize about its effect on crime. For example, religious groups with incompatible beliefs may elect to ignore or tolerate the beliefs of one another. Groups with competing economic interests may carve out spheres of influence so that direct competition is limited. And, in perhaps the most extreme case, groups with incompatible interests/values may elect to live largely separate lives in different parts of the same country.

Types of Group Conflict. Conflict involves groups with incompatible interests and/or values, with the members of one group trying to advance their values or interests by inflicting blameworthy harm on those in the other group because of their group status. Blameworthy harms are defined in the broad manner indicated in chapter 2. They involve voluntary and intentional acts— committed without legitimate justification or excuse—that violate rights identified in the international human rights law. Intentional acts include not only deliberate acts but also reckless and negligent acts, as well as the failure to act when there is an obligation to do so in the international law. Blameworthy harms are synonymous with oppression, and *oppression based on group status is the defining feature of group conflict.*

There are many ways for one group to oppress another, with multiple forms of oppression often being employed. The integrated theory should develop a systematic classification of the types of oppression. This effort will of course overlap with the effort to more fully define blameworthy harms (see chap. 2). As an illustration of how to proceed, I briefly describe several types of oppression below. Oppression may be categorized in a variety of ways. I focus on the major purposes of the oppression and the particular acts intended to achieve these purposes, although a given act often serves more than one purpose. It is important to note that most types of oppression may occur at several levels, including the state, institutional, organizational, community, and interpersonal levels. For example, educational discrimination against blacks may result from policies that characterize educational institutions in general, from the practices of particular schools, and from the prejudices of particular teachers. Related to this, the degree to which oppressive acts are organized may vary. At one extreme, group leaders may carefully plan and carry out a massive campaign of oppression against the members of another group (e.g., the Holocaust). At the other, oppression may result from the largely uncoordinated activities of scattered group members.

- Oppressors deliberately harm others in the direct pursuit of their interests and values. A wide range of harms fall into this category, including physical harm, the theft and destruction of property, threats, emotional abuse, and (possibly) efforts to indoctrinate. To give a few examples: Members of one religious group kill those in another to advance their religious values. Members of one ethnic group forcibly take the homes and land of those in another to expand their territory. A conquering army enslaves those in the subject population to advance their economic interests. A husband coerces his wife—through threats and emotional abuse—to obey his commands. The methods of inflicting harm, however, may be more subtle. For example, husbands may induce obedience in their wives thru verbal persuasion that relies on prejudicial beliefs (e.g., the Bible states that wives should obey their husbands).
- Oppressors pursue their interests/values with little regard for the harm that may result, particularly to those in less powerful groups. Here oppressors do not deliberately cause harm, but harm results from their negligent or reckless behavior. For example, corporate officials—intent on increasing their profits—neglect the impact of their actions on the environment, working conditions, and consumer safety.

- Oppressors prevent those in the oppressed group from threatening their interests and values. A range of actions may be taken here. Oppressors may exercise *greater control* over those in the oppressed group, attempting to discourage threatening behavior. This control may be exercised by formal organizations, such as the police, school, and work. And it may be exercised by informal groups, such as family members, peers, and neighbors. While the acts of control may not be oppressive in and of themselves (e.g., arrest and imprisonment), they are applied in a discriminatory manner, thereby meeting the definition of oppression. Related to this, oppressors may use their power to *criminalize the threatening acts* of those in oppressed groups, as well as ensure that such acts are consistently and severely sanctioned. Oppressors may also *limit the power* of those in the oppressed group. For example, oppressors may limit such things as voting rights, free speech, the right to organize, and the right to protest. Oppressors may also deny access to those resources that provide power, such as financial resources and the media. Further, oppressors may *segregate* those in oppressed groups, confining them to certain areas or limiting their interaction with oppressors. Blacks, for example, have been forced to live in certain communities, are imprisoned at relatively high rates, and are discouraged from having intimate contact with whites. Finally, oppressors may *kill or physically harm* those in oppressed groups.
- Oppressors prevent or make it difficult for those in oppressed groups to pursue their interests and values, thereby indirectly making it easier for oppressors to achieve their interests/values. A range of acts fall into this category, depending on the interests/values under consideration. Consider the desire for economic success. Oppressors may *limit the ability* of oppressed individuals to achieve this goal. For example, oppressors may restrict access to the educational system or provide inferior schooling. Oppressors may *undermine the willingness* of oppressed individuals to pursue this goal. This might be done by harassing oppressed individuals who strive for economic success, convincing them that they are undeserving of such success, or encouraging them to pursue alternative goals, such as nurturing others. And oppressors may *limit opportunities* for economic success, even if oppressed individuals are willing and able to pursue such success. This might be accomplished through discrimination in the hiring and promotion process, or by providing less pay for comparable work.
- Oppressors justify or excuse the harm they cause. Oppressors may exercise control over information sources to *conceal or misrepresent the harms* they cause. They may use their power to ensure that the *blameworthy harms they*

cause are legal or are only mildly sanctioned. And they may promote values and beliefs that *justify or excuse these harms*. These beliefs usually deny or minimize the harm caused; claim that the harm is unavoidable or unintended; argue that the harm is in the service of some greater good (e.g., God or country); or claim that those in the oppressed group deserve to be treated in a negative manner (e.g., they are dangerous, lazy, or weak). As Bandura (1990) points out, the de-humanization of those in oppressed groups is an especially potent mechanism for the justification of oppression (also see Quillian, 2006; Reiman, 2006; Sykes and Matza, 1957). The process of oppression, then, often generates negative stereotypes about those in the oppressed group.[16] While these stereotypes originate out of the efforts of oppressors to justify or excuse the harm they cause, they frequently take on a life of their own once created. That is, these stereotypes directly encourage negative treatment of those in the oppressed group—over and above that negative treatment motivated by a desire to advance ones interests/values (e.g., Johnson and Betsinger, 2009).

There are clearly many types of oppression, and the integrated theory should extend and refine this list. Also, researchers need to examine whether certain types of oppression tend to occur together, permitting the identification of major types of conflict. This is a critical task, since different types of conflict may have different effects on the extent and nature of crime. As an example, consider gender and race conflict in the United States. Both females and blacks experience many of the types of oppression listed. But there are important differences in the nature of their oppression, with such differences at least partly explaining why the rate of serious crime is relatively low among females and high among blacks.

The oppression of females is *paternalistic* in nature. In particular, males want to protect and provide for the basic needs of females but also want to regulate their behavior—including their rights and duties. This paternalistic orientation stems from the fact that males have close emotional ties to females but view females as weak, in need of protection, and suited largely for childbearing and domestic labor (see Morash, 2006). By contrast, the oppression of blacks is *antagonistic* in nature. Whites want to protect themselves *from* blacks, through segregation, exclusion, and sanction. This antagonistic orientation stems from the fact that many whites dislike blacks and view them as threat to both their safety and economic well-being (see Buckler et al., 2009). (This scheme draws on Fiske et al., 2002). These different orientations are reflected in the specific types of oppression to which females (especially white females) and blacks are subject. To give two examples:

- Both females and blacks are especially subject to social control by their oppressors. In the case of females, however, the control is largely informal and indirect–reflecting their close ties to males, perceived weakness, and presumed domestic inclinations. In particular, females are closely supervised by parents and spouses, restricted to the domestic sphere, and socialized to be submissive and caring. Informal and indirect control of this type is quite effective at controlling crime (Agnew, 2009). In the case of blacks, the control is largely formal and direct, reflecting their weak ties to whites and perceived threat. In particular, blacks are subject to formal control by the criminal justice system, with a focus on detecting and severely sanctioning criminal acts. This type of control is less effective at reducing crime; in fact, it may increase crime when applied in a discriminatory or harsh manner (Sherman, 1993).
- Females and blacks are likewise subject to occupational discrimination. In the case of (white) females, such discrimination increases financial dependence on spouses and the likelihood of remaining at home, with a focus on childcare and household maintenance. These effects reduce their opportunities for most types of crime, as well as increasing the ability of males to exercise control over them. (This pattern is of course changing with the increase in single-parent families headed by females). In the case of blacks, occupational discrimination does not result in confinement to the domestic sphere. Further, blacks are not able to compensate for their material deprivation in the same manner as many females. As a result, such discrimination increases crime.

The Extent of Group Conflict. It is important to estimate the extent as well as type of conflict. Researchers have developed methods for at least roughly estimating the extent of certain types of oppression. For example, researchers can estimate the extent to which group differences in income or incarceration rates are due to discrimination (see Quillian, 2006). However, it is difficult to make comparisons across groups in terms of the total amount of oppression experienced. Groups experience somewhat different types of oppression, and we lack a common metric that allows for comparisons across types. As Purdie-Vaughns and Eibach (2008:380) state: "How does one quantify suffering in a way that would permit comparisons among rape, unjustified incarceration, chronic poverty, racial profiling, hate-crime victimization, and social exclusion." Nevertheless, gross comparisons can sometimes be made. The most severe instances of group oppression involve multiple *types* and severe *levels* of oppression directed at *most or all peo-*

ple in the oppressed group. Using these rough criteria, it is clear that some groups are more oppressed than others. Consider, for example, the social control and discrimination to which females are subject. Women in the United States are subject to more control than men and face educational and occupational discrimination; but this control and discrimination fall far short of that encountered by women in parts of Afghanistan. Here the Taliban prohibit woman from exposing any part of their skin, from working outside their home, from venturing outside their home without a male escort, and from being educated (Morash, 2006:234; also see Hunnicutt, 2009; Ogle and Batton, 2009).

The "Real" and Perceived Nature of Conflict

Group conflict is distinguished by the oppression of one group by another, with this oppression ultimately motivated by group differences in interests/ values. But critical theorists recognize that individuals in oppressed groups may be unaware of both the oppression they experience and their "true" interests. Many females, for example, do not believe that they are oppressed by men. And they often fail to realize that it is in their interest to have the same opportunities as men (Davis and Robinson, 1991; Hunnicutt, 2009). Rather, these females believe that is in their interest to serve men and assume major responsibility for childcare and household maintenance. This is not surprising. Those in powerful groups often conceal their oppression and encourage those in oppressed groups to adopt a "false" view of their interests; it is easier to oppress those who are unaware of their oppression (see Reiman and Leighton, 2010, for an excellent discussion). But we must still classify such relations as oppressive, despite the views of the oppressed. To do otherwise is to become a party to the oppression.

This argument, however, raises a very difficult question: If the victims of oppression deny that they are being oppressed, on what basis can criminologists claim that oppression exists (see Meyers, 2006)? I believe that the definition of group conflict provides the answer: Group conflict or oppression occurs when one group inflicts blameworthy harm on another, regardless of whether those in the oppressed group are aware of or troubled by such harm. Blameworthy harm was defined in chapter 2, with this definition drawing heavily on the international human rights law. In defining harm, the human rights law makes certain assumptions about the rights or the "true" interests of people. And, for reasons discussed in chapter 2, such assumptions represent the most solid foundation on which to define blameworthy harm.

To illustrate, the United Nations Convention on the Elimination of All Forms of Discrimination against Women states that discrimination is a harm to be eliminated. Article 1 of the Convention defines discrimination against women as "any distinction, exclusion, or restriction made on the basis of sex which has the effect or purpose of impairing or nullifying the recognition, enjoyment or exercise by women, irrespective of their marital status, on a basis of equality of men and women, of human rights and fundamental freedoms in the political, economic, social, cultural, civic or any other field" (United Nations, 2010). That document and others elaborate on this definition. For example, it states that women have "the right to equal remuneration, including benefits, and to equal treatment in respect of work of equal value." Thus, drawing on this document, we have grounds to argue that women have a true interest in the elimination of discrimination and that the discrimination they experience is a form of oppression. For example, if women receive less pay for equal work, then oppression exists—even if such oppression is denied or accepted by those experiencing it.

It should be emphasized that the views of those in oppressed groups are important. In particular, it makes a great deal of difference whether they are aware of their oppression. Awareness is a key determinant of their reaction to oppression. Generally speaking, we would expect that awareness increases the likelihood of resistance to oppression, with resistance sometimes taking the form of crime. Oppression, however, still affects group members even if they are unaware of it. For example, individuals may be unaware of the occupational discrimination they experience, but the poverty that results from such discrimination still increases the likelihood of crime.[17]

Explaining Variation in the Nature and
Extent of Consensus/ Conflict

A large body of research from several fields deals with the factors affecting variation in group relations, particularly the factors promoting group conflict.[18] The arguments made in this research are quite diverse and sometimes contradictory, posing a challenge to those seeking to pull them together into a unified whole. Nevertheless, the integrated theory should present a systematic description of those factors affecting variation in the nature and extent of group relations. As an illustration of how to proceed, I list *certain* of these factors below.

- *Human nature.* Human nature helps explain why societies show evidence of both consensus and conflict. Human nature partly accounts for the fact that most individuals—regardless of group membership—condemn the unconditional use of violence and theft and are disposed to cooperate with others (see chap. 4). Human nature, however, also underlies group conflict. While people show some social concern, this concern is greatest for the members of their in-group. People are strongly inclined to divide others into in-groups and out-groups, to favor their in-group, and to show hostility toward out-groups, particularly when they threaten in-group interests.[19] Human nature is of less help in explaining the variation in consensus and conflict over time and across societies, but may still play some role here. In particular, human nature influences how group members react to environmental factors, such as status threats and conditions of scarcity.[20]
- *The nature of the groups involved in conflict,* including group salience, cohesion, similarity in interests/values, and organization. We would expect conflict to be more likely to the extent that people identity with the groups to which they belong, are closely tied to other group members, share core values and interests with them, and are able to coordinate actions.[21] It is important to keep in mind that certain of these factors may vary over both the short– and long-term. For example, ones racial status may be quite salient at certain times, but less so at others.
- *Degree and nature of incompatibility between the interests and values of different groups.* We would expect conflict to be more likely to the extent that the incompatibility involves most or all of the core interests and values of group members, is high in degree, is of long duration, and is expected to continue into the future. This is the case with those group conflicts that have been the focus of criminologists, including class, gender, and race/ethnic conflicts. Further, as indicated in the discussion of gender versus race conflict, the nature of the incompatibility influences the nature of the conflict.[22]
- *Differences in power.* As indicated earlier, more powerful groups are inclined to oppress less powerful groups, in large part because they can get away with it (see the discussion of the costs and benefits of oppression below). I earlier mentioned how power is measured and certain of the factors influencing group power, such as group size, resources, and organization. As an example of the importance of power, consider gender conflict. Men often oppress women using physical violence. However, violence against women is less likely in societies where women have more power; for example, they have more educational, occupational, and economic

resources; have greater decision-making authority in the household; work outside the home; and participate in the political arena. Further, women who have social ties to others are less likely to be victims of violence than those who are isolated (Morash, 2006).

- *Perceived threats, especially unjust threats.* Oppression is more likely when one group perceives another as threat, particularly when the threat is seen as unjust. As noted above, several factors may contribute to the perception of threat, with much attention focusing on the size of the group with incompatible interests/values. Beyond that, we would expect "threatening" statements and acts on the part of one group to elicit perceptions of threat in another. For example, Chamlin (2009) found that a riot in Cincinnati provoked a police crackdown on blacks. Further, we might expect perceptions of threat to increase as valued resources become scarcer. For example, an increase in the unemployment rate may lead groups to view one another as economic threats (see King and Wheelock, 2007; Young, 1999; Zagefka et al., 2007). The integrated theory, however, should attempt to develop a reasonably precise description of those conditions and acts likely to be seen as threatening and unjust (see Agnew, 2001, 2006a). Further, it is important to remember that perceptions of threat not only depend on the nature of the "threatening" act but also on such things as the nature of media coverage and the characteristics of the perceivers (e.g., Carter et al., 2009; Davis and Robinson, 1991).

- *Alternatives to conflict.* While the above factors increase the likelihood of group conflict, they may sometimes result in other outcomes such as competition, tolerance, and avoidance. Whether conflict results is partly a function of the availability of these alternatives. In particular, is it possible for groups to compete or resolve their disputes in a fair manner (e.g., through fair elections)? Is there cultural support for the tolerance of incompatible values/interests (see Young, 1999)? Can satisfactory arrangements for the avoidance of conflict be negotiated?

- *Disposition for conflict.* The disposition for conflict is strongly influenced by values and beliefs. Does the oppressing group justify or excuse certain blameworthy harms. For example, do group members believe that one should respond to provocations or insults with violence. Also, how do group members view those in other groups. Oppression is especially likely if these others are seen as deserving of oppression, perhaps because they are viewed as weak, lazy, threatening, or subhuman. The nature of such views, as indicated earlier, can also influence the nature of the oppression (e.g., paternalistic versus antagonistic). In addition, disposition is influenced by the actions and statements of third parties. Oppression is more likely when it is supported by others. As an illustration of these points, violence against women is most common in households where traditional gender attitudes are strongest and in societies where gender stratification is most extreme (Hunnicutt, 2009; Morash, 2006). Also, men are more likely to oppress women when they have friends who model oppression, present beliefs favorable to oppression, and reinforce oppression (Morash, 2006).

- *Costs and benefits of conflict.* Finally, conflict is more likely when its costs are seen as low and its benefits as high. A range of factors are relevant here. One cost is *sanction and/or moral condemnation from the state* and others. For example, violence against women is less likely when it is consistently sanctioned and when programs are available to support and advocate for the victims of violence (Morash, 2006). Another cost is *retaliation by the oppressed group.* Conflict should be less likely when the oppressed group is able to retaliate in a meaningful way, perhaps because of its size, resources, organization, or support from others. Still another cost has to do with *the emotional and material ties between groups.* Conflict should be less likely when the members of one group have strong emotional ties with those in another, perhaps because they have much interpersonal contact with one another. Conflict is still possible here, however, as noted in the discussion of gender conflict, although the close ties influence the nature of the conflict. Also, conflict should be less likely when it will impose high material costs on the oppressors. This may occur because the oppressors are involved in cooperative endeavors with those in the oppressed group (e.g., they do business with one another). Conversely, conflict should be more likely when it is expected to benefit the oppressors. Benefits include material resources, such as money and land, increased status, and greater power.

Not All Group Members Are Alike

The previous discussion focuses on groups and assumes that there are differences across groups in such things as interests/values, power, perceptions of threat, and experiences with discrimination. It assumes, for example, that blacks on average experience more discrimination than whites. Much data support these assumptions, but at the same time it is important to note that not all group members are alike. Some men, for example, hold very traditional gender role attitudes, while others strongly favor gender equality (e.g., Hunnicutt, 2009). Group members, in fact, differ on most of the factors listed above. Among other things, they differ on the salience of their group membership, the extent to which they share group interests and values, the degree to which they feel threatened by other groups, their ability to successfully pursue their interests in the competitive arena, their disposition for conflict, and the costs and benefits of conflict for them. It is critical for the integrated theory to recognize such differences, since they influence the likelihood that particular individuals will become involved in group conflict, either as oppressors or oppressed.[23]

The Importance of Multiple Group Memberships (or Intersectionality)

The intersection of group memberships strongly shapes the extent and nature of conflict. Consider the example involving gender and race oppression, where gender was discussed separately from race. Individuals are not simply males or females or whites or blacks. For example, black females are viewed and treated differently than are white females. Among other things, black females are seen as more threatening and less in need of protection. Also, they are less likely to be confined to the private sphere (home). Reflecting these facts, white women have high rates victimization in and around the home, but low rates elsewhere; black women have high rates both at home and elsewhere (Morash, 2006:70). Similar points can be made regarding the intersection of gender and class (Hagan, 1989) and other group dimensions (Dillon, 2010).

At the most basic level, taking account of intersectionality means examining the different combinations of group memberships. For example, it means examining whether individuals with particular intersections of race/ethnicity, class, gender, and age (e.g., young, black, lower-class males) are especially likely to experience discrimination in the criminal justice system. At the same time, researchers should attempt to build a theory of intersectionality. This theory would predict and explain the effect of particular intersections on outcome variables, including crime and treatment by the criminal justice system.

As an illustration, there are two major theories about how particular types of intersections affect levels of oppression. The double-jeopardy perspective states that people with multiple subordinate-group identities will experience more oppression than those with a single subordinate group identity. For example, black females will experience more oppression than black males. Black females, in particular, will experience those oppressions associated with both a subordinate racial and gender status (see Hancock, 2007; Purdie-Vaughns and Eibach, 2008). And, in fact, research suggests that individuals with multiple subordinate-group identities fare worse on several indicators of oppression, such as wages and occupational status (e.g., Madene, 2009). Another perspective, however, argues that individuals with a single subordinate-group identity often bear the brunt of oppression directed at their group. Such individuals are taken as prototypical representatives of the group and are therefore targeted. So black males will experience more oppression than black females. There is some support for this view as well. For example, black males face more discrimination in the criminal justice system and more often report that they are the victims of discrimination (e.g., Doerner and Demuth, 2010; Purdie-Vaughns and Eibach, 2008; Steffensmeier et al., 1998).

A compromise position argues that it is unproductive to ask who experiences more oppression overall: those with multiple subordinate-group identities or those with one. The amount oppression experienced may vary across social circumstances. For example, black males may experience more discrimination in the criminal justice system, but black females may experience more discrimination in other spheres. Also, researchers should focus on differences in the types of oppression experienced. For example, Purdie-Vaughns and Eibach (2008) argue that those with single subordinate identities are more likely to experience direct discrimination targeting that group (e.g., hate crimes based on that group identity). Those with multiple subordinate identities are more likely to experience "intersectional invisibility" or the failure to be recognized as full members of their constituent groups. That is, they are often marginalized within each of the groups to which they belong. Criminologists can contribute to the development of such theoretical work on intersectionality by exploring the effect of various group identities on outcomes such as crime, victimization and discrimination in the criminal justice system.

Further, the integrated theory should not only consider intersectionality from the perspective of individuals. As noted, it should also consider the patterning of group affiliations across the society. The critical question here would seem to be the extent to which subordinate group affiliations overlap. We might expect more conflict when the overlap is high (e.g., those in subordinate race/ethnic groups fully overlap with those in subordinate religious groups). Among other things, high overlap may increase the incompatibility in interests/values between subordinate and superordinate groups, undermine the emotional and material ties between these groups, and increase perceptions of threat.

In sum, the integrated theory draws on both the consensus perspective and a range of critical perspectives as well as associated literatures. It focuses on a variety of groups and values/interests, emphasizing the importance of an intersectional approach. It argues that there is a core consensus in all societies, but beyond that the degree and nature of consensus/conflict varies across societies and over time. And the theory describes the different types of consensus and conflict as well as the factors influencing variation in consensus/conflict. The next section describes the implications of the theory for the causes and control of crime as well as issues that the integrated theory should address.

The Integrated Theory and the Causes and Control of Crime
The Causes of Crime

The integrated theory recognizes the existence of both consensus and conflict, and therefore incorporates the causes identified by both perspectives. Many such causes are listed in the previous section, and additional causes are suggested in the discussions of the nature of consensus/conflict and the factors affecting variation in consensus/conflict.

Macro-Level Causes. Certain of these causes involve features of the larger social environment. These causes influence or index macro-levels of control, the likelihood of group conflict or oppression, the processes of oppression, and the consequences of oppression. A partial list includes:

- Social disorganization at the community and societal level
- Incompatible interests and values between groups
- Group differences in power
- Indicators of group threat, including the relative size and power of groups, threatening statements and acts by groups, the scarcity of valued resources, and perceptions of threat
- The availability of alternatives to group conflict, including free elections, an impartial court system, and mechanisms to ensure open and fair competition
- The failure to provide social supports, such as income, food, housing, and health supports (see Cullen, 1994)
- Discrimination in the family, educational, religious, economic, political, and criminal justice systems. This discrimination may manifest itself in numerous ways; among other things, certain groups may be denied resources, opportunities, and rights, and privileges, may be subject to greater control, and may be saddled with certain duties
- Absolute and relative material deprivation (e.g., income inequality, percentage of group members below the poverty line)

- Groups differences in strains, such as criminal victimization and homelessness
- The exclusion and segregation of certain groups (e.g., housing segregation)
- Coercive methods of control, including policies involving mass imprisonment, forced or constrained labor, dispossession, and violence (see Colvin, 2000)
- Certain cultural beliefs and values, such as an emphasis on the unrestrained pursuit of material interests, justifications/excuses for blameworthy harms of various types, and negative stereotypes regarding certain groups, including the de-humanization of group members
- Group differences in alienation from major institutions, perceptions of injustice, and emotions such as anger and hopelessness

These factors usually increase crime, including core crimes and often the other types of crime described in chapter 2. But certain of these factors may in fact reduce crime. This is especially true for those factors that involve excessive control, particularly informal control, and the limitation of opportunities for certain types of crime. Certain of these causes, such as material deprivation and social disorganization, have been the subject of much research (Pratt and Cullen, 2005). Others have been neglected in crime research.

Individual-Level Causes. The integrated theory also incorporates a range of individual-level causes. Certain of these causes derive from the consensus perspective, particularly low self – and social control. The integrated theory should also consider those causes described by such mainstream theories as strain, social learning, rational choice, opportunity, and bio-psychological theories (see Agnew, 2009; Cullen and Agnew, 2011 for overviews). Certain of these theories (or versions of them) are compatible with the consensus perspective, others with the conflict perspective, and still others with both perspectives (see Einstadter and Henry, 2006; Taylor et al., 1973). But all of the causes identified by these theories are easily incorporated into the integrated theory, which again recognizes both consensus and conflict. In addition, the integrated theory points to certain individual-level causes that have been neglected by criminologists. Some of these causes involve individual traits, such as alienation from major social institutions, a sense of injustice, and emotions such as anger, fear, and hopelessness. These causes also involve types of strain seldom examined in mainstream criminology, such as discriminatory experiences with school officials, employers, and police; perceptions of threat from other groups; and partner abuse. Further, they include values such as hostile attitudes toward other groups and the "win at any cost" orientation that often develops when group conflict is high. And they include indicators of power and autonomy (see Agnew, 1990; Tittle, 1995; Wright et al., 1999).

Self-Interest and Social Concern. The integrated theory should also incorporate the key points made about human nature in chapter 4. In particular, the theory should recognize that people show both social concern and self-interest; that the degree of concern and self-interest vary; and that this variation is likely related to crime. Social concern and self-interest can be readily incorporated into the integrated theory. While the variation in social concern and self-interest is in part biologically based, it is also influenced by the level of consensus/conflict in a society. Most notably, consensus fosters social concern (see chap. 4), while conflict fosters self-interest (e.g., Bonger, 1969: Messner and Rosenfeld, 2007).

The Relationship between Causes. The integrated theory should do more than provide an expanded list of the causes of crime. The theory should also describe the relationship between these causes, thereby providing a better sense of why they vary and how they work together to cause crime. One major contribution the theory can make in this area is to link macro– and micro-level causes. Conflict theories focus on the larger social environment and often neglect the individual-level mechanisms by which the larger environment leads people to engage in crime. Mainstream theories, including those based on the consensus perspective, focus on individual-level causes and often neglect the impact of the larger social environment on such causes. Since the integrated theory draws on both the conflict and consensus perspectives, it provides a good vehicle for cross-level integration.

The Context in Which the Causes Operate. Most crime theories simply list one or a few causes, and assume that these causes apply to all people and all types of crime (or at least all types of core crime). The integrated theory, however, suggests that the applicability of the causes sometimes depends on the nature of the society, the groups to which people belong, and the type of crime being explained. It is therefore critical that criminologists devote more attention to contextual issues when explaining crime. As indicated, societies differ in the extent and nature of consensus/conflict. And this difference has *some* effect on the causes of crime that are most applicable. To give an obvious example, causes such as racial discrimination, perceptions of racial threat, and feelings of injustice are more relevant in societies where racial conflict is high. Also, the causes differ somewhat across groups, particularly across more and less advantaged groups. Certain causes may apply to some groups but not others (e.g., social power, poverty). Group affiliation also affects the level and nature of those causes to which group members are exposed (e.g., the level and nature of criminal victimization). And group affiliation sometimes conditions the effect of the causes on crime. Finally, certain causes may be more applicable to some types of crime than others. For example, low self-control is more applicable to the explanation of core crimes than to corporate crimes (Benson and Moore, 1992).

The integrated theory, however, needs to more fully describe how context matters. This is of course a major task, especially when issues of intersectionality are considered. At the same time, this task points to the major strengths of the theory. Since the theory incorporates and extends the key arguments from both the consensus and conflict perspectives, it is capable of explaining crime in a range of societies. It can also explain crimes by the members of both superordinate and subordinate groups. And it can explain the different types of crime listed in chapter 2. These types include the core crimes that are the focus of consensus theorists and mainstream criminologists more generally. And they include several types of crime that are not easily explained by the consensus perspective, such as unrecognized blameworthy harms and repressive state crimes (e.g., environmental pollution, the production of unsafe products, genocide). Such crimes typically emerge out of group conflict, and they reflect the efforts of powerful groups to advance their interests and values through the oppression of others.

Conditioning Variables. Most causes generally increase the likelihood of crime, but the causes do not always lead to crime. For example, individuals and groups may respond to material deprivation by (1) accepting such deprivation as justified; (2) suffering in silence; (3) working to reduce their deprivation through legal channels, such as the political process; (4) engaging in illegal protest; (5) engaging in civil war or guerilla activities; and/or (6) engaging in certain types of crime. And if individuals and groups do respond with crime, they may engage in crime to reduce their oppression (e.g., theft, drug selling to obtain money); express resistance to oppression (e.g., vandalism, civil disobedience); seek revenge against oppressors; or pursue interests not directly related to their oppression. The response taken is shaped or conditioned by a range of factors. The integrated theory should describe those factors that condition the response to the causes of crime. Some suggestions have already been provided. For example, a criminal response to material deprivation is more likely when individuals have few legal coping options, have little to lose from crime, hold beliefs favorable to crime, and have opportunities for crime (also see Agnew, 2006a, 2010b).

The Role of Bounded Agency. The integrated theory should also recognize that the response to the causes of crime is influenced by the exercise of agency. As discussed in chapter 3, agency is more likely to be exercised by some individuals than others, and the exercise of agency influences both the level of crime and the amount of variation around that level. The integrated theory should also build on chapter 3 by more fully describing how the larger social environment and group affiliation influence the exercise of agency. In particular, there is good reason to believe that the level of consensus/conflict in a society and group characteristics have a large effect on all of the factors affecting agency. These factors (see chap. 3) include the motivation to alter one's behavior; the belief that one can produce desired change; the possession of those resources necessary for the exercise agency (e.g., creativity, broad knowledge, autonomy, power); and location in environments that have weak or countervailing constraints, provide numerous opportunities for agency, and encourage agency.

As an illustration, there is some reason to believe that lower-class individuals are more likely than higher-class individuals to be in a state of "drift" (see Matza, 1964: chap. 3). On the one hand, they are more likely to experience a range of strains, including family, school, peer, and work problems; thus, they should be motivated to alter their behavior (Agnew, 2006a:142–46). Further, they are more often in environments where social control is low and/or they face countervailing constraints, providing the freedom to exercise agency. On the other hand, lower-class individuals are lower in self-efficacy and less likely to possess many of the traits and resources necessary for the exercise of agency, such as creativity, broad knowledge, and power (Kohn, 1977: Thoits, 2006). So lower-class individuals have the desire and freedom to engage in agentic behavior, but lack the capacity, placing them in a state of drift.

Controlling Crime

The integrated theory can shed light on the control as well as the causes of crime. In particular, the forces described in the integrated theory influence the nature and operation of the criminal justice system. The extent and nature of consensus/conflict influences what is and is not defined as a crime by the state. It influences the types of crime on which justice officials focus their efforts; for example, it influences the attention devoted to corporate crimes. It influences the extent to which the system focuses on crime control strategies such as punishment, rehabilitation and prevention, and altering the larger social environment. And it influences the extent and nature of discrimination in the system. Researchers should elaborate on these ideas; more fully describing the ways in which the nature and extent of consensus/conflict influences various features of the criminal justice system. The result will be a single theory that explains both the causes of and the response to crime.

The integrated theory also suggests a range of approaches to reducing crime; approaches reflecting both the consensus and conflict perspectives. Issues involving the inability and unwillingness to abide by the social consensus are likely to be present in all societies. So efforts to increase self- and social control should be a central part of all policy initiatives. As indicated earlier, a range of initiatives involving rehabilitation, prevention, and the criminal justice system have shown some success here. But the integrated theory also draws heavily on the conflict perspective. And to the extent that group conflict is present, efforts to control crime must also focus on reducing such conflict. Several initiatives were earlier suggested in this area, with these initiatives targeting the causes, mechanisms, and consequences of group conflict.

Conclusion

Some criminologists assume that society is characterized by consensus; people hold similar values; pursue shared and interdependent interests; agree on the "rules of the game" when they do compete; and generally get along with one another. Other criminologists assume that society is characterized by conflict; groups hold conflicting values and interests, and those in more powerful groups oppress others as they promote their values and advance their interests. There is some support for each of these positions. There is a core consensus; with the vast majority of people condemning core crimes and cooperating to at least some degree in certain areas. Beyond that, the extent and nature of consensus/conflict varies. It varies according to the groups being considered, the interests/values in question, the society, and the time period. This chapter presented the foundation for an integrated consensus/conflict theory, one which describes the groups and interests/values that criminologists should consider, the major types of consensus and conflict, and the factors influencing the nature and extent of consensus/conflict. This theory points to a range of causes at the social and individual level-including some that have been neglected in the discipline. And it has the potential to explain the different types of crime discussed in chapter 2, as well the nature and operation of the criminal justice system.

6

The Nature of Reality

*Is There an Objective Reality That
Can Be Accurately Measured?*

Postmodernists fundamentally disagree that there is such a thing as objective truth. Instead, all knowledge is subjective, shaped by personal, cultural, and political views . . . knowledge is made up simply of "claims to truth" [from Foucault]. They believe that knowledge and truth are "socially constructed." This means that there is no independent reality outside the minds and practices of those who create and re-create it. Knowledge is artificial, an outcome of humans making distinctions and judging . . . one set of ideas as superior to another. . . . Part of the postmodern critique involves the "resurrection of subjugated knowledges," the excluded, neglected, and marginal knowledges discounted by dominant social constructions. It involves including other voices.

—Lanier and Henry, *Essential Criminology*

Previous chapters have dealt with the assumptions that criminologists make about the nature of crime, people, and society. As indicated, these assumptions have a fundamental impact on the causes of crime that are considered and the crime control strategies that are recommended. Once these causes and strategies are identified, criminologists must determine whether they affect crime. This is accomplished through a process of empirical research, with criminologists collecting and analyzing data from the larger world. Criminologists, however, take two rather different approaches to the collection and analysis of data, and these different approaches are rooted in the different assumptions they make about the larger world or "reality."

Positivistic criminologists assume that there is an objective reality, that it is possible to obtain reasonably accurate measures of it, and that this reality is the primary determinant of behavior-including crime. These criminologists obtain data on the larger world through several methods, with the most common being large-scale surveys. The respondents in such surveys are asked about the extent of their crime and those variables believed to cause crime, such as self-control, attachment to parents, and association with delinquent peers. Positivistic criminologists are aware that the responses they receive may provide an inaccurate or biased view of reality. As a result, they employ a range of techniques designed to *minimize bias*, with the goal of developing the single best measures of crime and its causes. Most criminological research published in mainstream journals fits this model. Typically, there will be single measures of crime and each of the causes of crime being considered (although these measures may be comprised of multiple items or questions). Researchers often acknowledge that these measures are less than ideal. Nevertheless, they claim that such measures provide reasonably accurate indicators of those aspects of reality that are the major causes of crime.

Other criminologists, frequently called "constructionists," emphasize that peoples' views of reality are socially constructed. In particular, those views are shaped by their characteristics and experiences, including the values they hold and the people they interact with. In fact, some claim that there is no objective "reality" out there to describe, as reflected in the quote at the beginning of this chapter. Instead, there are only multiple subjective realities, corresponding to the different views of the world that people hold. Further, constructionists argue that it is critical for criminologists to carefully examine these subjective views. These views—although shaped by personal characteristics and experiences—are the primary determinants of behavior, including crime. For example, individuals may believe that they are doing well in school, even though their school grades indicate otherwise (Agnew and Jones, 1988). This belief, although mistaken, may nevertheless affect their likelihood of engaging in crime–even after "objective" measures of school performance are considered. This mistaken belief, for example, may reduce their level of subjective strain. So constructionists argue that we should *not* try to minimize bias and develop the single best measures of reality; rather, we should embrace the biased views of individuals and examine their effects, including their effect on crime. This task is best accomplished through intensive interviews with and the close observation of a small number of people, a process that allows researchers to more fully describe how people view the world and the effects of these views.

So we have two rather different views of reality; one assumes that there is an objective reality, that it can be accurately measured, and that it is the major determinant of crime. The other assumes that there are multiple subjective realities and that subjective views are the major determinant of crime. And each has different implications for how we study crime. The first two sections of this chapter describe these differing views, certain of the evidence related to them, and their implications for research. The third section proposes a compromise between the "objective reality" and "multiple-subjective reality" views; what I call the "multiple-perspectives approach."

On the one hand, I argue that there is an objective reality "out there," that it is possible to measure it in ways that *minimize* bias, and that it exerts an important effect on crime. On the other hand, I argue that it is also important to take account of the subjective views of different individuals. Although biased, such views may impact crime even after measures of objective reality are considered. An approach for constructing "reduced-bias" measures of reality *and* separately considering the effects of individual views is described. The final section argues that this approach will substantially improve our ability to explain and control crime, since crime is a function of both objective conditions and the subjective views of individuals. Further, I argue that considering the relationship between different views of the world can also improve our ability to explain and control crime. For example, I argue that crime is more likely when parents and juveniles hold different views of their family life.

The Assumption of an Objective Reality That Can Be Accurately Measured

Most mainstream criminology is based on the "positivistic approach." This approach assumes that there is an objective reality which can be accurately measured and that this reality is the major determinant of crime. It is the task of researchers to test their theories against this reality.[1] In doing so, researchers attempt to develop the single best measures of this reality. This reality is comprised of a range of objects, including the larger social environment (e.g., the level of neighborhood poverty), the more immediate environment (e.g., the nature of family and peer groups), the acts that individuals engage in and are subject to (e.g., child abuse), individual traits (e.g., low self-control), attitudes (e.g., beliefs regarding crime), and biological factors (e.g., level of serotonin).

Positivistic criminologists collect data on this reality mainly through the use of surveys, which allow them to examine large, representative samples of respondents; readily measure most of the objects that comprise reality; and avoid many of the ethical and practical problems associated with experiments (see Agnew, 2009). Therefore, positivistic criminologists rely heavily on the reports or views of survey respondents when measuring reality. These reports are generally treated as indicators of objective reality (what Presser, 2009, calls "narrative as record"). However, it is recognized that they are often inaccurate or biased. For example, respondents may state that they engage in less crime than is actually the case, perhaps in an effort to make themselves look good. This bias is seen as undesirable, and positivistic criminologists take steps to reduce or eliminate it. Positivistic criminologists recognize also that there are some aspects of reality which cannot be measured with respondent reports, including certain features of the larger social environment (e.g., gross national product) and of the individual's biology (e.g., brain structure and functioning). These features of reality are estimated in other ways, such as the use of statistical compilations and biological tests. Again, the aim is to produce the single best (i.e., unbiased) measures of reality.

That said, it is important to note that positivistic criminologists are sometimes interested in measuring the subjective views of respondents (what Presser, 2009, calls "narrative as interpretation"). Deterrence theorists, for example, are interested in estimating both the "true" likelihood of punishment and the likelihood of punishment *as seen by the respondent* (see Agnew, 2009, for an overview). Deterrence theorists recognize that respondents frequently overestimate the true likelihood of punishment, but argue that the respondent's view of punishment also affects crime. Likewise, general strain theory (GST) states that researchers should measure both "objective" and "subjective" strains. That is, researchers should determine if respondents have experienced events and conditions that are generally disliked (objective strains), and researchers should measure how respondents subjectively view such strains. It is recognized that the same objective strain, such as a divorce, may be viewed differently by different people. For example, some may view their divorce as the worst thing that ever happened to them, while others may view it as a cause for celebration. GST states that both objective and subjective strains impact crime (Agnew, 2006a).

So positivistic criminologists do not deny the importance of subjective views. But such views are seen as *one part* of the much larger reality they want to measure. And the goal is to measure most aspects of this reality in an objective manner; that is, in a way that minimizes the biases in subjective views or does not rely on subjective views. For example, the focus is on measuring "actual" or "true" levels of self-control, parental supervision, peer delinquency, and neighborhood poverty, along with the perceived likelihood of punishment. Reflecting this fact, positivistic criminologists devote much effort to estimating the accuracy of the responses they receive, determining why such responses are sometimes inaccurate, and developing methods to increase their accuracy. In doing so, they draw heavily on the work of psychologists and sociologists, who have devoted much attention to the validity or accuracy of the measures they employ. I next provide a brief overview of certain of this work.

Research on the Accuracy of Respondent Reports

Agreement between Different Respondents. One way in which the accuracy of respondent reports is examined is by comparing the reports that different respondents provide about the same phenomena. For example, children, parents, and teachers might all be asked to describe the child's level of self-control. If respondent reports accurately describe reality, the different reports should all be very similar. However, the reports usually have only a modest correlation with one another. In the classic study in this area, Achenbach et al. (1987) conducted a meta-analysis of the reports of different respondents regarding the emotional and behavioral problems of children and adolescents. The average size of the correlation between reports depended on the respondents being compared (juveniles, parents, teachers, peers, and mental health workers were examined). Most correlations were in the .20s, suggesting that the reports of one type of respondent explain less than 10 percent of the variation in the reports of another type of respondent regarding the same variable.

More recent research has confirmed these findings with a broader range of variables.[2] As Achenbach et al. state (1987:227): "it is clear that no one type of informant typically provides the same data as any other type of informant." If that were not enough, it is sometimes the case that respondents do not even agree with themselves. In particular, respondents often give different reports about the same phenomena when interviewed on separate occasions (Wikman, 2006). A variety of factors influence the correlation between respondent reports, such as the visibility of the variable that is being described.[3] For example, respondents are more likely to agree with one another if they are describing a variable such as sex than a variable such as intelligence.

The Effect of Respondent Reports on Outcome Variables. Researchers have also examined the accuracy of respondent reports by comparing their effect on outcome variables, such as crime. If the reports of different respondents are accurate, we would expect them to have similar effects on outcome variables. However, they often have different effects (e.g., De Los Reyes and Kazdin, 2005; Ladd and Kochenderfer-Ladd, 2002; Offord et al., 1996). For example, Loeber et al. (1991) focused on child, parent, and teacher reports of the child's level of hyperactivity/inattention, oppositional behavior, and conduct problems. The reports of different respondents often had different effects on outcomes such as school suspension, school retention, special class placement, and police conduct—all measured one year later. To illustrate, the Time 1 child reports of hyperactivity/inattention had a correlation of .0 with Time 2 police contacts, while the parent reports of hyperactivity/inattention had a correlation of .18 (also see Larzelere and Patterson, 1990; Loeber et al., 1990).

Related to this, it is frequently the case that reports from one type of respondent have a significant effect on outcomes such as crime, even after we take account of the reports from other respondents (Achenbach et al., 2005). For example, Krohn et al. (1992) examined the effect of parent and adolescent reports of family processes on delinquency. They looked at reports of family attachment, communication, supervision, consistency of discipline, and positive parenting, among other things. They found that taking account of the parental reports of these family processes about doubled their ability to explain delinquency, *after* the adolescent reports were considered. And taking account of the adolescent reports almost doubled their ability to explain delinquency, *after* the parent reports were considered.

Respondent Reports Compared to "Gold Standard" Measures. The above studies compare the reports of different respondents with one another. In a few cases, it has been possible to compare respondent reports to what are known as "gold standard" measures of a variable; that is, measures believed by those in the scientific community to be highly accurate. Research suggests that respondent reports are often only weakly to moderately correlated with such measures (Achenbach et al., 2005:371). For example, the correlations between biological measures of drug use and the reports of respondents regarding their drug use are often modest in size (Achenback et al., 2005: 371; Magura and Kang, 1996). Related to this, memory researchers have asked respondents about events that they know the respondents have and have not experienced. Such researchers have found that respondents often forget about events that have happened to them and sometimes remember events that have not happened to them. This occurs for a variety of reasons: the passage of time, preoccupation with a distracting issue when the event occurred, and the suggestibility of many individuals (see Renk et al., 2007). Based on his review of the memory research, Gazzaniga (2005:120) states that: "Of all the things we remember, the truly amazing fact is that some of them are true" (also see Renk et al., 2007).

The Importance of Factors beyond the Individual's Conscious Awareness. Finally, a growing body of research suggests that individuals are not consciously aware of many of the factors that affect their behavior (see Dijksterhuis, 2010, for an overview). For example, individuals are often unaware of the biases they hold toward the members of other groups. These "implicit" biases have been measured in several ways, including psychophysiological measures. And research suggests that they affect the behavior of the individuals who hold them (e.g., Hewstone et al., 2002; Quillian, 2006). More generally, research suggests that much human behavior is performed in response to environmental stimuli that we are not consciously aware of. As Bargh and Chartrand (1999:466) state, "the external environment can direct behavior non-consciously through a two-stage process: automatic perceptual activity that then automatically creates behavioral tendencies." A series of experiments confirm this. For example, experimenters will non-consciously activate stereotypes by presenting individuals with words related to the stereotype (e.g., stereotypes regarding the elderly will be activated by words such as "wrinkle" and "Florida"). Individuals presented with such words are then more likely than those in a control group to act in accord with stereotypes during later, unrelated tasks (also see the discussion of rationality in chap. 4).

Sources of Bias in Respondent Reports

Given these findings, researchers have examined why respondent reports are so often inaccurate or biased. Three major sources of bias have been identified.

First, *respondents may not accurately and fully report what they "know" to researchers.* There is a large literature on how the nature of the research process may lead to distorted reports. In some cases, respondents deliberately provide biased reports to researchers. For example, researchers sometimes find evidence for a "social desirability effect," with respondents under-reporting behaviors and traits that are socially condemned and over-reporting those that are approved. To illustrate, juveniles sometimes withhold information about delinquent acts they have committed (Loeber et al., 1990, 1991; Peets and Kikas, 2005). And parents often present an overly favorable image of their child-rearing practices (e.g., Schwarz et al., 1985). In other cases, researchers fail to provide respondents with the opportunity to fully report what they know. Qualitative researchers, in particular, have been critical of survey research methods, which often ask respondents to describe their beliefs or attitudes by indicating whether they agree or disagree with a simple statement (e.g., "Do you like school"). It is said that such statements fail to capture the often complex nature of respondent views.

Second, *respondents may have limited information about certain aspects of the world*, most often because these aspects are not readily observable by them. As a result, respondents cannot provide accurate reports even if they want to and are given ample opportunity to do so. In particular, respondents often have limited information on (a) their own internal biological states (e.g., levels of serotonin); (b) the internal biological and psychological states of others (e.g., the beliefs of others); (c) behavior that occurs in situations beyond their view (e.g., parents may have limited information on the behavior of their children at school); and (d) a range of macro-social variables that are difficult to accurately estimate based on individual observations (e.g., the probability of arrest in a community). In other cases, however, information about a variable is often readily observable, such as the sex of an individual. So we would expect respondent reports to be more accurate here.

Third, *a range of factors affect how respondents perceive, interpret, and recall what they do observe*. As a result, respondents may provide biased reports even if they have full information about some aspect of the world. Those factors contributing to bias include personality traits. For example, some individuals have a negative attributional bias, such that they are more likely to interpret the ambiguous acts of others as deliberate provocations (Dodge and Schwartz, 1997). So an accidental bump may be interpreted as a deliberate shove by such people. Those factors contributing to bias also include emotional states. For example, there is some evidence that depressed parents are more likely to view their children's behavior in a negative light (De Los Reyes and Kazdin, 2005; Richters, 1992). Biasing factors include beliefs, attitudes, and values; including the stereotypes that people hold. For example, we are more likely to notice and remember information that confirms our stereotypes (Snyder and Uranowitz, 1978). Biasing factors include a self-serving bias, such that individuals tend to perceive, interpret, and recall events in ways that enhance their identity and serve their interests. Parents, for example, frequently describe family processes in a more positive manner than both children and trained independent observers.[4] Biasing factors include the desire to conform. As noted in chapter 4, respondents show a strong tendency to agree with the judgments of others, even when there is good evidence that such judgments are mistaken. Many additional sources of bias have been identified (see Renk, 2005; Renk et al., 2007). Further, evidence suggests that these biases often differ across individuals and socio-demographic groups, (e.g., De Los Reyes and Kazdin, 2005; Gazzaniga, 2005; Tein et al., 1994). Some individuals, for example, are more inclined to conform than others.

In sum, there is much reason to doubt the accuracy of respondent reports. Nevertheless, the large share of positivistic research relies on such reports— typically reports from the individuals whose crime is being explained. Positivistic researchers, however, regularly note the potential problems with such reports and the need for better measures. Most are not in a position to develop such measures, given their reliance on survey research conducted by others. Some positivistic criminologists, however, have taken steps to minimize the biases in respondent reports, drawing heavily on the work of positivistic researchers in other fields.[5]

Efforts to Minimize Bias

Certain of the efforts taken to minimize bias focus on the nature of the survey process, with researchers developing techniques to help ensure that respondents will more honestly and fully report what they know. For example, researchers try to establish better rapport with respondents, so they will feel more comfortable reporting sensitive information. Researchers also provide ways to report such information in a confidential manner, such as responding to questions on a laptop computer. And they provide opportunities for respondents to provide more detailed responses (e.g., Ferrell et al., 2008; Groves et al., 2009; Wikman, 2006). Researchers have also attempted to estimate and correct for certain types of bias. For example, they sometimes employ validity or "lie" scales in their surveys in an attempt to determine whether respondents are giving random or deceptive responses (see Achenback et al. 2005:362–63).

Another strategy for reducing bias involves collecting information from multiple types of respondents. For example, a researcher seeking to explain juvenile crime might interview not only a sample of juveniles but also one of the parents, one of teachers, and certain of the friends of these juveniles. These others may report certain information that the juvenile conceals (e.g., school misbehavior), may have information not available to the juvenile (e.g., family income), and their perceptions may differ from those of the juvenile. That is not to say that the reports of these others are unbiased, but rather that their biases differ somewhat from those of the juvenile. As such, their reports can supplement those of the juvenile, providing a more complete and perhaps accurate picture of reality.

Researchers have also tried to reduce bias by supplementing respondent reports with information from other sources. Information may be obtained from *official records*, such as school, police, and court records. These records often reveal information that respondents are unaware of or unwilling to reveal, such as failing grades or arrests (e.g., Agnew and Jones, 1988; Mosher et al., 2002). Information may also be obtained by *observing respondents*, both in the laboratory and in the field. For example, juveniles may be asked to interact with their parents in a lab setting, playing games or performing certain tasks. Independent observers then evaluate the quality of parent-child relations on several dimensions, such as level of warmth (e.g., Larzelere and Patterson, 1990; Noller and Callan, 1988). Or independent observers may rate the aggressiveness of children by observing them play during recess at school (e.g., Williams, 1986). Further, information may be obtained through *physiological or psychological tests*, such as intelligence tests or saliva tests for drug use. Finally, information may be obtained through *laboratory or field experiments*. For example, one study surveyed employers about their hiring practices *and* conducted a field experiment, in which blacks and whites applied for jobs with these employers (Pager and Quillian, 2005). The researchers discovered that some employers who claimed to be unbiased nevertheless favored white applicants.

The measures based on these information sources are useful, frequently affecting outcome variables even after respondent reports are considered (e.g., Larzelere and Patterson, 1990). But at the same time, the measures from these sources are biased as well. For example, consider the observations of independent observers. Independent observers are usually trained to rate individuals in a way that minimizes many of the biases listed. As Lorber (2006:336) states: "Observers are shown multiple samples of each behavior of interest and [told] how to discriminate among them. . . . Multiple cycles of practice, review, and critique ensue, until observers reach a target level of agreement." Nevertheless, bias occurs. Assessments by independent observers are especially subject to the second type of bias (limited information about a factor), since their ratings are usually based on observations made in a single setting. Also, the presence of observers may influence the behavior of those being observed. Further, observers are subject to the third set of biases (the ways respondents perceive, interpret, and recall what they observe). For example, the ratings of observers are sometimes affected by their prejudices (see Gonzales et al., 1996; Sessa et al., 2001). The other methods of measuring "reality" listed above are likewise biased in various ways. In fact, there are substantial literatures on the biases in official records, field observations, and experiments (e.g., Ferrell et al., 2008; Mosher et al., 2002; MacDonald, 2010).

The biases in these different information sources, however, often differ from one another and from the biases in respondent reports, such as the reports of juveniles, parents, and teachers. Given this fact, researchers argue that we can combine these various reports to get a more accurate image of reality. There has been much research on how to best combine these reports, with many favoring the creation of what are known as *latent variables* through the use of confirmatory factor analysis.[6] I won't go into technical detail here, but the logic is as follows: It is assumed that each of the reports reflect "reality" to some extent. The reports from these sources therefore partly agree or overlap. This overlap is said to represent the best measure of reality. Each report also contains what is known as "measurement error," which is due to the types of bias listed earlier. The nature of this error is assumed to differ somewhat across reports, however. Confirmatory factor analysis allows researchers to create latent variables that reflect the *overlap* between the different reports—with the measurement error removed.

The latent variable approach is not problem-free, however. It assumes that there are no shared biases between *all* of the different information sources. An example of a shared bias would be the tendency of respondents, parents, *and* official records to *under-estimate* the respondent's level of crime. Also, most applications of this approach treat the unique information provided by each source as measurement error. It is usually not possible to separate this unique information into its component parts, namely that part which provides accurate, but unique information about a variable and that part which reflects biases in the information source.[7] In particular, an information source may provide accurate data on an aspect of the real world that is not provided in other sources (see Achenbach et al., 1987). For example, this may occur because a particular type of respondent has access to information not available to other respondents (e.g., teachers have unique information regarding a juvenile's school behavior and performance). Such information may aid in the explanation of crime, even though it is not known by others, including the juvenile being examined.

Nevertheless, the latent variable approach, while not perfect, allows researchers to minimize the biases described earlier. Criminologists sometimes make use of this approach, and research relying on latent variables is usually better able to explain the variance in crime.[8] But the fact that such research requires data from multiple information sources limits its use. It is costly and difficult to obtain such data, especially when examining a large, representative sample of respondents. Even so, data from multiple sources has been successfully obtained in several large-scale surveys, making it possible for researchers to construct more accurate—although still imperfect— measures of reality.[9]

The Assumption of Multiple-Subjective Realities

The "objective reality" approach has been challenged by criminologists who draw on several perspectives, including symbolic interactionism, labeling theory, phenomenology, ethnomethodology, postmodernism, cultural criminology, and certain feminist and conflict theories.[10] These perspectives differ from one another in important ways, but they all argue that one's view of reality is socially constructed. That is, individuals learn how to perceive and interpret the world through their interactions with others. For example, individuals learn to categorize and interpret acts in certain ways. Anderson (1999) provides an illustration in his ethnographic study of a poor, inner-city community. Residents are taught that looking at someone for an excessive amount of time constitutes "staring," and that stares should sometimes be interpreted as challenges, particularly when one young male stares at another.

Constructionists argue that the subjective views of individuals are strongly influenced by their group affiliations, including their class, gender, age, and race/ethnicity. Individuals in the same group are exposed to similar influences and so develop similar views of the world. Also, they have similar interests, which also shape their views. Whites, for example, frequently develop a worldview that justifies their privileged position (see chap. 5). Certain worldviews, however, may come to dominate others. These views spread throughout the society and are reflected in its major institutions, such as the family, school, work, and political system. This is especially true of those views promoted by the members of powerful groups (chaps. 2 and 5 in this book provide several illustrations of this point). Most notably, powerful groups are usually able to convince others that certain behaviors should be viewed as harmful. And the views of these powerful groups are reflected in the criminal justice system. But at the same time, constructionists argue that the subjective views of individuals are also somewhat unique. As individuals interact with one another, they sometimes struggle to make sense of the world. And they often develop their own accounts or interpretations of what is happening. So constructionists would not challenge the evidence suggesting that parents, juveniles, teachers, and others often view the same phenomena in different ways. In fact, this is exactly what constructionists would expect.

Further, constructionists argue that the socially constructed views of individuals are the primary determinants of behavior. This is the case even if such views are biased or inaccurate. For example, an individual may mistakenly interpret the stare of another as a challenge, but this mistaken interpretation nevertheless drives behavior. The person being "stared" at, for example, may respond with violence. (Recall the popular sociological insight: "If people view a situation as real, it is real in its consequences.") Given this, constructionists do not view the biases inherent in respondent views as "measurement error" that is to be minimized. Rather, constructionists embrace the biased views of respondents, making them the central focus of analysis. This is reflected in the approach that constructionists take when studying crime.

Unlike positivists, constructionists do not try to develop the single best measures of particular variables. Rather, they examine the subjective views of those people involved in the production of crime. In particular, a complete explanation of crime should take account of the views of all of the major actors involved in its production. A study of juvenile crime, for example, might consider the views of juveniles, parents, and teachers, among others. We would expect all such views to have independent effects on crime, even if the different respondents are describing the "same" aspect of "reality" (e.g., juveniles and parents are each describing levels of parental supervision). Reflecting this fact, constructionists would take great satisfaction in those studies that find that our ability to explain crime is substantially improved when we separately consider the views that different individuals hold of the same phenomena.

When studying crime, constructionists examine the nature of respondent views, how they emerge, and the manner in which they influence crime. For example, labeling theorists examine how certain acts come to be viewed as crimes, including acts that cause relatively little harm. They examine why some individuals are more likely than others to be viewed and treated as criminals. And they examine how individuals respond when they are labeled as criminals. Often, labeled individuals come to view themselves as criminals and engage in crime as a result (see Agnew, 2009; Cullen and Agnew, 2011). The focus, then, is not on describing "objective reality" but on understanding how individuals view the world and the consequences of such views.

Constructionists favor the use of what are known as "qualitative methods" in examining individual views. Rather than sampling a large number of individuals and asking each a set of predetermined questions, it is best to closely examine a smaller number of individuals. Ideally, these individuals should be intensively interviewed, with ample opportunity for them to speak in their own words; they should be observed in natural settings, such as home, school, and the community; and an effort should be made to understand the larger social influences to which they are subject. For example, one should closely examine the media influences to which they are exposed. As Ferrell et al. (2008:205) state, criminology should "grasp the phenomenology of everyday life: the experiences of joy, humiliation, anger, and desperation, the seductions of transgression and vindictiveness, the myriad forms of resistance and the repressive nature of acquiescence." This goal is not accomplished by tabulating the responses to closed-ended questions on a survey, questions such as "do you like your mother." Rather, it is accomplished through immersion in the everyday world and the close study of those involved in crime. And constructionists have produced many excellent qualitative studies of crime that follow this strategy (e.g., Anderson, 1999; Katz, 1988; Miller, 2001).

But again, constructionists differ from one another in important ways. Most believe that there is an objective reality "out there," and some will even make efforts to measure aspects of it when discussing the social construction of respondent views. For example, there may be an effort to describe how neighborhood characteristics—such as level of poverty—help shape the views that residents hold regarding violence (e.g., Anderson, 1999). Such constructionists, however, stress that views of reality are socially constructed and that socially constructed views are the major determinants of behavior (see Liska and Messner, 1999). Other constructionists, particularly postmodernists, argue that there is no such thing as objective reality—a view reflected in the quote at the start of this chapter. My focus in this chapter is on the first group of constructionists; it is not possible to integrate postmodernist and positivistic approaches because they are diametrically opposed.[11]

The Multiple Perspectives Approach

We have, then, two rather different views of reality. The positivistic view assumes that there is an objective reality than can be accurately measured, with positivistic researchers developing the single best measures of this reality. Such measures are said to be the major determinants of behavior. The constructionist view assumes that there are multiple subjective realities, with constructionist researchers separately considering the views of different respondents. And these subjective views are said to be the major determinants of behavior. The research described earlier provides some support for both views. The reports from different respondents and information sources do overlap somewhat–suggesting that there may be an objective reality "out there." Building on such overlap, the research on latent variables suggests that it is possible to construct what might be called "reduced-bias measures" of reality. In addition, it is occasionally possible to develop "gold standard measures" of certain aspects of reality; with there being some reason to believe that such measures are highly accurate. And these latent variables and gold standard measures affect behavior, even after subjective views are taken into account. Further, there are certain important aspects of reality that cannot be measured in terms of the respondent reports that constructionists employ, yet there is good evidence that such aspects exist and strongly affect behavior (e.g., levels of serotonin in the brain, social and cultural features of the total society). So there is some reason to maintain the assumption that there is an objective reality and continue in our efforts to accurately measure it. But at same time, there is strong evidence that individuals often hold different views of the "same" reality, and that studies that separately consider such views are able to substantially improve our ability to explain crime.

The Multiple Perspectives Approach (MPA) therefore draws on both the positivistic and constructionist approaches, incorporating the advantages of each. Drawing on the positivistic approach, it assumes that there is an objective reality. That is, people *really* do possess certain characteristics, live in certain types of environments, and have certain experiences. Or, in the words of Pinker (2002:203), "the world really does contain ducks, who really do share properties." And while it may not be possible to measure this reality in a way free of all biases, it is possible to construct reduced-bias measures of it. Drawing on the constructionist approach, it argues that the subjective views of respondents are also important. While such views are affected by a range of factors beyond objective reality, they nevertheless guide behavior. So they too affect outcome variables, even after reduced-bias measures of reality are taken into account.

The MPA describes a general strategy for taking account of both reduced-bias measures of reality and the subjective views of respondents. This strategy is similar to the "mixed methods" approach that many behavioral and social scientists have come to advocate in recent years (see Tashakkori and Teddlie, 2003, for an excellent overview). It builds on the mixed method approach in certain ways, however; particularly in its suggestion that researchers examine the relations between the reports from different information sources—with these relations having an independent effect on outcome variables such as crime. The components of the MPA are as follows:

1. *Researchers should consider the views of key respondents when measuring crime variables.* Key respondents include the individual whose crime is being examined (the "target individual") and others likely to have a substantial impact on this individual's criminal behavior. These others include members of the target individual's primary group (e.g., parents, spouse, close friends) and representatives from those secondary groups that impact the individual—especially those who have much contact with the individual (e.g., teachers, employers). The respondents selected will to some extent depend on the variable being examined. For example, the individual's employer should ideally be consulted when measuring commitment to work but not when measuring attachment to spouse. Related to this, the value of different respondent reports in explaining crime will likely vary from variable to variable. Research and theory will help determine which reports are most relevant for which variables.[12] While the collection of data from multiple respondents may seem a daunting task, it is typically the case that data from only a few types of respondents are necessary. For juveniles, such respondents might include the primary caregiver, a teacher, and a close friend.

2. *Researchers should take steps to maximize the completeness and honesty of respondent reports.* This can be done by using those strategies described in the literatures on quantitative and qualitative research.[13] Also, researchers should consider using both large-scale surveys *and* qualitative methods, including focus groups and intensive interviews with a sub-sample of the individuals being surveyed.[14] The qualitative data provide more complete information on respondent views, allowing one to better interpret the meaning of the survey responses. The survey data provide some sense of the generalizability of the qualitative results.

3. *Where possible and desirable, researchers should also obtain independent assessments of the target individual's standing on variables.* These assessments may be based on official records, ratings by trained independent observers, physiological or psychological tests, experiments, content analyses, and other methods. Such assessments should not only focus on the individual's characteristics and immediate environment, but also on the larger social forces which impact the individual (see chap. 5). As such, data may also be obtained from statistical complications and archives. While such assessments frequently suffer from a range of biases, these biases often differ from those in respondent reports. The assessments therefore provide another valuable source of information regarding the target individual's standing on variables (see Jick, 1979). In a few cases, the assessments may even provide "gold standard measures" (see page 172). As a general rule, researchers seeking to measure a variable should consider the strengths and weakness of different information sources, including respondent reports and independent assessments, and try to select sources that complement one another (see Tashakkori and Teddlie, 2003).

4. *Researchers should create "reduced-bias" measures of key variables, with such measures usually based on the overlap or shared variation between the different information sources (respondent reports and independent assessments).* The reduced-bias measures may be created through the use of confirmatory factor analysis, with the resulting latent variables reflecting the overlap between information sources. It should be kept in mind that while latent variables minimize the effect of biases, they are not free of bias. A latent variable may reflect the shared biases of all the information sources that contribute to its construction (it is possible to control for biases shared by some of the information sources, however). Further, the information sources may provide incomplete data regarding the variable in question. The overlap between sources, then, may not fully reflect variation in the "true" variable. Nevertheless, the latent variable typically provides a better indicator of variation in the "true" variable than reports from a single information source or the simple combination of sources. In the few cases where "gold standard" measures are available, they may be used in place of latent variables.

5. *Researchers should examine the effect of both the reduced-bias measures and the individual respondent reports on outcome variables, including crime.* This allows researchers to determine whether the subjective views of respondents affect outcome variables after the reduced-bias measures are taken into account (and vice versa). These subjective views are composed of two

parts: (1) the unique information possessed by the respondent regarding the true level of a variable and (2) the biases of the respondent. Unfortunately, it is usually not possible to distinguish between these two components. It is possible, however, to examine the effect of respondent reports on outcome variables, with the latent variables controlled. This is the case even if the latent variables include the respondent reports as component parts (for an example, see Herrenkohl and Herrenkohl, 2007; also see Renk, 2005).

6. *Researchers should explore the sources of individual views.* In particular, researchers should examine the extent to which the views of respondents are influenced by the views of other respondents, other information sources, and latent variables. We would expect that an individual's perception of a variable would be influenced by the actual level of the variable; that is, the reduced-bias or latent variable. We would also expect that the individual's perceptions would be influenced by the perceptions of close others. For example, the mother's view of the child's delinquency may be influenced by the father's view, even after taking account of the actual level of delinquency. Respondent views may also be influenced by other information sources, such as an official record of delinquency. Further, respondent views may be influenced by the characteristics of the respondents, such as their personality traits, emotional states, beliefs, and socio-demographic characteristics (see the sources of bias listed above). Likewise, respondent views may be influenced by the characteristics of target individuals, such as their race/ethnicity and gender. Research in this area can shed much light on how the views of respondents are socially constructed. It can also shed light on related topics, such as labeling theory (see pages 179-180).

7. *Researchers should examine the relationship between the different information sources, including the relationship between respondent reports, other information sources (e.g., official records, observational data, laboratory tests), and latent variables.* For example, researchers should examine whether juveniles and parents have similar views of parenting practices, whether juvenile reports of their delinquency agree with those from official records, and whether juvenile reports of their peers' delinquency agree with the latent variable measuring peer delinquency. These relationships can be viewed as emergent variables and researchers should examine their effect on outcome measures, including crime. As discussed in the next section, certain types of relationships may increase the likelihood of crime and influence the effectiveness of crime control efforts.

It is recognized that full implementation of the Multiple Perspectives Approach would pose difficulties in data collection and analysis, although it is certainly within the realm of current capabilities. Researchers, however, may implement portions of the approach with several existing data sets. Many data sets, for example, measure particular variables with data from two or more types of respondents, such as target individuals, parents, teachers, and peers. Researchers employing such data sets often focus on just one type of respondent, typically the target individual, or they simply combine measures from different respondents. As suggested, researchers can make much better use of such data in their efforts to explain crime. At a minimum, researchers should attempt to create reduced-bias measures using the procedure described above, and examine the separate effects of both the reduced-bias measures and the individual respondent reports on crime.

Advantages of the Multiple Perspectives Approach

At the most basic level, the Multiple Perspectives Approach allows researchers to better measure the causes of crime by providing data from multiple information sources. This is especially important in those circumstances where there is reason to believe that target individuals are unaware of or grossly misperceive the factors that affect their behavior. For example, target individuals may not be conscious of the fact that others reinforce their aggressive behavior (see Patterson et al., 1992, for examples). The research by Krohn et al. (1992) suggests that the effect of using multiple information sources can be dramatic. They doubled the amount of variance they were able to explain in delinquency when they supplemented juvenile reports of family life with reports from parents.

Beyond that, the MPA has the advantage of examining the impact of both objective (reduced-bias) and subjective measures. At present, researchers usually only examine the effect of subjective measures, typically reports from target individuals. Since there is reason to believe that both objective and subjective measures affect crime, the MPA should dramatically improve efforts to explain and control crime. Further, the MPA allows researchers to explore the relations between information sources, something rarely done in current research. Particular types of relations may impact crime, over and above the effects of the individual information sources.

Crime as a Function of Both Subjective
Views and "Objective Reality"

There is reason to believe that behavior is influenced by both subjective views and objective reality. Individuals base their actions on their views, even if such views are mistaken. But at the same time, the real world imposes constraints on action and influences individuals in ways that they are unaware of or misperceive. As noted earlier, certain perspectives suggest that both objective reality and subjective views are important—with the importance of objective reality stemming *partly* from its influence on subjective views. For example, many social learning theorists argue that crime is a function of both its *perceived* costs and benefits and its actual costs and benefits (with actual costs often influencing perceived costs). And strain theorists focus on the importance of both objective strains and the subjective perception of those strains. Other perspectives, however, argue that subjective views *or* objective reality is the primary determinant of behavior. But even here, a good case can be made that both subjective views and objective reality are important and should therefore be considered when explaining crime.

Consider the variable of self-control, seen by some as the leading cause of crime (see Pratt and Cullen, 2000). Self-control refers to the ability of individuals to restrain themselves from acting on their immediate desires and impulses. Researchers should attempt to create an objective (or reduced-bias) measure of self-control, perhaps constructing a latent variable with information from several sources: juvenile reports, a parent report, a teacher report, a peer report, the observations of an independent observer, and/or a laboratory test (see Piquero et al., 2008). And researchers should also separately consider the reports of different respondents. All or most of these measures, both objective and subjective, may affect crime. The respondent's objective level of self-control may affect crime since those who are less able to restrain themselves are more likely to respond to temptations and provocations with crime. But the subjective measures may be important as well. Individuals who believe they are low in self-control may be less likely to make an effort to exercise such control, even after their "true" level of self-control is taken into account. The views of others may also be important. For example, conventional peers who view juveniles as low in self-control may be more likely to reject these juveniles—thus leading to association with delinquent peers. The consideration of both objective and subjective views should therefore improve our ability to explain crime.

A Note on the Definition of Crime

The focus on both objective and subjective measures is quite compatible with the definition of crime presented in chapter 2. Crimes were defined as acts that cause blameworthy harm, are condemned by the public, and/or are sanctioned by the state. That part of the definition involving "blameworthy harm" asserts that there are acts that are crimes in all places and at all times, regardless of how they are perceived (an "objective" definition of crime). At the same time, this definition recognizes that the subjective views of individuals and groups are important; and so the "constructionist" portion of the definition states that criminologists should also examine acts that are condemned by the public and/or sanctioned by the state. Further, criminologists were urged to explore the relationship between the objective definition of crime and subjective views of crime (e.g., why is it that certain blameworthy harms are not condemned or sanctioned).

The Relationships between Information Sources

Researchers should also examine the relationships between information sources. Particular types of relationships have important implications for the causes and control of crime, with several examples presented below.

Context-Specific versus General Offenders. The major schemes for classifying offenders focus on the frequency of offending, the seriousness of offending, and the patterning of offending over the life course (e.g., adolescence-limited versus life-course persistent offending) (Agnew, 2009). Another distinction, however, has been neglected. Some offenders may limit their crimes to particular contexts, such as family, school, peers, or work. Others may commit crimes across a range of contexts. Certain researchers have noted this possibility; for example, suggesting that the behavior of juveniles may shift dramatically across contexts, with delinquency being most likely in the company of peers.[15] Comparing the reports of the individual's offending across sources such as parents, teachers, and peers is perhaps the best method of determining whether offenders are context-specific or generalists. We would expect the causes of context-specific offending to differ somewhat from those of generalist offending. Generalist offending is likely motivated by characteristics of the individual that transcend contexts, such as personality traits and poverty. Context-specific offending is likely motivated by the level of social control, strain, social learning for crime, and criminal opportunities in particular contexts (e.g., De Coster and Kort-Butler, 2006). For example, many corporate and state criminals are context-specific offenders, responding to the pressures and opportunities in their particular positions. The distinction between context-specific and generalist offending also has important policy implications, since different interventions are required for each.

A Neglected Source of Strain. Researchers may find that respondents who are in close interaction with one another have very different views of reality. For example, parents may report that they give their children much freedom, while their children may report that their parents are overly strict. These disagreements may contribute to conflict or strain between individuals, particularly if they involve core goals, values, identities, or activities. As constructionists point out, individuals must share similar views of reality if they are to peacefully interact (see Einstadter and Henry, 2006). Researchers have rarely investigated the effect of discrepancies in informant reports, but limited data suggest that discrepancies between parents and juveniles are associated with higher levels of family stress, family conflict, and delinquency (Ferdinand et al., 2004: Tein et al., 1994).

Disagreements Reflecting Low Social Control. Certain relationships among respondent reports suggest low social control. Perhaps the best example is where the target individual reports high levels of delinquency, but other informants report that the target individual is low in delinquency. This combination suggests that others are not effectively monitoring the target individual. We would expect target individuals who fall into this category to be at higher risk for maintaining or increasing their levels of delinquency than comparable individuals whose delinquency has become known to conventional others.

Labeling. The use of multiple information sources can shed much light on labeling theory. Labeling theory argues that crime is most likely among individuals who are viewed and treated as criminals by others (Agnew, 2009; Cullen and Agnew, 2011). Such individuals develop a criminal self-concept, are mistreated by others, and are cut off from conventional others and institutions. Further, labeling theory states that whether individuals are labeled as criminals is only partly a function of their level of crime. Labeling is also influenced by factors such as their race, class, and gender. These arguments are best tested through the examination of reports from multiple informants. For example, we might examine how others view the target individual's level of crime. If labeling theory is correct, the views of these others should be influenced by a range of factors in addition to the target individual's true level of crime. In addition, the views of these others should have a substantial effect on how they treat the target individual; for example, those who view the target individual as a criminal should be more likely to engage in rejecting behavior. The views of others should also influence whether the target individual views herself as a criminal, after taking account of the target individual's true level of crime. Finally, the views of these individuals should influence the target individual's *subsequent* level of crime, after taking account of the target individual's *current* level of crime.

An Unrecognized Need for Help. The examination of the relationship between information sources may also aid in the effort to control crime. For example, the analysis of different information sources may reveal an unrecognized need for help. This unrecognized need may take several forms. First, target individuals may report that they are high in strain, low in control, and/or high in delinquent peer association. But others around the target individual, such as parents and teachers, may fail to report these criminogenic factors. This suggests that others are unaware that the target individual is in need of assistance. Second, target individuals may not report any problems, but serious problems may be revealed by other information sources, such as parents, teachers, and independent assessments. This suggests that target individuals do not realize that they need help (see the excellent discussion of this issue in De Los Reyes and Kazdin, 2005). Third, target individuals and others may disagree about the nature of those problems that need to be addressed. This is in fact a common problem among those in treatment. For example, juveniles, parents, and treatment staff often hold different views about the nature and source of the problems that need correction (Hawley and Weisz, 2003). The use of the MPA can help identify those in need of treatment and the problems to be treated.

Conclusion

The Multiple Perspectives Approach draws on both positivistic and constructionist approaches. It suggests a new approach for the collection and analysis of data, one with the potential to substantially improve the explanation and control of crime. Criminologists typically measure variables with data from a single informant, usually the individual whose crime is being explained. Much data, however, suggest that this approach is seriously flawed, sometimes producing misleading results and explaining much less variance in outcome measures than research using multiple information sources. The MPA recommends that criminologists collect data from the target individual, members of the target individuals primary group (e.g., parents, peers), key members of the target individual's secondary groups (e.g., teachers, employers), and—where possible and desirable—other sources (e.g., official records, independent observations, experiments). Drawing on positivistic and constructionist approaches, the MPA describes a strategy for creating "reduced-bias measures" of variables through the combination of these information sources *and* examining the separate effects on these sources on the target individual's crime. The MPA also focuses on the relationships between information sources, arguing that particular types of relationships are especially relevant to the explanation and control of crime. Thus, as in previous chapters, this chapter argues that the integration of insights from different perspectives substantially improves our ability to explain and control crime.

7

A Unified Criminology

> If theory A asserts X and theory B asserts not-X, it would seem
> impossible to bring them together in a way pleasing and satis-
> factory to both, and also pointless to try.
> —Hirschi, "Exploring Alternatives to Integrated Theory"

I began this book by stating that criminology is a divided discipline, comprised of theories and perspectives that are at odds with one another. These theories and perspectives focus on different types of crime, identify different causes, employ different methods, and/or make different recommendations for controlling crime. Criminologists have responded to this division in several ways. They test these theories and perspectives, hoping to identify those that are true and those that are false. As Bernard and Snipes (1996) point out, this effort has largely failed: one would be hard pressed to identify a theory that has been falsified. Most theories appear to have *some* merit, explaining a portion of the variation in some crime. Criminologists also attempt to integrate certain of these theories. But none of the integrations has attracted wide support; partly because they reflect the divided nature of the field, combining a small number of related theories and ignoring others. And, perhaps most commonly, criminologists set up shop in their own corner of the discipline; mostly ignoring the work of criminologists in other areas, but occasionally drawing on or attacking it.

Differences in Underlying Assumptions

I argued that the division in criminology is not easily resolved because it has deep roots. It is based on the different assumptions that criminologists make about the nature of crime, people, society, and reality. In particular, some criminologists assume that crime involves violations of the criminal law, while others disagree, proposing alternative definitions. Some assume that crime is determined by forces beyond the individual's control, while others claim that individuals have some choice over whether to engage in crime. Some assume that individuals are self-interested; others that they are socially concerned; and still others that they are blank slates, shaped by social forces. Some assume that society is characterized by a consensus over core values and interests, with people generally getting along; while others state that society is characterized by conflict, with some groups oppressing others. And some assume that there is an objective reality that can be accurately measured, while others argue that there are multiple subjective realities.

These assumptions have a fundamental impact on the types of acts that are viewed as crimes, the causes that are examined, the methods that are employed, and the recommendations that are made for controlling crime. That is to say, the discipline of criminology is built on these assumptions. To give a few examples from previous chapters: The assumption that crime involves violations of the criminal law leads many criminologists to focus on "street crimes," such as personal violence and theft, and to ignore many intentional acts that cause far more harm than such crimes (see chap. 2). The assumption that individuals are self-interested leads criminologists to focus on those factors that restrain the pursuit of interests, such as self- and social control; while the assumption that individuals are socially concerned leads to a focus on those factors that pressure or entice individuals into crime, such as strains and approval from peers (see chap. 4). And the assumption that there is an objective reality leads to efforts to develop the single best measures of that reality, while the assumption that there are multiple subjective realities leads to efforts to better understand the subjective views of individuals (see chap. 6).

These differences in underlying assumptions are most pronounced between mainstream and critical perspectives. However, there are also major differences in the assumptions made by mainstream theories and by critical theories. But despite the importance and pervasiveness of these differences, they are seldom discussed, particularly by mainstream criminologists, and they are rarely the object of systematic evaluation. There is a good reason for this. It was not possible to properly evaluate these assumptions until recently. For example, the data on human nature was of poor quality. As a result, it was possible for some to claim that people are self-interested, pointing to the many cruel acts committed in the pursuit of personal interests; others to claim that people are socially concerned, pointing to the many kind acts committed, even at some personal cost; and still others to claim that people are blank slates, pointing to the many differences among individuals and groups. And there was no good way to adjudicate between these claims. Recent developments in several areas, however, have made it possible to better evaluate the underlying assumptions of crime theories and perspectives.

All Underlying Assumptions Have Some Support

There has been much recent research on the topics of agency and determinism, the nature of human nature, consensus and conflict models of society, and biases in individual perception. Also, there has been rapid growth in the international human rights law and the scholarship associated with this law. Much of the work in these areas has been carried out by biologists, psychologists, anthropologists, political scientists, and sociologists. With certain notable exceptions, criminologists have not yet taken account of this work. This is understandable; the explosive growth in criminology has made it difficult for criminologists to keep abreast of developments in their own field, let alone other fields. Prior chapters summarized the relevant developments in these other fields and discussed their implications for the underlying assumptions of criminology.

The core argument to emerge from each of these chapters is that there is some truth to each of the underlying assumptions made by criminologists, but that each assumption only captures a part of the truth. In particular, a good case can be made that crime should be defined as acts that cause blameworthy harm, are publicly condemned, and/or are sanctioned by the state. There is reason to believe that crime is strongly influenced by factors beyond the individual's control, but that it also reflects the exercise of agency, with a range of factors influencing the degree of agency exercised. Research suggests that individuals are socially concerned, self-interested, and learn much from others, with the strength of these traits varying across individuals and social circumstances. Societies appear to be characterized by both consensus and conflict, with a range of factors influencing the extent and nature of consensus/conflict. And there is some basis for arguing that there is an objective reality that can be measured in ways that reduce the effect of individual biases, but that it is also important to take account of the subjective views of individuals.

In brief, we live in a complex and variable world. The assumptions that underlie particular crime theories and perspectives are overly simplistic, each reflecting only a part of this world. As a result, each theory or perspective typically has some support, but falls far short of providing a complete explanation of crime. Further, the very different assumptions that underlie particular theories and perspectives makes it impossible to integrate them-so that criminologists might better explain crime and advocate for its control. As the quote by Hirschi at the beginning of this chapter indicates, one cannot integrate theories that assert X with those that assert not-X. For example, how does one integrate theories claiming that crime is fully determined by forces beyond the individual's control with those claiming that crime is the result of choice? How does one integrate theories claiming that people are self-interested with those that claim that they are socially concerned? Or how does one integrate perspectives claiming that society is characterized by consensus with those claiming it is characterized by conflict? Before we can build an integrated or unified theory of crime, the differences in underlying assumptions must be resolved.

A New Set of Underlying Assumptions

Drawing on the recent work just described, a new set of underlying assumptions was presented. These assumptions integrate and extend the assumptions made by existing theories and perspectives. As such, they provide a foundation on which to build a unified criminology, one capable of more fully explaining a broader range of crimes. I provide a brief summary of these assumptions below and their implications for criminology (see the chapters indicated for fuller discussions, including the evidence and other justifications for these assumptions).

The Nature of Crime

There is of course no research that can definitively determine the nature of crime, since the nature of crime is a matter of definition. The advantages and disadvantages of several definitions were discussed, and it was argued that crime is best defined as (1) *acts which cause blameworthy harm,* (2) *are condemned by the public, and/or* (3) *are sanctioned by the state.* Defining acts as blameworthy harms has always been problematic, since it is difficult to define blameworthiness and harm in ways that are independent of the values and political agendas of criminologists. (At the same time, it is important to note that the legal definition of crime partly reflects the values and agendas of powerful groups.) The rapid growth of the international human rights law, however, provides criminologists with a more solid foundation for defining blameworthy harms. While the international law is a political creation, it transcends the politics of particular states, reflects much debate between agents with a range of perspectives, and includes most of the harms that have attracted the attention of critical criminologists. At the same time, there is also good reason to define crimes in terms of public condemnation and state sanction.

The three dimensions identified in the above definition encourage criminologists to devote greater attention to the origins and nature of their subject matter. For example, criminologists are encouraged to ask why certain blameworthy harms are not condemned or sanctioned by the state, as well as why certain relatively harmless acts are condemned and sanctioned. Relatedly, these dimensions provide criminologists with a new mission: making the public and policy makers more aware of those blameworthy harms that are not condemned and sanctioned. Finally, these dimensions provide the basis for a new typology of criminal acts, with seven types of crime identified. This typology directs attention to certain neglected types of crime. It points to certain very general causes of these crimes (e.g., individuals are ignorant of or deny the harm caused by their acts). And it suggests that there may be some differences in causes and control strategies across types of crime (see chap. 2).

Determinism and Agency

There has been much debate over whether crime is the result of agency or is fully determined by forces beyond the individual's control. Agency involves making choices and taking actions that are not fully determined by such forces; which is to say that the individual could have chosen and acted differently. The research does not allow us to definitively prove the existence of determinism or agency. But it does provide some reason to believe that behaviors fall along a continuum, ranging from fully determined to somewhat agentic. Further, research and theory suggest that individuals exercise greater agency when they (a) are motivated to alter their behavior, (b) believe they can produce desired change, (c) have the traits and resources necessary to exercise agency (e.g., creativity, broad knowledge, autonomy, power), and (d) are in environments that have weak or countervailing constraints, provide numerous opportunities for agency, and encourage agency.

While researchers cannot definitely prove that agency exists, they can investigate the implications of the above arguments. Among other things, we would expect behavior to be more unpredictable and somewhat more likely to involve crime when conditions favor the exercise of agency. Therefore, taking account of those factors that influence the exercise of agency will allow criminologists to better explain both the level of crime *and* the amount of variation (unpredictability) around this level. Further, there is reason to believe that the exercise of agency is subject to guidance. In fact, those most likely to exercise agency may be especially subject to influence, since they are open to change, inclined to conscious deliberation, and better able to act on the choices they make. The policy implications of this argument were discussed. Finally, the arguments regarding agency support the definition of crime that was presented. We cannot blame individuals for their behavior unless we assume that they have at least some responsibility for it, which is to say that they exercise some agency (see chap. 3).

Human Nature

Research suggests that people show some concern for others, especially kin and members of their in-group. This concern involves a desire for close ties with and the respect of others, empathy for them, a reluctance to cause direct harm to innocent others, an inclination to help innocent others in need, a desire to cooperate with others who reciprocate in an equitable manner, and a strong inclination to conform. This social concern is shown even at some personal cost to the individual, but considerations of self-interest are also important. People take account of the costs and benefits of possible actions, particularly crime. (Their rationality, however, is limited and other factors also influence the decision to engage in crime.) Further, the pursuit of self-interest is especially important in certain circumstances, including competition among males for rank, competition over scarce resources, and interactions with those in out-groups. Finally, people have a strong inclination and ability to learn from others, and do in fact learn much from others. Among other things, the above inclinations for social concern and self-interest are specified, modified, and stressed to varying degrees in social groups. So people show evidence of social concern, self-interest, *and* social learning—with the strength of these traits varying across individuals and social circumstances.

This more complex view of human nature suggests that all theories of crime are relevant, including those that focus on the constraints to crime and on the motivations for crime. It also suggests that criminologists need to pay much attention to bio-psychological factors, since the underlying traits that cause crime vary across individuals for reasons that are in part biologically based. Related to this, criminologists should attempt to better measure the traits of social concern and self-interest and examine their effect on crime. Further, criminologists should pay more attention to those social circumstances that foster social concern and self-interest; they too should impact crime. There is also reason to believe that levels of social concern and self-interest can be deliberately altered, suggesting a range of policy interventions. Finally, the research on human nature provides some support for the definition of crime presented in chapter 2, suggesting that people are naturally inclined to view some acts as blameworthy and harmful. The research also supports the arguments regarding bounded agency in chapter 3, suggesting that individuals are inclined to pause and deliberate before engaging in most of the acts defined as crimes. Such deliberation is at the heart of agency (see chap. 4).

Consensus and Conflict

There is reason to believe that all functioning societies are characterized by a core consensus; with people condemning the unconditional use of personal violence and theft and cooperating in certain areas, such as defense from external threats. Beyond that, the extent and nature of consensus and conflict vary. The outline of an integrated consensus/conflict theory was presented. Conflict involves the oppression of one group by another, with oppression involving the infliction of blameworthy harm (as defined in chap. 2). A range of blameworthy harms or types of oppression were listed. Those factors influencing the extent and nature of conflict were described. And the reasons why conflict influences crime were discussed. Group conflict generally increases crime among both oppressors and oppressed, although certain types of conflict may reduce crime among the oppressed. Drawing on the integrated theory, a list of social and individual-level variables predicted to affect crime was presented. These variables deal with the ability and willingness to participate in the consensus; as well as the causes, mechanisms, and consequences of group conflict. While many of these variables play a central role in current consensus and conflict theories (e.g., self-control, poverty), others are neglected in current research (e.g., discrimination) (see chap. 5).

The Nature of Reality

There is reason to believe that there is an objective reality that affects behavior, including crime. At the same time, it is difficult to accurately measure this reality, particularly since individual reports of it are biased for several reasons. Some progress, however, has been made in developing "reduced-bias" measures of this reality. Such measures focus on the overlap or shared variance between different information sources; including reports from different types of respondents (e.g., juveniles, parents, teachers) and other information sources (e.g., independent assessments by trained observers, experiments, official records). Researchers, however, should not rely solely on these reduced-bias measures. It is also important to consider the subjective views of different types of respondents. Research and theory suggest that they also affect behavior, even after researchers take account of reduced-biased measures. Further, researchers should examine the relations between the different information sources (e.g., between juvenile and parental reports of the same factor, or between reduced-biased measures and the subjective views of respondents). Particular types of relationships may affect crime, over and above the individual effects of their component parts. Employing these measurement approaches should substantially improve efforts to explain and control crime (see chap. 6).

Next Steps

Examining the Proposed Underlying Assumptions

The underlying assumptions described above should of course be discussed and empirically examined. While these assumptions are integrative in nature, it is likely than many will object to them. Many criminologists, in particular, not only assert that an assumption is true (e.g., people are self-interested) but also assert that other assumptions are false (e.g., people are *not* socially concerned). The integrated assumptions listed capture the positive assertions of most theories and perspectives but deny the negative assertions. I believe that the evidence supports this approach, but others may read the evidence differently. I therefore encourage criminologists to examine the literatures I describe in more detail and actively discuss the assumptions proposed. Such discussion, as well as the ongoing research in these literatures, will likely result in the refinement and revision of these assumptions.

Related to this, the proposed assumptions should be empirically examined. It is possible to test the validity of certain of these assumptions or, more commonly, to examine their utility by exploring their implications. The previous chapters contain numerous suggestions for empirical research. Many of these suggestions, in fact, point to major new areas of research for the discipline. For example, chapter 2 identifies seven general categories of crime and suggests that criminologists examine the extent to which their causes are similar and different. Chapter 3 suggests that criminologists not only examine differences in the level of crime but also differences in the amount of variation around that level. Chapter 4 suggests that criminologists directly measure the components of social concern and self-interest, estimate their effects on crime, and examine the biological and social factors that influence variation in them. Chapter 5 presents numerous propositions regarding those factors influencing the extent and nature of both consensus/conflict and crime. And chapter 6 suggests that criminologists make use of a range of information sources when studying crime, including reduced-bias measures and the subjective views of different types of respondents, and explore the relations between these sources.

Exploring Additional Assumptions

This book focuses on what I believe are the major underlying assumptions of the discipline, with these assumptions responsible for much of the division in the field. But criminologists make still other assumptions, many of which also have a large impact on the discipline. Most notably, criminologists make assumptions about the disciplinary status of those variables that affect crime. Until recently, mainstream criminologists focused on social-psychological variables, including features of the individual's immediate environment (e.g., family, school, peer group) and socially determined features of the individual (e.g., beliefs regarding crime). Most psychological characteristics were ignored, along with the biological factors influencing these characteristics. In fact, many criminologists argued that biological and psychological factors had little role to play in the explanation of crime (see Andrews and Wormith, 1989; Raine, 1993). Features of the larger social environment were also neglected in mainstream criminology. And the physical environment was ignored by virtually all criminologists.

Perhaps the major change in criminology over the last quarter century has been the dramatic expansion in the disciplinary range of those causes that are considered. Mainstream criminologists now devote more attention to psychological characteristics and the biological factors contributing to such characteristics (see Wright et al., 2008). Likewise, mainstream criminologists devote more attention to the larger social environment, including community – and societal-level variables (e.g., Messner and Rosenfeld, 2007; Pratt and Cullen, 2000: Sampson et al., 1997). And even features of the physical environment have begun to receive some attention (Bottoms and Wiles, 2002). These changes reflect the fact that criminology has become more interdisciplinary in nature, drawing on a broader range of scholars and more readily incorporating outside research. But certain types of causes are still neglected by mainstream criminologists. These include physical features of the individual, such as physical size, strength, and appearance (e.g., Agnew, 1984; Felson, 1996; Messerschmidt, 2004); the interactional patterns leading up to crime (Short, 1998); certain of the quasi-social consequences of crime, such as pain and thrills (e.g., Katz, 1988; McCarthy and Hagan, 2005); and certain features of the natural environment, such as weather and climate (Cheatwood, 2009).

Another underlying assumption has to do with the variation in variables. Until recently, criminologists assumed that the variables that cause crime are fairly stable over time. Little consideration was given to long-term changes in these variables, evident over the life-course of individuals. And little attention was paid to situational changes in these variables. This too has changed. Much attention is now devoted to changes in the causes of crime over the life-course (see Piquero and Mazerolle, 2001). Likewise, researchers devote significant attention to the manner in which certain causes—such as level of supervision—change from situation to situation (see Felson, 2002). Criminologists, however, still neglect short-term changes in the causes of crime, some of those changes lasting from hours to weeks (see Agnew, 2006b, 2011; Horney et al., 1995). For example, criminologists neglect daily or weekly changes in variables such as strain, parental supervision, and self-control.

Yet another assumption has to do with the manner in which variables affect crime. Mainstream criminologists tend to assume that variables have linear, additive, and lagged effects on crime. That is, they assume that a given change in a variable always results in the same amount of change in crime (a linear relationship). They assume that the effect of a variable on crime does not depend on the level of other variables (additive effect). And they assume that it takes some time for a variable to influence crime (lagged effect). This last assumption is reflected in the quantitative research on crime, where longitudinal studies typically examine whether variables measured at one point in time affect crime at a later point in time—typically one year later. But as certain criminologists have noted, there is sometimes good reason to assume that some effects are nonlinear, interactive, and/or contemporaneous (Agnew, 2005, 2006a; Tittle, 1995). For example, a strain may not affect crime until it passes a certain threshold level (nonlinear effect). The effect of the strain on crime may be conditioned or influenced by other variables, such as coping skills and resources (interactive effect). And the effect of the strain on crime may be immediate (contemporaneous effect). Criminologists should devote greater attention to these assumptions. And I am sure that additional assumptions can be identified.

A Unified Theory of Crime

The ultimate goal of this book is to lay the foundation for a unified theory of crime, one that examines a broad range of crimes and incorporates the key arguments of all major theories and perspectives. These include control and motivational theories; mainstream and critical theories; and classical, positivistic, and constructionist perspectives. The rationale for this unified theory informs virtually every page of this book: there is reason to believe that each of the theories and perspectives in criminology has some relevance. Therefore, the best explanation of crime will be one that incorporates all major theories and perspectives.

The construction of such a theory will of course be a major undertaking. The theory must include a broad range of causes, including biological, social-psychological, and social factors. It must describe how these causes are related to one another and work together to affect crime (e.g., Agnew, 2005; Bernard and Snipes, 1996; Messner et al., 1989). It must explain not only between-individual differences in crime but also within-individual differences over the life course, situational differences, and group differences— including societal differences. Further, this theory must explain both the level of crime and the amount of variation around this level (see chap. 3). In addition, it must devote much attention to context. That is, it must consider the type of crime being explained (see chap. 2). It must take account of the nature of the society, particularly the nature and extent of consensus and conflict. Likewise, it must consider the position of individuals and groups within the society (see chap. 5). There is good reason to believe that these contextual factors influence the causes that are most relevant, the level of these causes, and sometimes the effect of these causes. And, once the theory is in a form where it can be tested, researchers must examine both objective and subjective measures-as well as the relations between measures (see chap. 6).

Constructing such a theory will be a gradual process, involving the contributions of a broad range of individuals, since it requires expertise in a broad range of areas. The pursuit of such a theory, however, is critical given the current state of criminology. As noted earlier, current theories are able to explain only a small portion of the variance in crime. Further, the amount of variance explained has not increased in recent years (Weisburd and Piquero, 2008). This is the case even though criminology is awash in theories, with new theories emerging at a rapid rate (see Bernard and Snipes, 1996). It seems doubtful that the development of yet another theory will significantly advance the discipline. Rather, we should recognize that each of the existing theories in criminology has some contribution to make to the explanation of crime; but that a full explanation of crime requires that we find a way to integrate and build on the key insights of these theories. This book has hopefully contributed to this mission by suggesting a set of underlying assumptions that draw on the positive contributions of all these theories and perspectives—thereby providing a more solid foundation for a unified theory of crime.

Notes

NOTES TO CHAPTER 1

1. See Agnew, 1993; Gottfredson and Hirschi, 1990; Greenberg, 2008; Hirschi, 1977; Kornhauser, 1978.

2. For examples, see Colvin, 2000; Elliott et al., 1985; Thornberry, 1987; Tittle, 1995.

3. For examples, see Greenberg, 1993; Henry and Lanier, 2001, 2006; MacLean and Milovanovic, 1997; Schwartz and Hatty, 2003; Taylor et al., 1973; Vold et al., 2002; Walton and Young, 1998.

NOTES TO CHAPTER 2

1. For overviews of how criminologists define crime and the rise of the legal definition, see Gibbons and Farr, 2001; Greer and Hagan, 2001; Henry and Lanier, 2001; Kramer, 1982; Michael and Adler, 1933; Schwendinger and Schwendinger, 2001; Tappan, 1947; Taylor et al., 1973.

2. For criticisms of the legal definition of crime, see Barak, 1998; Greer and Hagan, 2001; Henry and Lanier, 2001; Hillyard and Tombs, 2004; Kramer, 1982; Lanier and Henry, 2004; Lynch and Michalowski, 2006; Schwendinger and Schwendinger, 1970; Sellin, 1938; Sutherland, 1939, 1940, 1944; Taylor et al., 1973; Turk, 1982.

3. See Box, 1983; Chambliss and Zatz, 1993; Lynch and Michalowski, 2006; Reiman and Leighton, 2010; Schwendinger and Schwendinger, 2001; Sutherland, 1944.

4. Also see Box, 1983; Hillyard and Tombs, 2004; Kauzlarich and Kramer, 1999; Kramer, 1982.

5. For additional examples, see Barak et al., 2001; Box, 1983; Hillyard et al., 2004; Lynch and Michalowski, 2006; Sutherland, 1940; Tift and Sullivan, 2001.

6. Some question the focus on group crime, claiming that it is ultimately individuals who decide to engage in crime and carry out criminal acts. It is argued, however, that it is reasonable to view groups such as corporations and states as "actors" in their own right (see Kauzlarich and Kramer, 1998; Matthews and Kauzlarich, 2007). Such groups often persist over time, outliving the people who belong to them. Groups develop goals, norms, and routines that are distinct from those of the individuals in them. Groups are often treated in a distinct manner from the individuals in them; for example, groups are subject to a distinct set of rules (e.g., the laws governing corporations). Groups make "collective" decisions, with these decisions being the result of the interaction between group members, structured by the goals and norms of the group. And group crime is often committed to further the goals of the group; for example, it is committed to increase corporate profits. Given these arguments, it is said that any definition of crime should explicitly recognize group as well as individual crime.

7. Also see Box, 1983; Chambliss, 1999; Green and Ward, 2004; Hillyard et al., 2004; Matthews and Kauzlarich, 2007; Passas and Goodwin, 2004b; Reiman and Leighton, 2010; Tift and Sullivan, 2001; Ward, 2004.

8. For examples, see Barak, 1994; Galliher, 1989; Green and Ward, 2004; Hillyard and Tombs, 2004; Hillyard et al., 2004; Kramer, 1982; Kramer and Michalowski, 2005; Passas and Goodwin, 2004b; Pemberton, 2007; Ward, 2004.

9. For examples, see Barak, 1994; Friedrichs and Friedrichs, 2002; Green and Ward, 2000, 2004; Hagan and Greer, 2002; Kauzlarich and Kramer, 1998; Kramer and Michalowski, 2005; Maier-Katkin et al., 2009; Matthews and Kauzlarich, 2007; Passas and Goodwin, 2004a.

10. For further information, see Blau and Moncada, 2009; Brooks, 2008; Callaway and Harrelson-Stephens, 2007; Hagan and Greer, 2002; Levy and Sznaider, 2006; Merry, 2006; Normand and Zaidi, 2008; Office of the United Nations High Commissioner for Human Rights, 2008; the websites for Amnesty International and Human Rights Watch.

11. See Blau and Moncada, 2009; Brooks, 2008; Callaway and Harrelson-Stephens, 2007; Hagan and Greer, 2002; Levy and Sznaider, 2006; Normand and Ziadi, 2008.

12. For further information, see Blau and Moncada, 2009; Brooks, 2008; Callaway and Harrelson-Stephens, 2007; Horowitz and Schnabel, 2004; Normand and Zaidi, 2008.

13. See Bronitt, 2008; Fletcher, 2007; Lacey, 2007; Reiman and Leighton, 2010.

14. There are certain problems when applying the criteria for blameworthiness to groups. As Pemberton (2007:38–39) states with respect to one type of group, "Corporations are large organizations with complex divisions of labor, and consequently the harms that corporations produce encompass large chains of decision-making and actions. The allocation of responsibility for harm within such organizations raises difficult moral and philosophical questions." Some progress, however, has been made in identifying responsible actors, namely those who "create policies and regimes which lead to harm" (Pemberton, 2007:39).

Also, while criminologists draw heavily on the criminal law in defining blameworthiness, some argue for a broader of definition of blameworthiness. In particular, some claim that *morally indifferent behavior* is frequently blameworthy (see especially Pemberton, 2004, 2007). Moral indifference may assume several forms (see Box, 1983; Cohen, 2001; Pemberton, 2004, 2007; Reiman and Leighton, 2010). Sometimes the *perpetrators* of harm show moral indifference. In particular, the perpetrators do not intend to cause harm but are indifferent to the harmful consequences of their actions (or inactions). This indifference may occur even though they know (or have a duty to know) that their actions cause harm. In this case, moral indifference may overlap with criminally negligent or reckless behavior. An example is the lack of concern/ action shown by corporate directors over the unsafe working conditions they create in the pursuit of profit (see Reiman and Leighton, 2010). This indifference may also stem from a "reasonable" lack of awareness of the harm they cause or its immorality. Perhaps the harm that results is not visible or is socially defined as excusable or justifiable. For example, most individuals engage in activities that pollute the environment, such as driving large SUVs and consuming meat from factory farms. But certain of these activities are viewed as justifiable or excusable, and there is little awareness of the harm caused by other of these activities. This type of moral indifference is usually not defined as a violation of the criminal law.

Moral indifference may also involve the *bystanders* to harm (see Cohen, 2001). Most notably, individuals may be aware of the harm caused by others, but fail to intervene, even though intervention is possible. Prominent examples include the failure of government officials to intervene despite their knowledge of the Holocaust (6,000,000+ deaths) and the Rwandan genocide (800,000 deaths). In the criminal law, the failure to prevent harm caused by others is usually not a crime, unless one has a specific duty to intervene (e.g., a parent's duty to provide their children with adequate food, clothing, and shelter).

Some critical criminologists believe that we should adopt a very broad conception of moral indifference, arguing that moral indifference of the above types is responsible for much of the harm that occurs in the world (e.g., Box, 1983; Hillyard et al., 2004; Hillyard and Tombs, 2004; Pemberton, 2004, 2007). Other criminologists favor a more limited conception of moral indifference. Reiman (2006:363), for example, argues that there is a good reason why the failure to intervene is typically not defined as a crime: "Since there is always more one can do to prevent harms, little else would be morally permissible if we were held morally responsible for all the harms we don't prevent." An exception, of course, involves those with a specific duty to intervene. Reiman (2006) also argues that a broad concept of moral indifference is quite difficult to apply in practice. He gives the following example: a firm produces a product that was previously produced at higher cost by local artisans, causing the artisans to lose their jobs. Reiman asks who, if anyone, is morally responsible for this harm—the directors of the firm, the workers in the firm, and/ or the local consumers who chose not to buy from the artisans?

15. For overviews of the constructionist perspective, see Eistenstader and Henry, 2006; Goode, 1997; Liska and Messner, 1999; Tittle and Paternoster, 2000.

16. For selected studies and overviews, see Box, 1983; Cullen et al., 1987; Reiman and Leighton, 2010; Roberts et al., 2003; Surette and Otto; 2001.

17. Also see Greer and Hagan, 2001; Green and Ward, 2004; Matthews and Kauzlarich, 2007; Sellin, 1938.

18. For overviews of the international human rights law, see Blau and Moncada, 2007, 2009; Horowitz and Schnabel, 2004; Merry, 2006; and the United Nations website on human rights at http://www.un.org/en/rights/index.shtml

19. One might ask whether it is possible to rank these harms according to their level of severity. It would certainly seem like a rough ranking is possible. Henry and Lanier (2001: 232) provide some guidance here, stating that criminologists should take the number of victims into account and prioritize harms that kill and permanently injure over those which cause some "temporary loss of capability, money, property, or position." Further, work in criminology, economics, public health, and other areas is making much progress in measuring the physical, financial, and other harms caused by various acts (e.g., Hillyard and Tombs, 2004; Nutt et al., 2007; Passas and Goodwin, 2004b; Piquero et al., 2008; Reiman and Leighton, 2010; Sloan et al., 2004; Welsh et al., 2001). At the same time, there are difficulties involved, particularly when it comes to comparing the more intangible harms caused by different types of rights violations. For example, how does one compare the harm caused by the denial of free elections to that caused by the denial of religious freedom? In this area, the 1993 World Conference on Human Rights specifically rejected the notion that there is a hierarchy of rights, some more important than others. Conference representatives passed a resolution stating that "all human rights are universal, indivisible and interdependent and interrelated"

and that "the international community must treat human rights globally in a fair and equal manner, on the same footing, and with the same emphasis" (Office of the United Nations High Commissioner for Human Rights, 2008:7). The philosophical work on human rights also claims that the different rights are of equal value, all being "fundamental prerequisites for each human being leading a minimally good life" (Fagan, 2005:1). What is critical when it comes to defining crime, however, is not the ability to rank acts in a hierarchy according to the harm they cause; but rather the ability to identify acts that cause sufficient harm to warrant attention by criminologists. And the international law provides much guidance here.

20. The Covenant goes on to state that "if a state fails to meet these [obligations] because it does not have the resources, it must demonstrate that it has made every effort to use all available resources to satisfy, as a matter of priority, these core obligations." There are fairly specific guidelines about what is expected of states in this area, even in situation of scarce resources (Office of the United Nations High Commissioner for Human Rights, 2008). Also, states, must immediately implement certain rights, regardless of resources, such as the elimination of discrimination in areas such as health care, education, and work. To give another example, the *Rome Statute* states that military commanders can be held criminally responsible if the subordinates under their effective command commit the crimes described in the Statute. In particular, the crimes must occur as a result of the military commanders "failure to exercise control properly over such forces, where: (a) that military commander or person either knew or, owing to the circumstances at the time, should have known that the forces were committing or about to commit such crimes; and (b) that military commander or person failed to take all necessary and reasonable measures within his or her power to prevent or repress their commission or to submit the matter to the competent authorities for investigation and prosecution."

21. Criminologists using this definition will likely discover that it is difficult to precisely rank many behaviors on the three dimensions. This partly reflects the fact that the definition is in need of further development, particularly a fuller description of those behaviors viewed as harmful in the international law. It partly reflects the fact that there is some disagreement in the international law regarding the ranking of human rights violations; with the prevailing view being that different types of rights violations should be treated as equally serious. And it partly reflects the fact that even if researchers could precisely measure dimensions such as harm, blameworthiness, and condemnation; the dividing line between acts that should and should not fall under the domain of criminology will be somewhat arbitrary. For example, what percentage of the population must condemn an act in order for it to qualify as a "crime." And how does one take account of such things as the intensity of the condemnation and who condemns the act (e.g., should acts be given special consideration if they are condemned by a small, but very powerful group of people?) (see Tittle and Paternoster, 2000 for a discussion of certain of these issues). More work is clearly needed on the dimensions of crime before precise ratings can be made; nevertheless, the dimensions are sufficiently well developed to permit researchers to determine whether most acts can be classified as crimes and to distinguish more from less serious crimes.

22. For examples of such work, see Green and Ward, 2004; Hillyard and Tombs, 2004; Kauzlarich and Kramer. 1998; Passas and Goodwin, 2004b; Reiman and Leighton, 2010.

1. The focus of this chapter is on the exercise of agency by *individuals*, for discussion of collective agency, see Bandura, 2001; Sewell, 1992.

2. For overviews of the positivistic approach, see Agnew, 1995a; Beirne, 1993, Matza, 1964; Rafter, 2010; Taylor et al., 1973; Vold et al., 2002.

3. See Cullen and Agnew, 2006; Goldkamp, 1987; Gottfredson and Hirschi, 1987, 1990:47–84; Vold et al., 2002.

4. For examples, see Agnew, 1995a; Akers, 1990; Gottfredson and Hirschi, 1987, 1990; Morash, 2006; as well as the review in Clarke and Cornish, 1985.

5. See Farrall and Bowling, 1999; Giordano et al., 2002; Laub and Sampson, 2001; LeBel et al., 2008; Maruna, 2001; Shover, 1996.

6. At the same time, it is important to note that a majority of the public *also* believe that a range of other factors influence crime, including poverty, "a breakdown in families and school," the inability to achieve monetary success, learning beliefs that encourage law-breaking, and "the inability to control one's anger and other impulses" (Sims, 2003). So while most members of the public believe that individuals exercise some free choice, they recognize that many factors influence the choice to engage in crime.

7. For overviews and examples, see Bandura, 2001, 2006; Bertelsen, 2005; Dietz and Burns, 1992; Elder-Vass, 2007; Emirbayer and Mische, 1998; Gazzaniga, 2005; Hitlin and Elder, 2007; Hitlin and Long, 2009; Kane, 2002; Libet, 1999; Loyal and Barnes, 2001; Maasen et al., 2003; Pinker, 2002; Sewell, 1992; Tancredi, 2005.

8. Also see Gazzaniga, 2005; Libet, 1999; Prinz, 2003; Tancredi, 2005; Wegner, 2004.

9. See Bandura, 2006; Burns, 1992; Farrall and Bowling, 1999; Hitlin and Elder, 2007; Sewell, 1992.

10. For discussions regarding the nature of agency, see Agnew, 1995a; Bandura, 2001, 2006; Bayer et al., 2003; Bertelsen, 2005; Elder-Vass, 2007; Emirbayer and Mische, 1998; Goschke, 2003; Kane, 2002.

11. The exercise of such agency, although limited, is critical. Without the ability to adapt general habits/schema for action to a range of particular situations, social interaction would crumble. As sociologists note, this ability to adapt habitual behavior makes our social institutions possible—such as the family, school, and economy. At heart, social institutions refer to routinized systems of behavior. The institution of school, for example, is built around the routinized behavior of students, teachers, and others (e.g., students go to school each day at a certain time, attend classes, take exams). So in something of a paradox, the existence of agency makes the routinized behavior that underlies institutions possible. For fuller discussions, see Elder-Vass, 2007; Emirbayer and Mische, 1998; Farrall and Bowling, 1999; Goschke, 2003; Sewell, 1992.

12. For discussions of the factors influencing agency, see Bandura, 2001, 2006; Bayer et al., 2003; Clarke and Cornish, 1985; Emirbayer and Mische, 1998; Loyal and Barnes, 2001.

13. Psychologists, philosophers, and others have pointed out that it is common for people to believe that they have some control over their behavior and the world around them (Wegner, 2004). In particular, research has found that individuals tend to attribute their actions to their own free choice, even when there is compelling evidence that their actions were due to forces beyond their control (Wegner, 2004). Kane (2002:5) states, "From a

personal or *practical* standpoint, we see ourselves as free agents capable of influencing the world in various ways. Open alternatives seem to lie before us. We reason or deliberate among them and choose. We feel it is 'up to us' what we choose and how we act; and this means we could have chosen or acted otherwise."

14. See Agnew, 1995a; Bandura, 2001; Elder-Vass, 2007; Emirbayer and Mische, 1998.

15. Agnew (1990) lists several types of autonomy and the factors that contribute to each:

Emotional autonomy, defined as "freedom from an excessive need for approval, closeness, togetherness, and emotional support" from others (Hoffman, 1984:171). Emotional autonomy is said to be higher among those with certain psychological traits, such a low need for social approval, and those with wide social networks, such that emotional support is available from many sources.

Value autonomy, with values broadly defined to include beliefs, attitudes, opinions, and ideologies. Those high in value autonomy are able to transcend customary or common views of themselves and the world around them. Value autonomy is said to be higher among those high in creativity and intelligence, low in the need for social approval, and high in exposure to alternative values.

Functional autonomy, or "the ability to manage and direct one's practical and personal affairs without the help" of others. Factors such as money, knowledge/skills of various types, intelligence, creativity, and an automobile are important here.

Agnew (1990) identifies several types of power and the factors contributing to them.

Coercive power is based on the threat of negative sanctions. Individuals possess such power to the extent that others believe they are willing and able to apply negative sanctions, such physical force, verbal abuse, and taking valued possessions. Coercive power is a function of a range of factors, including physical strength, physical size and shape, fighting ability, displays of violence and strength in the past, and the adoption of an "aggressive demeanor" (see Anderson, 1999). These factors contribute to the individual's reputation as someone willing and able to employ physical force. Also important are verbal skills and past displays of verbal abuse. Further, individuals may increase their coercive power by drawing on their connections to others; that is, individuals may recruit powerful others to act on their behalf. In some cases, individuals may form ongoing alliances with others willing to engage in coercion. Adolescents, for example, frequently join gangs in an effort to increase their coercive power. Finally, certain individuals have access to the enormous coercive power of the state, including political leaders and certain members of the police and military.

Reward power is based on the ability to provide rewards. Individuals have such power to the extent that others believe they are able and willing to administer rewards such as money, material possessions, status, and needed assistance. Reward power is a function of such things as occupational position, disposable income, and prestige.

Legitimate power is based on shared norms indicating that "the power holder possesses an acknowledged right to command and the subjects an acknowledged obligation to obey" (Wrong, 1979:49). Parents, teachers, employers, the police, and state leaders usually possess much legitimate power–although this power is sometimes limited to certain categories of people and certain areas of life. Teachers, for example, usually possess much power over students with respect to school-related matters, but not with respect to family-related matters.

Referent power is based on the attraction of one person to another because of the latter's personal qualities. For example, adolescents may exert influence by taking advantage of their parent's love for them or their romantic partner's attraction to them.

The role of other individual traits in facilitating agency is less clear. For example, some argue that high self-control promotes agency, since individuals with this trait are more likely to resist acting on their impulses, engage in careful planning–considering the future consequences of different actions, and persevere in the face of obstacles (see Hitlin and Long, 2009). Others, however, suggest that certain of the traits associated with low self-control, such as risk taking, lack of concern for others, self-centeredness, and impulsiveness–increase the likelihood that individuals will defy convention and engage in independent thought and behavior (Agnew, 1989).

16. There is some reason to believe that many lower-class individuals may be in a state of drift. On the one hand, they are more likely to experience a range of strains, including family, school, peer, and work problems; so they should be motivated to alter their habits/schema for action (Agnew, 2006a:142–46). Further, they are more often in environments where social control is low and/or they face countervailing constraints, providing the freedom to exercise agency. On the other hand, lower-class individuals are lower in self-efficacy and less likely to possess many of the traits and resources necessary for the exercise of agency–such as creativity, broad knowledge, and power (Krohn, 1977; Thoits, 2006). A similar argument may apply to adolescents (see Agnew, 2003, 2006a). Adolescents experience more strains than children and adults. Among other things, they must navigate a complex social world; dealing with a large number of diverse others at school, managing romantic relationships for the first time, and trying to meet increased academic demands. Also, adolescents have significant freedom; they are isolated from adults, but not yet saddled with the responsibilities of adulthood. At the same time, they lack many of the abilities and resources that contribute to the exercise of agency. The result, then, is drift.

17. This corresponds to the methodological assumption of homoscedasticity: the variance of the dependent variable is assumed to be the same across all values of the independent variables.

18. See Elder-Vass, 2007; Emirbayer and Mische, 1998; Hiltin and Elder, 2007; Sewell, 1992.

19. Such individuals lack the capacity for self-direction; in particular, they are low in self-efficacy, creativity, breath of knowledge, and most forms of autonomy and power. Also, they are in environments where they are strongly constrained to engage in crime. Specifically, they face strains highly conducive to crime (Agnew, 2001, 2006a). They have strong ties to criminal others, who differentially reinforce crime, model crime, and teach beliefs favorable to crime. Their ties to pro-social others, however, are weak or nonexistent. They have abundant opportunities to engage in crime, but limited opportunities for pro-social behavior. And they are not encouraged to exercise agency; just the opposite, they are under much pressure to "conform," although they are conforming to the deviant norms and values in their environment.

20. See Cochran et al., 2008; Foglia, 1997; Pogarsky, 2002; Wright et al., 2004.

21. See Agnew, 2009; Cullen and Agnew, 2006; Braithwaite, 2002; Sherman, 1993.

1. For overviews of the self-interested/rational actor assumption, see Boudon, 2003; Clarke and Cornish, 1985; Einstader and Henry, 2006; Elster, 2009; Hayward, 2007; Jolls et al., 1998; Marini, 1992; Matsueda et al., 2006; McCarthy, 2002; Ward et al., 2006.

2. For discussions of bounded rationality, see Akers, 1990; Clarke and Cornish, 1985; Hayward, 2007; Jolls et al., 1998; Marini, 1992; Nagin, 2007; Piquero and Tibbetts, 2002; Ward et al., 2006.

3. See Clarke and Cornish, 1985; Cornish and Clarke, 1986; Gottfredson and Hirschi, 1990; Hirschi, 1969; Piquero and Tibbetts, 2002; Ward et al., 2006.

4. See Agnew, 2009; Cullen and Agnew, 2011; Hirschi, 1969; Sampson and Laub, 1993.

5. For discussions of the assumption that everyone is more or less equally motivated to engage in crime, see Agnew, 1993; Gottfredson and Hirschi, 1990:95; Greenberg, 2008; Hirschi, 1969:10-11; Kornhauser, 1978; Toby, 1957.

6. See Agnew, 2009; Akers, 1990, 1998; Matsueda et al., 2006; McCarthy, 2002.

7. Also see the discussions in Agnew, 1993; Cloward and Ohlin, 1960: 36-37; Einstader and Henry, 2006:154-156; Hirschi, 1969:4-5.

8. Wrong's (1961) classic article on "The Oversocialized Conception of Man in Modern Sociology" provides an excellent overview of these arguments (also see Hirschi, 1969: 4-5; Kornhauser, 1978).

9. It is important to note, however, that these criminologists do not deny that individuals are self-interested and rational. In fact, strain theorists recognize that strained individuals frequently turn to crime because they believe it is the best way to achieve their goals or otherwise reduce their strain. Strain theorists, however, assume that this self-interest exists against a backdrop of social concern. That is to say, they assume that there is a natural constraint to the criminal exercise of self-interest. As a result, individuals will only turn to crime when their interests are seriously threatened (i.e., they are under much pressure or strain). Further, many such individuals will not turn to crime unless they also have the support of close others (see Cloward and Ohlin, 1960; Cohen, 1955). Self-interest does not lead to crime simply when control is low or the "lid is off."

10. To complicate maters still further, social learning also draws on the notion of the socially concerned actor. In particular, it is said that social approval from others is a powerful reinforcer, suggesting that individuals may find such approval intrinsically reinforcing. As Akers (1985:45) states: "approving responses, recognition, status, and acceptance from significant others are universal social reinforcers for humans."

11. For overviews, see Dunbar et al., 2005; Fehr and Fischbacher, 2003; Fehr and Gintis, 2007; Gintis et al., 2008a,b; Hauser, 2006; Jolls et al., 1998; Pinker, 2002.

12. See Dunbar et al., 2005:124-26; Gazzaniga, 2008: 144-45; Harris, 1998; Hornsey et al., 2003; Pinker, 2002; Tomasello, 2009.

13. See Boudon, 2003; Elster, 2009; Fehr and Gintis, 2007; Gazzaniga, 2005; Gintis, 2008; Haidt, 2001; Hayward, 2007; Jolls et al., 1998; Marini, 1992; Nagin, 2007; Piquero and Tibbetts, 2002.

14. For overviews and selected studies, see Clarke and Cornish, 1985; Cornish and Clarke, 1986; Matsueda et al., 2006; McCarthy, 2002; Nagin, 1998; Piquero and Tibbetts, 2002.

15. For overviews, see Gazzaniga, 2005, 2008; Haidt, 2001; Hauser, 2006; Mikhail, 2007; Pinker, 2002, 2008; Tancredi, 2005.

16. See Bandura, 1990; Maruna and Copes, 2005; Matza, 1964; Sykes and Matza, 1957.

17. See Gazzaniga, 2008; Gert, 2009; Haidt, 2007; Haidt and Joseph, 2004; Hauser, 2006; Pinker, 2002, 2008; Wilson, 1993.

18. For overviews, see Bloom, 2010; Dunbar et al., 2005; Gazzaniga, 2008; Gopnik, 2009: Hauser, 2006; Tancredi, 2005; Tomasello, 2009; Wilson, 1993; Wright et al., 2008; Zahn-Waxler et al., 1992.

19. See Calkins and Degnan, 2006; Caspi et al., 2005; Cloninger, 2003; De Pauw et al., 2009:309; also see Lahey et al., 2008; McCrae et al., 2000.

20. For overviews of evolutionary psychology, see Bowles and Gintis, 2003; Crawford and Krebs, 2008; Dunbar et al., 2005; Duntley and Shackelford, 2008; Fehr and Fischbacher, 2003; Gazzaniga, 2008; Gintis et al., 2008a,b; Haidt, 2007; Hauser, 2006; Johnson et al., 2008; Krebs, 2008; Neuberg et al., 2010; Pinker, 2002; Tomasello, 2009. It should be noted that evolutionary psychology has provoked some controversy, particularly among certain sociologists and criminologists (e.g., Hamilton, 2008). Many of the criticisms leveled against evolutionary psychology, however, appear exaggerated or dated. In particular, most evolutionary psychologists now recognize that evolutionary processes select for general propensities (e.g., aggressiveness) rather than specific behaviors (e.g., robbing convenience stores). These propensities are usually responsive to environmental stimuli. For example, aggression is not displayed in all situations, but rather is more likely to be activated in certain situations–such as confrontations with members of an out-group. And while evolutionary processes sometimes select for traits that involve rapid, unconscious responses to certain stimuli (e.g., threats), they also select for traits that facilitate learning from others and adaptation to the environment. Evolutionary psychology, then, does not deny the importance of environmental influences; in fact, it helps explain why such influences play such a large role in the lives of humans.

21. See Gintis et al., 2008a; Johnson et al., 2008; Krebs, 2008; Neuberg et al., 2010; Pinker, 2002.

22. In making these arguments, some researchers explain the survival value of cooperation and helping behavior in terms of group-level as well as individual-level selection. That is, they claim that groups with a higher proportion of cooperative individuals are more likely to survive; thus the individuals in these groups are more likely to reproduce. Group level selection was discounted for many years. It was said that the selfish individuals in a given group would exploit the cooperative individuals, such that the group would eventually be overrun with selfish individuals. Recent data, however, suggest that group selection may help explain the evolution of socially concerned behavior under certain conditions. Among other things, there must be competition between groups and there must be movement of individuals between groups, so that the selfish individuals do not come to dominate a particular group (see Dunbar et al., 2005).

23. For overviews of the genetics research, see Baker et al., 2006; Bouchard, 2005; Caspi et al., 2005; Cloninger, 2003; Dick and Todd, 2006; Hauser, 2006; Lahey, et al., 2008; McCrae et al., 2000; Pinker, 2002; Ridley, 2004; Robinson and Beaver, 2009; Wright et al., 2008.

24. For overviews of the research on brain structure and functioning, see Blakemore et al., 2004; Lieberman, 2010; Pinker, 2002; Robinson and Beaver, 2009; Tancredi, 2005; Wright et al., 2008.

25. See Gazzaniga, 2005; Gintis, 2008; Greene and Haidt, 2002; Haidt, 2007; Pinker, 2002.

26. See Baker et al., 2006; Bateson, 2004; Dick and Todd, 2006; Dunbar et al., 2005; Guo et al., 2008; Nisbett, 2009; Pinker, 2002, 2004; Ridley, 2004; Robinson and Beaver, 2009; Rutter et al., 2006; Tancredi, 2005.

27. See Baker et al., 2006; Caspi et al., 2002; also see Robinson and Beaver, 2009; Rutter et al., 2006.

28. It should be noted that strain and social learning theories would still have some relevance even if there was no natural social concern. That is because most individuals, including offenders, are subject to some social control. That is, most individuals have been socialized to condemn crime to some limited degree; have relationships and achievements, however meager, that might be jeopardized by crime; and are subject to sanction for crime. Motivation in the form of strain or expected reinforcement increases the likelihood they will act against these controls.

29. It should be noted that the research on human nature provides some insight into *why* certain events and conditions are experienced as stressful or are disliked. Many events and conditions pose a threat to the ability of individuals to survive and reproduce. Examples include intentional harms, particularly physical harms; inequitable or unfair treatment by others–including the failure to return favors and free-riding; the failure to obtain sufficient status or rank; the loss of close ties to others; and competition for scarce resources. Thus, the evolutionary process selects for individuals who have an aversion to these events and conditions. That is not to say, however, that all strains pose a threat to adaptive success; individuals may *learn* to dislike certain events and conditions.

30. It should be noted, however, that those high in self-interest may *sometimes act* in a socially concerned manner; for example, they may sometimes seek close ties with others or readily conform to those around them. But these acts do not reflect their underlying inclinations; rather, they are based on a consideration of their interests. Self-interested individuals seek close ties to others, for example, only when it is in their interest to do so.

31. There is also a second circumstance in which social concern *may* promote crime; situations where individuals free ride off the contributions of others, failing to reciprocate in an equitable manner. Those high in social concern have a strong sense of fairness, and so are inclined to punish these individuals, even at some cost to themselves. The other elements of social concern, however, may reduce the likelihood that such punishments are criminal in nature. Rather, those high in social concern may be more inclined to avoid free-riders or attempt to legally sanction them.

32. See especially Bandura, 1990; Maruna and Copes, 2005; Matza, 1964; Sykes and Matza, 1957.

NOTES TO CHAPTER 5

1. For overviews, see Akers and Hawkins, 1985; Akers and Sellers, 2008; Bernard, 1983; Chambliss and Zatz, 1993; Einstadter and Henry, 2006; Lanier and Henry, 2004; Liska and Messner, 1999; Lynch and Michalowski, 2006; Taylor et al., 1973; Vold et al., 2002.

2. For excellent overviews of the consensus perspective, see Akers and Hawkins, 1975; Akers and Sellers, 2008; Bernard, 1983; Chambliss and Zatz, 1993; Dillon, 2010; Kornhauser, 1978; Liska and Messner, 1999; Taylor et al., 1973; Vold et al., 2002; Wrong, 1961.

3. For excellent overviews, see Akers and Sellers, 2008; Arrigo and Williams, 2010; Barak et al., 2001; Bernard, 1983; Box, 1983; Bobo and Hutchings, 1996; Burgess-Proctor, 2009; Chambliss and Zatz, 1993; Cullen and Agnew, 2011; Currie, 1997, 1998; DeKeseredy, 2011; Einstadter and Henry, 2006; Gabbidon, 2010; Greenberg, 1993; Hagan, 1989; Hunnicutt, 2009; Lanier and Henry, 2004; Lynch and Michalowski, 2006; MacLean and Milovanovic, 1997; Ogle and Batton, 2009'; Quinney, 1977; Reiman and Leighton, 2010; Schwartz and Hatty, 2003; Taylor et al., 1973; Vold et al., 2002; Walton and Young, 1998; Young and Matthews, 1992.

4. See Barak et al., 2001; Burgess-Proctor, 2006; Dillon, 2010; Morash, 2006.

5. For discussions on how group values and interests might be altered, see Aberson and Haag, 2007; Crisp and Beck, 2005; Hewstone et al., 2002; Nelson, 2009; Otten et al., 2009.

6. For overviews of the evidence on the consensus and conflict perspectives, see Akers and Sellers, 2008; Akers and Hawkins, 1975; Bernard, 1983; Colvin, 2000; Cullen and Agnew, 2011; DeKeseredy, 2011; Kornhauser, 1978; Lynch et al., 2006; Vold et al., 2002.

7. For overviews, see Lynch and Michalowski, 2006; Quillian, 2006; Reiman and Leighton, 2010; Roscigno, 2007; Rothenberg, 2007.

8. For overviews and recent studies, see Barkan, 2009; Buckler et al., 2009; Chamlin, 2009; Eitle and Monahan, 2009; Greenberg and West, 2001; Keen and Jacobs, 2009; King and Wheelock, 2007; Kubrin et al., 2009; Liska and Messner, 1999; Lynch and Michalowski, 2006; Rosenstein, 2008; Unnever and Cullen, 2007; Western, 2006.

9. For overviews and recent studies, see Barak et al., 2001; Barkan, 2009; Doerner and Demuth, 2010; Johnson and Betsinger, 2009; Kubrin et al., 2009; Lynch and Michalowski, 2006; Mitchell, 2005; Reiman and Leighton, 2010.

10. For summaries of the research in this area, see Agnew, 2009; Colvin, 2000; Currie, 1997, 1998; Lynch and Michalowski, 2006.

11. For overviews and selected research, see Agnew, 2005, 2006a, 2009; Barak et al., 2001; Barkan, 2009; Baumer and Gustafson, 2007; Colvin, 2000; Cullen and Agnew, 2011; Lynch and Michalowski, 2006; Messner et al., 2008; Pratt and Cullen, 2005; Pratt and Lowenkamp, 2002; Reiman and Leighton, 2010; Savage et al., 2008; Unnever et al., 2009; Western, 2006.

12. See Agnew, 2006a; Blazak, 2001; Brezina, 1999; Broidy and Agnew, 1997; Cohen, 1955; Greenberg, 1977; Messerschmidt, 1993; Tittle, 1995.

13. For examples, see Dillon, 2010; Morash, 2010; Kramer and Michalowski, 2005; Rothe et al., 2009.

14. This type of consensus bears much in common with Durkheim's concept of "mechanical solidarity" (see Lukes, 1973).

15. This type of interdependence bears much in common with Durkheim's concept of "organic solidarity" (see Lukes, 1973).

16. See Bobo and Hutchings, 1996; King and Wheelock, 2007; Rosenstein, 2008; Zagefka et al., 2007.

17. Related to this, researchers should recognize that group members may perceive oppression when there is none. For example, many whites in neo-Nazi organizations believe they are being oppressed by Jews who are said to control the government and other major institutions (Blazak, 2001). Although mistaken, such beliefs may contribute to crime, including hate crimes against Jews.

18. For overviews, see Dovidio and Gaertner, 2010; De Dreu, 2010; Hamilton, 2007; Hewstone et al., 2002; Huddy, 2004; Nelson, 2009; Otten et al., 2009; Schaller and Neuberg, 2008; Yzerbyt and Demoulin, 2010.

19. See chapter 4 and Dovidio and Gaertner, 2010; Hewstone et al., 2002; Otten et al., 2009; Schaller and Neuberg, 2008; Yamagishi and Mifune, 2009.

20. Also, as noted in chap. 4, it should be kept in mind that social factors influence the degree and nature of social concern and self-interest-including the acts that are viewed as harmful, the justifications and excuses that are accepted for causing harm, and who is seen as worthy of social concern. It is reasonable to suppose that such factors will also influence the nature and extent of consensus/conflict in a society.

21. As an example, see the following sources for discussions of the research on group salience and conflict, see Crisp and Beck, 2005; De Dreu, 2010; Huddy, 2004; Otten et al., 2009; Stone and Crisp, 2007; Vignoles and Moncaster, 2007.

22. A central question is what factors influence the degree and nature of incompatibility between the interests/values of different groups. Biological factors may play a role in certain cases, such as gender and age conflicts (e.g., Davies and Shackelford, 2008; Pinker, 2002; Schaller and Neuberg, 2008; Wright et al., 2008). But such factors are only part of the explanation, as reflected in the variation in gender and age relations across societies and over time. History and contemporary social arrangements likely play the major role in influencing incompatibility. Although determining the reasons for incompatibility is not a core task for criminologists, the integrated consensus/conflict theory should certainly draw on those larger literatures that deal with this issue.

23. The theory must also take account of the origins of such individual differences, drawing on the research in other fields. For example, why are some individuals more likely than others to hold negative stereotypes of those in different groups. Among other things, this information is likely to suggest policy initiatives.

NOTES TO CHAPTER 6

1. See Einstadter and Henry 2006; Ferrell et al., 2008; Liska and Messner, 1999; Rafter, 2010; Tashakkori and Teddlie, 2003; Vold et al., 2002.

2. See Achenbach, 2006; Achenbach et al., 2005; De Los Reyes and Kazdin, 2005; Desimone, 2006; Loeber et al., 1991; Tein et al., 1994.

3. See Achenbach et al., 1987; De Los Reyes and Kazdin, 2005; Kenny, 1991; Tein et al., 1994.

4. See Gonzales et al., 1996; Noller and Callan, 1988; Pinker, 2002; Schwarz et al., 1985.

5. For examples, see Krohn et al., 1992; Larzelere and Patterson, 1990; Matsueda and Anderson, 1998.

6. See Achenbach et al., 2005; Cook and Goldstein, 1993; Matsueda and Anderson, 1998; Meyers et al., 2006; Renk et al., 2007; Tein et al., 1994; van der Valk et al., 2001; Wikman, 2006.

7. For further discussion, see Cook and Goldstein, 1993; Heath et al., 1992; Rowe and Kandel, 1997; van der Valk et al., 2001.

8. For examples, see Caspi et al., 1994; Farrington et al., 1996; Larzelere and Patterson, 1990; Loeber et al., (1991); Patterson et al., 1992; Rowe and Kandel, 1997; also see Krohn et al., 1992.

9. For examples, see the Cambridge Study in Delinquent Development; the National Survey of Children, Youths, and Adults; the National Youth Survey; and the Project on Human Development in Chicago Neighborhoods. Information on these and other data sets that draw on multiple sources of information is available through the website of the Inter-University Consortium on Political and Social Research (ICPSR) at http://www. icpsr.umich.edu/icpsrweb/ICPSR/index.jsp. Also see Achenbach et al., 2005; Lorber, 2006.

10. For overviews of these perspectives, see Dabney et al., 2002; Dillon, 2010; Einstadter and Henry, 2006; Ferrell et al., 2008; Henry, 2009; Henry and Lanier, 2001; Lanier and Henry, 2004; Liska and Messner, 1999; Morash, 2006; Polizzi, forthcoming; Presser, 2009; Tashakkori and Teddlie, 2003.

11. Nevertheless, the integrated perspective I advance in this chapter does at least partly incorporate certain of the recommendations of postmodernist scholars. In particular, we should examine the views of a range of individuals and groups, including the powerless whose voices are seldom heard; we should probe the origin and meaning of such views; and we should be very cautious about privileging one set of views over another.

12. For research and suggestions in this area, see Harkness et al., 1995; Kraemer et al., 2003; Ladd and Kochenderfer-Ladd, 2002; Loeber et al., 1990; Renk, 2005; Rowe and Kandel, 1997.

13. For discussions, see Dabney et al., 2002; Dodson et al., 2007; Ferrell et al., 2008; Groves et al., 2009.

14. For an overview of such mixed-method approaches, see Tashakkori and Teddlie, 2003; for examples, see Jick, 1979; Gioradano et al. 2002, Hagan and McCarthy, 1997; Sampson and Laub, 1993.

15. See Anderson, 1999; Horney et al., 1995; Matza, 1964; Osgood et al., 1996; also see Akers, 1998, on the concept of discriminative stimuli.

Bibliography

Aberson, Christopher L., and Sarah C. Haag. 2007. Contact, Perspective Taking, and Anxiety as Predictors of Stereotype Endorsement, Explicit Attitudes, and Implicit Attitudes. *Group Processes and Intergroup Relations* 10:179–201.

Achenbach, Thomas M. 2006. As Others See Us: Clinical and Research Implications of Cross-Informant Correlations for Psychopathology. *Current Directions in Psychological Science* 15:94–98.

Achenbach, Thomas M., Rebecca A. Krukowski, Levent Dumenci, and Marsha Y. Ivanova. 2005. Assessment of Adult Psychopathology: Meta-Analyses and Implications of Cross-Informant Correlations. *Psychological Bulletin* 131:361–82.

Achenbach, Thomas M., Stephanie H. McConaughy, and Catherine T. Howell. 1987. Child/Adolescent Behavioral and Emotional Problems: Implications of Cross-Informant Correlations for Situational Specificity. *Psychological Bulletin* 101:213–32.

Adler, Freda, Gerhard O. Mueller, and William S. Laufer. 2007. *Criminology.* New York: McGraw-Hill.

Agnew, Robert. 1984. Appearance and Delinquency. *Criminology* 22:421–40.

———. 1989. Delinquency as a Creative Enterprise. *Criminal Justice and Behavior* 16:98–113.

———. 1990. Adolescent Resources and Delinquency. *Criminology* 28:535–66.

———. 1993. Why Do They Do It? An Examination of the Intervening Mechanisms between "Social Control" Variables and Delinquency. *Journal of Research in Crime and Delinquency* 30:245–66.

———. 1995a. Determinism, Indeterminism, and Crime: An Empirical Exploration. *Criminology* 33:83–109.

———. 1995b. Testing the Leading Crime Theories: An Alternative Strategy Focusing on Motivational Processes. *Journal of Research in Crime and Delinquency* 32:363–98.

———. 1998. The Causes of Animal Abuse: A Social Psychological Analysis. *Theoretical Criminology* 2:177–210.

———. 2001. Building on the Foundation of General Strain Theory: Specifying the Types of Strain Most Likely to Lead to Crime and Delinquency. *Journal of Research in Crime and Delinquency* 38:319–61.

——— 2003. An Integrated Theory of the Adolescent Peak in Offending. *Youth and Society* 34:263–99.

———. 2005. *Why Do Criminals Offend? A General Theory of Crime and Delinquency.* New York: Oxford University Press.

———. 2006a. *Pressured Into Crime: An Overview of General Strain Theory.* New York: Oxford University Press.

———. 2006b. Storylines as a Neglected Causes of Crime. *Journal of Research in Crime and Delinquency* 43:119–47.

———. 2009. *Juvenile Delinquency: Causes and Control.* New York: Oxford University Press.

———. 2010a. Controlling Crime: Recommendations from General Strain Theory. In *Criminology and Public Policy: Putting Theory to Work,* edited by Hugh D. Barlow and Scott H. Decker, 25–55. Philadelphia: Temple University Press.

———. 2010b. A General Strain Theory of Terrorism. *Theoretical Criminology* 14:131–54.

———. 2011. Crime and Time: The Temporal Patterning of Crime Variables. *Theoretical Criminology,* forthcoming.

Agnew, Robert, and Diane Jones. 1988. Adapting to Deprivation: An Examination of Inflated Educational Expectations. *Sociological Quarterly* 29:315–37.

Agnew, Robert, Nicole Leeper Piquero, and Alex Piquero. 2009. General Strain Theory and White-Collar Crime. In Simpson, *Criminology of White-Collar Crime,* 35–60.

Ajzenstadt, Mimi. 2009. The Relative Autonomy of Women Offender's Decision Making. *Theoretical Criminology* 13:201–25.

Akers, Ronald L. 1990. Rational Choice, Deterrence, and Social Learning Theory in Criminology: The Path Not Taken. *Journal of Criminal Law and Criminology* 81:653–76.

———. 1998. *Social Learning and Social Structure: A General Theory of Crime and Deviance.* Boston: Northeastern University Press.

———. 2010. Nothing Is as Practical as a Good Theory: Social Learning Theory and the Treatment and Prevention of Delinquency. In Barlow and Scott H. Decker, *Criminology and Public Policy,* 84–105.

Akers, Ronald L., and Richard Hawkins. 1985. *Law and Control in Society.* Englewood Cliffs, NJ: Prentice Hall.

Akers, Ronald L., and Christine S. Sellers. 2008. *Criminological Theories.* New York: Oxford University Press.

Amnesty Internal. 2010. *China Human Rights.* http://www.amnestyusa.org/china/page.do?id=1011134.

Anderson, Elijah. 1999. *Code of the Street.* New York: W. W. Norton.

Anderson, Linda A., and Susan C. Whiston. 2005. Sexual Assault Education Programs: A Meta-Analytic Examination of Their Effectiveness. *Psychology of Women Quarterly* 29:374–88.

Andrews, D. A., and J. S. Wormith. 1989. Personality and Crime: Knowledge Destruction and Construction in Criminology. *Justice Quarterly* 6:289–309.

Arrigo, Bruce A. 2006. Postmodern Theory and Crime. In *The Essential Criminology Reader,* edited by Stuart Henry and Mark M. Lanier, 224–33. Boulder, CO: Westview.

Arrigo, Bruce A., and Christopher R. Williams. 2010. Contemporary Retrospective on Conflict and Radical Theories. In *Criminological Theory,* edited by Heith Copes and Volkan Topalli, 401–12. New York: McGraw-Hill.

Auerhahn, Kathleen. 1999. The Split Labor Market and the Origins of Antidrug Legislation in the United States. *Law and Social Inquiry* 24:411–40.

Baker, Laura A., Serena Bezdjian, and Adrian Raine. 2006. Behavioral Genetics: The Science of Antisocial Behavior. *Law and Contemporary Problems* 69:7–46.

Bandura, Albert. 1990. Selective Activation and Disengagement of Moral Control. *Journal of Social Issues* 46:27–46.

———. 2001. Social Cognitive Theory: An Agentic Perspective. *Annual Review of Psychology* 52:1–26.

———. 2006. Toward a Psychology of Human Agency. *Perspectives on Psychological Science* 1:164–80.

Barak, Gregg. 1994. Crime, Criminality, and Human Rights: Toward an Understanding of State Criminality. In *Varieties of Criminology,* edited by Gregg Barak, 253–68. Westport, CT: Praeger.

———. 1998. *Integrating Criminologies.* Boston: Allyn and Bacon.

Barak, Gregg, Jeanne M. Flavin, and Paul S. Leighton. 2001. *Class, Race, Gender, and Crime.* Los Angeles: Roxbury.

Bargh, John A., and Tanya L. Chartrand. 1999. The Unbearable Automaticity of Being. *American Psychologist* 54:462–79.

Bargh, John A., and Melissa J. Ferguson. 2000. Beyond Behaviorism: On the Automaticity of Higher Mental Processes. *Psychological Bulletin* 126:925–45.

Barkan, Steven E. 2009. The Value of Quantitative Analysis for a Critical Understanding of Crime and Society. *Critical Criminology* 17:247–59.

Bateson, Patrick. 2004. The Origins of Human Differences. *Daedalus* 133(4): 36–46.

Batson, C. Daniel. 1990. How Social an Animal? The Human Capacity for Caring. *American Psychologist* 45:336–46.

Bayer, U. C., M. J. Ferguson, and P. M. Gollwitzer. 2003. Voluntary Action from the Perspective of Social-Personality Psychology. In Maasen, *Voluntary Action* 86–114.

Baumeister, Roy F., and Mark R. Leary. 1995. The Need to Belong: Desire for Interpersonal Attachments as a Fundamental Human Motivation. *Psychological Bulletin* 117:497–529.

Baumer, Eric P., and Regan Gustafson. 2007. Social Organization and Instrumental Crime: Assessing the Empirical Validity of Classic and Contemporary Anomie Theories. *Criminology* 45:617–64.

Beckett, Katherine, and Theodore Sasson. 2000. *The Politics of Injustice: Crime and Punishment in America.* Thousand Oaks, CA: Sage.

Beirne, Piers, 1993. *Inventing Criminology.* Albany: State University of New York Press.

Berkowitz, Leonard. 1994. Guns and Youth. In *Reason to Hope,* edited by Leonard D. Eron, Jacquelyn H. Gentry, and Peggy Schlegel, 251–79. Washington, DC: American Psychological Association.

Bennett, William J., John J. DiIulio Jr., and John P. Waters. 1996. *Body Count: How to Win America's War Against Drugs and Crime.* New York: Simon and Schuster.

Benson, Michael L. and E. Moore. 1992. Are White-Collar and Common Offenders the Same? An Empirical and Theoretical Critique of a Recently Proposed General Theory of Crime. *Journal of Research in Crime and Delinquency* 29:251–72.

Bernard, Thomas J. 1983. *The Consensus-Conflict Debate.* New York: Columbia University Press.

Bernard, Thomas, J., and Jeffrey B. Snipes. 1996. Theoretical Integration in Criminology. *Crime and Justice: A Review of Research* 20:301–48.

Bernburg, Jon Gunnar, and Marvin Krohn. 2003. Labeling, Life Chances, and Adult Crime. *Criminology* 41:1287–1318.

Bertelsen, Preben. 2005. *Free Will, Consciousness, and Self.* New York: Berghahn Books.

Bijleveld, Catrien, Aafke Morssinkhof, and Alette Smeulers. 2009. Counting the Countless: Rape Victimization during the Rwandan Genocide. *International Criminal Justice Review* 19:208–24.

Blakemore, Sarah-Jayne, Joel Winston, and Uta Frith. 2004. Social Cognitive Neuroscience: Where Are We Heading? *TRENDS in Cognitive Sciences* 8 (5): 216–22.

Blau, Judith, and Alberto Moncada. 2007. It Ought to Be a Crime: Criminalizing Human Rights Violations. *Sociological Forum* 22:364–71.

———. 2009. *Human Rights Primer.* Boulder, CO: Paradigm Publishers.

Blazak, Randy. 2001. White Boys to Terrorist Men. *American Behavioral Scientist* 44:982–1000.

Bloom, Paul. 2010. The Moral Life of Babies. *New York Times Magazine,* May 9, 44–49, 56, 62–63, 65.

Bobbitt-Zeher, Donna. 2007. The Gender Income Gap and the Role of Education. *Sociology of Education* 80:1–22.

Bobo, Lawrence, and Vincent Hutchings. 1996. Perceptions of Racial Group Competition: Extending Blumer's Theory of Group Position to a Multiracial Context. *American Sociological Review* 61:951–72.

Bolzendahl, Catherine I., and Daniel J. Meyers. 2004. Feminist Attitudes and Support for Gender Equality: Opinion Change in Women and Men, 1974–1998. *Social Forces* 83:759–90.

Bonczar, Thomas P. 2003. *Prevalence of Imprisonment in the U.S. Population, 1974–2001.* Washington, DC: Bureau of Justice Statistics, U.S. Department of Justice.

Bonger, Willem. 1969. *Criminality and Economic Conditions.* Bloomington: Indiana University Press.

Bottoms, Anthony E., and Paul Wiles. 2002. Environmental Criminology. In *Crime: Critical Concepts in Sociology,* edited by Philip Bean, 326–72. New York: Routledge.

Bouchard, Thomas J. Jr. 2005. Genes and Human Psychological Traits. In *The Innate Mind.* Vol. 3: *Foundations and the Future,* edited by Peter Carruthers, Stephen Laurence, and Stephen Stich, 69–89. Oxford: Oxford University Press.

Boudon, Raymond. 2003. Beyond Rational Choice Theory. *Annual Review of Sociology* 29:1–21.

Bowleg. Lisa, Jennifer Huang, Kelly Brooks, Amy Black, and Gary Burkholder. 2003. Triple Jeopardy and Beyond: Multiple Minority Stress and Resilience Among Black Lesbians. *Journal of Lesbian Studies* 7(4): 87–108.

Bowles, Samuel, and Herbert Gintis. 2003. The Origins of Human Cooperation. In *Genetic and Cultural Evolution of Cooperation,* edited by Peter Hammerstein, 1–17. Cambridge, MA: MIT Press.

Box, Steven. 1983. *Power, Crime, and Mystification.* London: Tavistock.

Braithwaite, John. 1989. *Crime, Shame and Reintegration.* Cambridge: Cambridge University Press.

———. 2002. *Restorative Justice and Responsive Regulation.* Oxford: Oxford University Press.

Brewer, Marilynn. 1999. The Psychology of Prejudice: Ingroup Love or Outgroup Hate? *Journal of Social Issues* 55:429–44.

Brezina, Timothy. 1999. Teenage Violence Toward Parents as an Adaptation of Family Strain. *Youth and Society* 30:416–44.

Broidy, Lisa, and Robert Agnew. 1997. Gender and Crime: A General Strain Theory Perspective. *Journal of Research in Crime and Delinquency* 34: 275–306.

Bronitt, Simon. 2008. Toward a Universal Theory of Criminal Law: Rethinking the Comparative and International Project. *Criminal Justice Ethics* 27:53–66.

Brooks, Thom. 2008. *The Global Justice Reader.* Malden, MA: Blackwell.

Brooks-Gunn, Jeanne, and Greg J. Duncan. 1997. The Effects of Poverty on Children. *Future of Children* 7:55–71.

Brown, Donald E. 1991. *Human Universals.* Philadelphia: Temple University Press.

———. 2004. Human Universals, Human Nature and Human Culture. *Daedalus* 133(4): 47–54.

Buckler, Kevin, Steve Wilson, and Patti Ross Salinas. 2009. Public Support for Punishment and Progressive Criminal Justice Policy Preferences: The Role of Symbolic Racism and Negative Racial Stereotype. *American Journal of Criminal Justice* 34:238–52.

Building Blocks for Youth. 2007. *No Turning Back.* http://www.buildingblocksforyouth.org.

Bunkley, Nick. 2010. Laboring to Survive. *New York Times,* January 6, B1,7.

Burgess-Proctor, Amanda. 2006. Intersections of Race, Class, Gender, and Crime. *Feminist Criminology* 1:27–47.

———. 2009. Looking Back, Looking Ahead: Assessing Contemporary Feminist Criminology. In Copes and Topalli, *Criminological Theory,* 431–43. New York: McGraw-Hill.

Calkins, Susan D., and Kathryn A. Degnan. 2006. Temperament in Early Development. In *Comprehensive Handbook of Personality and Psychopathology,* edited by Robert T. Ammerman, 64–84. Hoboken, NJ: John Wiley and Sons.

Callaway, Rhonda L., and Julie Harrelson-Stephens, eds. 2007. *Exploring International Human Rights: Essential Readings.* Boulder, CO: Lynne Rienner.

Carey, Benedict. 2006. When Death Is on the Docket, the Moral Compass Wavers. *New York Times,* February 7, D1, 6.

Carmichael, Stephanie, and Alex R. Piquero. 2004. Sanctions, Perceived Anger, and Criminal Offending. *Journal of Quantitative Criminology* 20:371–93.

Carter, J. Scott, Mamadi Corra, and Shannon K. Carter. 2009. The Interaction of Race and Gender: Changing Gender-Role Attitudes, 1974–2006. *Social Science Quarterly* 90:196–210.

Caspi, Avshalom, Joseph McClay, Terrie E. Moffitt, Alan Taylor, Ian W. Craig, Alan Taylor, and Richie Poulton. 2002. Role of Genotype in the Cycle of Violence in Maltreated Children. *Science* 297:851–54.

Caspi, Avshalom, Terrie E. Moffitt, Phil A. Silva, Magda Stouthamer-Loeber, Robert F. Krueger, and Pamela S. Schmutte. 1994. Are Some People Crime-Prone? *Criminology* 32:163–95.

Caspi, Avshalom, Brent W. Roberts, and Rebecca L. Shiner. 2005. Personality Development: Stability and Change. *Annual Review of Psychology* 56:453–84.

Chambliss, William J. 1973. The Saints and the Roughnecks. *Society* 11:34–41.

———. 1989. On Trashing Marxist Criminology. *Criminology* 27:231–38.

———. 1999. *Power, Politics, and Crime.* Boulder, CO: Westview.

Chambliss, William J., and Marjorie S. Zatz, eds. 1993. *Making Law.* Bloomington: Indiana University Press.

Chamlin, Mitchell B. 2009. Threat to Whom? Conflict, Consensus, and Social Control. *Deviant Behavior* 30:539–59.

Cheatwood, Derral. 2009. Weather and Crime. In *21st Century Criminology: A Reference Handbook*. Vol. 1, edited by J. Mitchell Miller, 51–58. Thousand Oaks, CA: Sage.

Clarke, Ronald V. 1995. Situational Crime Prevention. *Crime and Justice: A Review of Research* 19:91–150.

Clarke, Ronald V., and Derek B. Cornish. 1985. Modeling Offenders' Decisions: A Framework for Research and Policy. *Crime and Justice: An Annual Review of Research* 6:147–85.

Clarke, Ronald V., and John Eck. 2005. *Crime Analysis for Problem Solvers*. Washington, DC: Office of Community Policing Services, U.S. Department of Justice.

Clear, Todd. 2007. *Imprisoning Communities: How Mass Incarceration Makes Disadvantaged Neighborhoods Worse*. New York: Oxford University Press.

Cloninger, C. Robert. 2003. Completing the Psychobiological Architecture of Human Personality Development: Temperament, Character, and Coherence. In *Understanding Human Development: Dialogues with Lifespan Psychology*, edited by U. M. Staudinger and U. E. R. Lindenberger, 159–82. Boston: Kluwer Academic Publishers.

Cloward, Richard A., and Lloyd E. Ohlin. 1960. *Delinquency and Opportunity*. New York: Free Press.

Cochran, John K., Valentina Aleska, and Beth A. Sanders. 2008. Are Persons Low in Self-Control Rational and Deterrable? *Deviant Behavior* 29:461–83.

Cohen, Albert. 1955. *Delinquent Boys*. New York: Free Press.

Cohen, Albert K., and James F. Short, Jr. 1961. Juvenile Delinquency. In *Contemporary Social Problems*, edited by Robert K. Merton and Robert A. Nisbet, 77–126. New York: Harcourt, Brace, and World.

Cohen, Mark A., and Alex R. Piquero. 2009. New Evidence on the Monetary Value of Saving a High Risk Youth. *Journal of Quantitative Criminology* 25:25–49.

Cohen, Stanley. 2001. *States of Denial*. Cambridge: Polity Press.

Collins, Randall. 2008. *Violence: A Micro-Sociological Theory*. Princeton, NJ: Princeton University Press.

———. 2009. The Micro-Sociology of Violence. *British Journal of Sociology* 60:566–76.

Colvin, Mark. 2000. *Crime and Coercion: An Integrated Theory of Chronic Criminality*. New York: St. Martin's Press.

Conger, Rand D. 1976. Social Control and Social Learning Models of Delinquent Behavior. *Criminology* 14:17–54.

Cook, William L., and Michael J. Goldstein. 1993. Multiple Perspectives on Family Relationships: A Latent Variable Model. *Child Development* 1377–88.

Cooper, Jonathan A., Anthony Walsh, and Lee Ellis. 2010. Is Criminology Moving Toward a Paradigm Shift? Evidence from a Survey of the American Society of Criminology. *Journal of Criminal Justice Education* 21:332–47.

Cornish, Derek B., and Ronald V. Clarke. 1986. *The Reasoning Criminal*. New York: Springer-Verlag.

Cottrol, Robert J. 1998. Submission Is Not the Answer: Lethal Violence, Microcultures of Criminal Violence and the Right to Self-Defense. *University of Colorado Law Review* 69(4): 1029–80.

Crawford, Charles, and Dennis Krebs. 2008. *Foundations of Evolutionary Psychology*. New York: Lawrence Erlbaum Associates.

Crisp, Richard J., and Sarah R. Beck. 2005. Reducing Intergroup Bias: The Moderating Role of Ingroup Identification. *Group Processes and Intergroup Relations* 8:173–85.

Cropley, David H., James C. Kaufman, and Arthur J. Cropley. 2008. Malevolent Creativity: A Functional Model of Creativity in Terrorism and Crime. *Creativity Research Journal* 20:105–15.

Cullen, Francis T. 1994. Social Support as an Organizing Concept for Criminology. *Justice Quarterly* 11:527–59.

Cullen, Francis T., and Robert Agnew. 2010. *Criminological Theory: Past to Present.* New York: Oxford University Press.

Cullen, Francis T., Bruce G. Link, Lawrence F. Travis, III, and John F. Wozniak. 1985. Consensus in Crime Seriousness: Empirical Reality or Methodological Artifact? *Criminology* 23:99–118.

Cullen, Francis T., William J. Maakestad, and Gary Cavender. 1987. *Corporate Crime Under Attack: The Ford Pinto Case and Beyond.* Cincinnati, OH: Anderson Publishing.

Cullen, Francis T., John Paul Wright, and Kristie B. Blevins. 2008. *Taking Stock: The Status of Criminological Theory.* New Brunswick, NJ: Transaction.

Currie, Elliott. 1997. Market, Crime and Community. *Theoretical Criminology* 1:147–72.

———. 1998. Crime and the Market Society: Lessons from the United States. In *The New Criminology Revisited*, edited by Paul Walton and Jock Young, 130–42. New York: St. Martin's Press.

Dabney, Dean A., Michael McSkimming, and Bruce L. Berg. 2002. The Active Interview: Applications for Crime and Deviance Research. *Free Inquiry in Creative Sociology* 30:149–63.

Davies, Alastair P. C., and Todd K. Shackelford. 2008. Two Human Natures: How Men and Women Evolved Different Psychologies. In Crawford, *Foundations of Evolutionary Psychology*, 261–80.

Davis, Nancy J., and Robert V. Robinson. 1991. Men's and Women's Consciousness of Gender Inequality: Austria, West Germany, Great Britain, and the United States. *American Sociological Review* 56:72–84.

Daynard, Richard A. 2004. The Cigarette Industry. In *It's Legal but It Ain't Right: Harmful Social Consequences of Legal Industries*, edited by Nikos Passas and Neva Goodwin, 28–42. Ann Arbor: University of Michigan Press.

Decker, Scott H., and Barrik Van Winkle. 1996. *Life in the Gang.* Cambridge: Cambridge University Press.

De Coster, Stacy, and Lisa Kort-Butler. 2006. How General Is General Strain Theory? Assessing Issues of Determinacy and Indeterminacy. *Journal of Research in Crime and Delinquency* 43:297–325.

De Dreu, Carsten K. W. 2010. Social Conflict. In *Handbook of Social Psychology.* Vol. 2, edited by Sasna T. Fiske, Daniel T. Gilbert, and Gardner Lindzey, 983–1023. New York: Wiley.

DeKeseredy, Walter S. 2011. *Contemporary Critical Criminology.* London: Routledge.

DeLisi, Matt, John Paul Wright, Michael G. Vaughn, and Kevin M. Beaver. 2009. Copernican Criminology. *Criminologist* 34(1): 14–16.

De Los Reyes, Andres, and Alan E. Kazdin. 2004. Measuring Informant Discrepancies in Clinical Child Research. *Psychological Assessment* 16:330–34.

———. 2005. Informant Discrepancies in the Assessment of Child Psychopathology: A Critical Review, Theoretical Framework, and Recommendations for Further Study. *Psychological Bulletin* 131:483–509.

de Mesquita, Bruce Bueno. 2009. *The Predictioneer's Game: Using the Logic of Brazen Self-Interest to See and Shape the Future.* New York: Random House.

De Pauw, Sarah S. W., Ivan Mervielde, and Karla G. Van Leeuwen. 2009. How Are Traits Related to Problem Behavior in Preschoolers? Similarities and Contrasts between Temperament and Personality. *Journal of Abnormal Child Psychology* 37:309–25.

Desimone, Laura M. 2006. Consider the Source: Response Differences among Teachers, Principals, and Districts on Survey Questions about Their Education Policy Environment. *Educational Policy* 20:640–76.

de Waal, Frans B. M. 2005. *Our Inner Ape.* New York: Riverhead.

———. 2006a. *Primates and Philosophers: How Morality Evolved.* Princeton, NJ: Princeton University Press.

———. 2006b. The Most Bipolar Ape. *General Psychologist* 41(1): 9–10.

Dick, Danielle M., and Richard D. Todd. 2006. Genetic Contributions. In Ammerman, *Comprehensive Handbook of Personality and Psychopathology*, 16–28.

Dietz, Thomas, and Tom R. Burns. 1992. Human Agency and the Evolutionary Dynamics of Culture. *Acta Sociologica* 35:187–200.

Dijksterhuis, Ap. 2010. Automaticity and the Unconscious. In Fiske, *Handbook of Social Psychology*, vol. 1, 228–67.

Dillon, Michelle. 2010. *Introduction to Sociological Theory.* Malden, MA: Wiley-Blackwell.

Dodge, Kenneth A., and D. Schwartz. 1997. Social Information Processing Mechanisms in Aggressive Behavior. In *Handbook of Antisocial Behavior,* edited by David M. Stoff, James Breiling, and Jack D. Maser, 171–80. New York: Wiley.

Dodson, Lisa, Deborah Piatelli, and Leah Schmalzbauer. 2007. Researching Inequality through Interpretive Collaborations: Shifting Power and the Unspoken Word. *Qualitative Inquiry* 13:821–43.

Doerner, Jill K., and Stephen Demuth. 2010. The Independent and Joint Effects of Race/Ethnicity, Gender, and Age on Sentencing Outcomes in U.S. Federal Courts. *Justice Quarterly* 27:1–27.

Dombrink, John, and Daniel Hillyard. 2007. *Sin No More: From Abortion to Stem Cells, Understanding Crime, Law, and Morality in America.* New York: New York University Press.

Domhoff, G. William. 2005a. *Basics of Studying Power.* http://sociology.ucsc.edu/whorulesamerica.

———. 2005b. *The Class-Domination Theory of Power.* http://sociology.ucsc.edu/whorulesamerica.

———. 2005c. Power at the Local Level: Growth Coalition Theory. http://sociology.ucsc.edu/whorulesamerica.

———. 2006. C. Wright Mills 50 Years Later. *Contemporary Sociology* 35:547–50.

———. 2010. Wealth, Income, and Power. http://sociology.ucsc.edu/whorulesamerica.

Dovidio, John F., and Samuel L. Gaertner. 2010. Intergroup Bias. In Fiske, *Handbook of Social Psychology,* vol. 2, 1084–1121.

Dowdall, George W. 2005. White Gains from Black Subordination. *Review of Black Political Economy* 32:65–86.

Dunbar, Robin, Louise Barrett, and John Lycett. 2005. *Evolutionary Psychology: A Beginner's Guide.* Oxford: Oneworld Publications.

Duntley, Joshua D., and Todd K. Shackelford. 2008. Darwinian Foundations of Crime and Law. *Aggression and Violent Behavior* 13:373–82.

Durkheim, E. 1938. *The Rules of Sociological Method*. Chicago: University of Chicago Press.

Dye, Thomas R. 2002. *Who's Running America?* Englewood Cliffs, NJ: Prentice Hall.

Einstadter, Werner, and Stuart Henry. 2006. *Criminological Theory: An Analysis of its Underlying Assumptions*. Lanham, MD: Rowman and Littlefield.

Eitle, David, and Susanne Monahan. 2009. Revisiting the Racial Threat Thesis: The Role of Police Organizational Characteristics in Predicting Race-Specific Drug Arrest Rates. *Justice Quarterly* 26:528–61.

Elder-Vass, Dave. 2007. Reconciling Archer and Bourdieu in an Emergentist Theory of Action. *Sociological Theory* 25:325–46.

Elliott, Delbert S., David Huizinga, and Suzanne S. Ageton. 1985. *Explaining Delinquency and Drug Use*. Beverly Hills, CA: Sage.

Ellis, Lee, Jonathon A. Cooper, and Anthony Walsh. 2008. Criminologists' Opinions about Causes and Theories of Crime and Delinquency: A Follow-Up. *Criminologist* 33:23–26.

Elster, Jon. 2009. *Reason and Rationality*. Princeton, NJ: Princeton University Press.

Emirbayer, Mustafa, and Ann Mische. 1998. What Is Agency? *American Journal of Sociology* 103:962–1023.

Fagan, Andrew. 2005. Human Rights. *Internet Encyclopedia of Philosophy*. http://www.iep.utm.edu/hum-rts/

Farah, Martha J. 2005. Neuroethics: The Practical and the Philosophical. *TRENDS in Cognitive Sciences* 9:34–40.

Farrall, Stephen, and Benjamin Bowling. 1999. Structuration, Human Development, and Desistance from Crime. *British Journal of Criminology* 39:253–68.

Farrington, David P., Rolf Loeber, Magda Stouthamer-Loeber, Welmoet B. Van Kammen, and Laura Schmidt. 1996. Self-reported Delinquency and a Combined Delinquency Seriousness Scale Based on Boys, Mothers, and Teachers. *Criminology* 34:493–517.

Farrington, David P., and Brandon C. Welsh. 2007. *Saving Children from a Life of Crime*. Oxford: Oxford University Press.

Fehr, Ernst, and Urs Fischbacher. 2003. The Nature of Human Altruism. *Nature* 425:785–91.

Fehr, Ernst, and Hervert Gintis. 2007. Human Motivation and Social Cooperation: Experiments and Analytical Foundations. *Annual Review of Sociology* 33:43–64.

Felson, Marcus. 2002. *Crime and Everyday Life*. Thousand Oaks, CA: Sage.

Felson, Richard B. 1996. Big People Hit Little People: Sex Differences in Physical Power and Interpersonal Violence. *Criminology* 34:433–52.

Feminist Majority Foundation. 2010. *Campaign for Afghan Women and Girls*. http://www.feminist.org/afghan/taliban_women.asp.

Ferdinand, Robert F., Jan van der Ende, and Frank C. Verhulst. 2004. Parent-Adolescent Disagreement Regarding Psychopathology in Adolescents from the General Population as a Risk Factor for Adverse Outcome. *Journal of Abnormal Psychology* 113:198–206.

Ferrell, Jeff, Keith Hayward, and Jock Young. 2008. *Cultural Criminology*. Thousand Oaks, CA: Sage.

Fiske, Susan T., Amy J. Cuddy, Peter Glick, and Jun Xu. 2002. A Model of (Often Mixed) Stereotype Content: Competence and Warmth Respectively Follow from Perceived Status and Competition. *Journal of Personality and Social Psychology* 82:878–902.

Fletcher, George P. 2007. *The Grammar of Criminal Law*. Oxford: Oxford University Press.

Foglia, Wanda D. 1997. Perceptual Deterrence and the Mediating Effect of Internalized Norms among Inner-City Teenagers. *Journal of Research in Crime and Delinquency* 34:414–42.

Freund, Peter, and George Martin. 2008. Fast Cars/Fast Food: Hyperconsumption and Its Health and Environmental Consequences. *Social Theory and Health* 6:309–22.

Friedrichs, David O., and Jessica Friedrichs. 2002. The World Bank and Crimes of Globalization: A Case Study. *Social Justice* 29:1–2, 13–36.

Gabbidon, Shaun L. 2010. *Criminological Perspectives on Race and Crime.* New York: Routledge.

Galliher, John F. 1989. *Criminology: Human Rights, Criminal Law, and Crime.* Englewood Cliffs, NJ: Prentice Hall.

Garcia, R. Marie, Ralph B. Taylor, and Brian A. Lawton. 2007. Impact of Violent Crime and Neighborhood Structure on Trusting Your Neighbors. *Justice Quarterly* 24:657–78.

Gazzaniga, Michael S. 2005. *The Ethical Brain.* New York: Dana Press.

———. 2008. *Human: The Science behind What Makes Us Unique.* New York: HarperCollins.

Gert, Bernard. 2004. *Common Morality.* Oxford: Oxford University Press.

Gettleman, Jeffrey. 2009. Kenya's Criminals Tap a Growth Industry: Kidnapping. *New York Times*, October 12, A4.

Gibbons, Don C., and Kathryn Ann Farr. 2001. Defining Patterns of Crime and Types of Offenders. In *What Is Crime? Controversies over the Nature of Crime and What to Do about*, edited by Stuart Henry and Mark M. Lanier, 37–64 Lanham, MD: Rowman and Littlefield.

Gintis, Herbert. 2008. Five Principles for the Unification of the Behavioral Sciences. http://www.umass.edu/preferen/gintis/NewUnity.pdf.

Gintis, Herbert, Samuel Bowles, Robert Boyd, and Ernst Fehr. 2008a. Gene-Culture Coevolution, and the Emergence of Altruistic Behavior in Humans. In Crawford, *Foundations of Evolutionary Psychology*, 313–29.

Gintis, Herbert, Joseph Henrich, Samuel Bowles, Robert Boyd, and Ernst Fehr. 2008b. Strong Reciprocity and the Roots of Human Morality. *Social Justice Research* 21:241–53.

Giordano, Peggy C., Stephen A. Cernkovich, and Jennifer L. Rudolph. 2002. Gender, Crime, and Desistance: Toward a Theory of Cognitive Transformation. *American Journal of Sociology* 107:990–1064.

Goldhagen, Daniel Jonah. 2009. *Worse than War: Genocide, Eliminationism, and the Ongoing Assault on Humanity.* New York: Public Affairs.

Goldkamp, John S. 1987. Rational Choice and Determinism. In *Positive Criminology*, edited by Michael R. Gottfredson and Travis Hirschi, 125–37. Newbury Park, CA: Sage.

Gonzales, Nancy A., Ana Mari Cauce, and Craig A. Mason. 1996. Interobserver Agreement in the Assessment of Parental Behavior and Parent-Adolescent Conflict: African American Mothers, Daughters, and Independent Observers. *Child Development* 67:1483–98.

Goode, Erich. 1997. *Deviant Behavior.* Upper Saddle River, NJ: Prentice Hall.

Gopnik, Alison. 2009. *The Philosophical Baby.* New York: Farrar, Straus and Giroux.

Goschke, Thomas. 2003. Voluntary Action and Cognitive Control from a Cognitive Neuroscience Perspective. In Maasen, *Voluntary Action*, 49–85.

Gottfredson, Michael R., and Travis Hirschi. 1987. The Positive Tradition. In Gottfredson, *Positive Criminology*, 9–22.

———. 1990. *A General Theory of Crime*. Stanford: Stanford University Press.

Green, Penny J., and Tony Ward. 2000. State Crime, Human Rights, and the Limits of Criminology. *Social Justice* 27:101–15.

———. 2004. *State Crime: Governments, Violence and Corruption*. London: Pluto Press.

Greenberg, David F. 1993. *Crime and Capitalism: Readings in Marxist Criminology*. Philadelphia: Temple University Press.

———. 2008. Motivation in Criminological Theory. Unpublished paper.

Greene, Joshua, and Jonathan Haidt. 2002. How (and Where) Does Moral Judgment Work? *TRENDS in Cognitive Sciences* 6:517–23.

Greenwood, Peter. 2006. *Changing Lives: Delinquency Prevention as Crime Control Policy*. Chicago: University of Chicago Press.

Greer, Scott, and John Hagan. 2001. Crime as Disrepute. In Henry, *What Is Crime?*, 207–26.

Grills, Amie E., and Thomas Ollendick. 2003. Multiple Informant Agreement and the Anxiety Disorders Interview Schedule for Parents and Children. *Child and Adolescent Psychiatry* 42:30–40.

Groves, Robert M., Floyd J. Fowler, Jr., Mick P. Couper, James M. Lepkowski, Eleanor Singer, and Roger Tourangeau. 2009. *Survey Methodology*. New York: Wiley.

Guo, Gang, Michael E. Roettger, and Tianji Cai. 2008. The Integration of Genetic Propensities into Social-Control Models of Delinquency and Violence among Male Youths. *American Sociological Review* 73:543–86.

Haederle, Michael. 2010. Trouble in Mind: Will the New Neuroscience Undermine Our Legal System? *Miller-McCune* (March-April):70–79.

Hagan, Frank E. 2008. *Introduction to Criminology*. Los Angeles: Sage.

Hagan, John. 1989. *Structural Criminology*. New Brunswick, NJ: Rutgers University Press.

———. 1985. *Modern Criminology: Crime, Criminal Behavior, and Its Control*. New York; McGraw-Hill.

Hagan, John, and Scott Greer. 2002. Making War Criminal. *Criminology* 40:231–64.

Hagan, John, and Ron Levi. 2007. Justiciability as Field Effect: When Sociology Meets Human Rights. *Sociological Forum* 22:372–80.

Hagan, John, and Bill McCarthy. 1997. *Mean Streets*. Cambridge: Cambridge University Press.

Hagan, John, Carla Sheed, and Monique R. Payne. Race, Ethnicity, and Youth Perceptions of Criminal Injustice. 2005a. *American Sociological Review* 70:381–407.

Hagan, John, Wenona Rymond-Richmond, and Patricia Parker. 2005b. The Criminology of Genocide: The Death and Rape of Dafur. *Criminology* 43:525–62.

Haidt, Jonathan. 2001. The Emotional Dog and Its Rational Tail: A Social Intuitionist Approach to Moral Judgment. *Psychological Review* 108:814–34.

———. 2007. The New Synthesis in Moral Psychology. *Science* 316:998–1001.

Haidt, Jonathan, and Craig Joseph. 2004. Intuitive Ethics: How Innately Prepared Intuitions Generate Culturally Variable Virtues. *Daedalus* 133(4): 55–66.

Hamilton, David L. 2007. Understanding the Complexities of Group Perception: Broadening the Domain. *European Journal of Social Psychology* 37:1077–1101.

Hamilton, Richard. 2008. The Darwinian Cage: Evolutionary Psychology as Moral Science. *Theory, Culture, and Society* 25(2): 105–25.

Hancock, Ange-Marie. 2007. When Multiplication Doesn't Equal Quick Addition: Examining Intersectionality as a Research Paradigm. *Perspectives on Politics* 5:63–79.

Harkness, Allan R., Auke Tellegen, and Niels Waller. 1995. Differential Convergence of Self-Report and Informant Data for Multidimensional Personality Traits: Implications for the Construct of Negative Emotionality. *Journal of Personality Assessment* 64:185–204.

Harris, Judith Rich. 1998. *The Nurture Assumption*. New York: Free Press.

Hauser, Marc D. 2006. *Moral Minds: How Nature Designed Our Universal Sense of Right and Wrong*. New York: HarperCollins.

Hawley, Kristin M., and John R. Weisz. 2003. Child, Parent, and Therapist (Dis)Agreement on Target Problems in Outpatient Therapy: The Therapist's Dilemma and Its Implications. *Journal of Consulting and Clinical Psychology* 71:62–70.

Hay, Carter, and Walter Forrest. 2006. The Development of Self-Control: Examining Self-Control Theory's Stability Thesis. *Criminology* 44:739–74.

Hayward, Keith. 2007. Situational Crime Prevention and Its Discontents: Rational Choice Theory versus the "Culture of Now." *Social Policy and Administration* 41:232–50.

Heath, A. C., M. C. Neale, R. C. Kessler, L. J. Eaves, and K. S. Kendler. 1992. Evidence for Genetic Influences on Personality from Self-Reports and Informant Ratings. *Journal of Personality and Social Psychology* 63:85–96.

Heidensohn, Frances. 1996. *Women and Crime*. Basingstoke, England: Macmillan.

Henry, Bill, Avshalom Caspi, Terrie E. Moffitt, and Phil A. Silva. 1996. Temperamental and Familial Predictors of Violent and Nonviolent Criminal Convictions: Age 3 to Age 18. *Developmental Psychology* 32:614–23.

Henry J. Kaiser Foundation. 2006. Race, Ethnicity and Health Care. Washington, DC: Henry J. Kaiser Foundation.

Henry, Stuart. 2009. Social Construction of Crime. In Miller, *21st Century Criminology*, 296–304.

Henry, Stuart, and Mark M. Lanier. 1998. The Prism of Crime: Arguments for an Integrated Definition of Crime. *Justice Quarterly* 15:609–27.

———. 2001. *What Is Crime? Controversies over the Nature of Crime and What to Do about It*. Lanham, MD: Rowman and Littlefield.

———. 2006. *The Essential Criminology Reader*. Boulder, CO: Westview.

Herrenkohl, Todd I., and Roy C. Herrenkohl. 2007. Examining the Overlap and Prediction of Multiple Forms of Child Maltreatment, Stressors, and Socioeconomic Status: A Longitudinal Analysis of Youth Outcomes. *Journal of Family Violence* 22:553–62.

Hewstone, Miles, Mark Rubin, and Hazel Willis. 2002. Intergroup Bias. *Annual Review of Psychology* 53:575–604.

Hillyard, Paddy, Christina Pantazis, Steve Tombs, and Dave Gordon. 2004. *Beyond Criminology: Taking Harm Seriously*. London: Pluto Press.

Hillyard, Paddy, and Steve Tombs. 2004. Beyond Criminology? In Hillyard, *Beyond Criminology*, 10–29.

Hirschi, Travis. 1969. *Causes of Delinquency*. Berkeley: University of California Press.

———. 1977. Causes and Prevention of Juvenile Delinquency. *Sociological Inquiry* 47:322–41.

———. 1989. Exploring Alternatives to Integrated Theory. In *Theoretical Integration in the Study of Deviance and Crime: Problems and Prospects*, edited by Steven F. Messner, Marvin D. Krohn, and Allen E. Liska, 37–50. Albany: State University of New York Press.

Hitlin, Steven, and Glen H. Elder Jr. 2007. Time, Self, and the Curiously Abstract Concept of Agency. *Sociological Theory* 25:170–91.

Hitlin, Steven, and Charisse Long. 2009. Agency as a Sociological Variable: A Preliminary Model of Individuals, Situations, and the Life Course. *Sociology Compass* 3:137–60.

Hoffman, Jeffrey A. 1984. Psychological Separation of Late Adolescents from their Parents. *Journal of Counseling Psychology* 31:170–78.

Horney, Julie D., Wayne Osgood, and Ineke Haen Marshall. 1995. Criminal Careers in the Short-Term: Intra-Individual Variability in Crime and Its Relation to Local Life Circumstances. *American Sociological Review* 60:655–73.

Hornsey, Matthew J., Louise Majkut, Deborah J. Terry, and Blake M. McKimmie. 2003. On Being Loud and Proud: Non-Conformity and Counter-Conformity to Group Norms. *British Journal of Social Psychology* 42:319–35.

Horowitz, Shale, and Albrecht Schnabel. 2004. *Human Rights and Societies in Transition: Causes, Consequences, Responses.* Tokyo: United Nations University Press.

Huddy, Leonie. 2004. Contrasting Theoretical Approaches to Intergroup Relations. *Political Psychology* 25:947–67.

Hunnicutt, Gwen. 2009. Varieties of Patriarchy and Violence against Women. *Violence against Women* 15:553–73.

International Lesbian, Gay, Bisexual, Trans, and Intersex Association, 2010. http://ilga.org.

ICRC. 2003. *International Humanitarian and International Human Rights Law.* Geneva: International Committee of the Red Cross. http://www.icrc.org/Web/Eng/siteengo.nsf/html/section_ihl_and_human_rights.

Jick, Todd D. 1979. Mixed Qualitative and Quantitative Methods: Triangulation in Action. *Administrative Science Quarterly* 24:602–11.

Johnson, Brian D., and Sara Betsinger. 2009. Punishing the "Model Minority": Asian-American Criminal Sentencing Outcomes in Federal District Courts. *Criminology* 47:1045–89.

Johnson, Dominic D. P., Michael E. Price, and Masanori Takezawa. 2008. Renaissance of the Individual: Reciprocity, Positive Assortment, and the Puzzle of Human Cooperation. In Crawford, *Foundations of Evolutionary Psychology,* 331–52.

Jolliffe, Darrick, and David P. Farrington. 2007. Examining the Relationship between Low Empathy and Self-Reported Offending. *Legal and Criminological Psychology* 12:265–86.

Jolls, Christine, Cass R. Sunstein, and Richard Thaler. 1998. A Behavioral Approach to Law and Economics. *Stanford Law Review* 50:1471–1550.

Kaiser, Cheryl R., and Brenda Major. 2006. A Social Psychological Perspective on Perceiving and Reporting Discrimination. *Law and Social Inquiry* 31:801–30.

Kane, Robert, ed. 2002. *The Oxford Handbook of Free Will.* Oxford, England: Oxford University Press.

Katz, Jack. 1988. *Seductions of Crime.* New York: Basic Books.

Kaufman James C., Jonathan A. Plucker, and John Baer. 2008. *Essentials of Creativity Assessment.* Hoboken, NJ: John Wiley and Sons.

Kauzlarich, David, and Ronald C. Kramer. 1998. *Crimes of the American Nuclear State.* Boston: Northeastern University Press.

Keen, Bradley, and David Jacobs. 2009. Racial Threat, Partisan Politics, and Racial Disparities in Prison Admissions: A Panel Analysis. *Criminology* 47:209–238.

Kenny, David A. 1991. A General Model of Consensus and Accuracy in Interpersonal Perception. *Psychological Review* 98:155–63.

King, Ryan D., and Darren Wheelock. 2007. Group Threat and Social Control: Race, Perceptions of Minorities and the Desire to Punish. *Social Forces* 85:1255–80

Kohn, Melvin. 1977. *Class and Conformity: A Study in Values.* Chicago: University of Chicago Press.

Koppel, Herbert. 1987. *Lifetime Likelihood of Victimization.* Washington, DC: U.S. Department of Justice, Bureau of Justice Statistics.

Kornhauser, Ruth Rosner. 1978. *Social Sources of Delinquency.* Chicago: University of Chicago Press.

Kraemer, Helena C., Jeffrey R. Measelle, Jennifer C. Ablow, Marilyn J. Essex, W. Thomas Boyce, and David J. Kupler. 2003. A New Approach to Integrating Data from Multiple Informants in Psychiatric Assessment and Research: Mixing and Matching Contexts and Perspectives. *American Journal of Psychiatry* 160:1566–77.

Kramer, Ronald C. 1982. The Debate over the Definition of Crime: Paradigms, Value Judgments, and Criminological Work. In *Ethics, Public Policy, and Criminal Justice,* edited by Frederick Elliston and Norman Brown, 33–58i. Cambridge, MA: Oelgeschlager, Gunn, and Hain.

Kramer, Ronald C., and Raymond J. Michalowski. 2005. War, Aggression, and State Crime. *British Journal of Criminology* 45:446–69.

Krebs, Dennis. 2008. How Selfish by Nature? In Crawford, *Foundations of Evolutionary Psychology,* 293–312.

Krohn, Marvin D., Susan B. Stern, Terence P. Thornberry, and Sung Joon Jang. 1992. The Measurement of Family Process Variables: The Effect of Adolescent and Parent Perceptions of Family Life on Delinquent Behavior. *Journal of Quantitative Criminology* 8:287–315.

Kubrin, Charis E., Thomas D. Stucky, and Marvin D. Krohn. 2009. *Researching Theories of Crime and Deviance.* New York: Oxford University Press.

Lacey, Nicola. 2007. Legal Constructions of Crime. In *The Oxford Handbook of Criminology,* edited by Mike Maguire, Rod Morgan, and Robert Reiner, 179–200. Oxford: Oxford University Press.

Ladd, Gary W., and Becky Kochenderfer-Ladd. 2002. Identifying Victims of Peer Aggression from Early to Middle Childhood: Analysis of Cross-Informant Data. *Psychological Assessment* 14:74–96.

Laham, Simon M. 2008. Expanding the Moral Circle: Inclusion and Exclusion Mindsets and the Circle of Moral Regard. *Journal of Experimental Social Psychology* 45:250–53.

Lahey, Benjamin B., and Irwin D. Waldman. 2007. Personality Dispositions and the Development of Violence and Conduct Problems. In *The Cambridge Handbook of Violent Behavior and Aggression,* edited by Daniel J. Flannery, Alexander T. Vazsonyi, and Irwin D. Waldman, 260–87. Cambridge: Cambridge University Press.

Lahey, Benjamin B., Carol A. Van Hulle, Kate Keenan, Paul J. Rathouz, Brian M. D'Onofrio, Joseph Lee Rodgers, and Irwin D. Waldman. 2008. Temperament and Parenting during the First Year of Life Predict Future Child Conduct Problems. *Journal of Abnormal Child Psychology* 36:1139–58.

Lanier, Mark M., and Stuart Henry. 2004. *Essential Criminology.* Boulder, CO: Westview.

Laub, John H., and Robert J. Sampson. 2001. Understanding Desistance from Crime. *Crime and Justice* 28:1–70.

Larzelere, Robert E., and Gerald R. Patterson. 1990. Parental Management: Mediator of the Effect of Socioeconomic Status on Early Delinquency. *Criminology* 28:301–24.

LeBel, Thomas P., Ros Burnett, Shadd Maruna, and Shawn Bushway. 2008. The "Chicken and Egg" of Subjective and Social Factors in Desistance from Crime. *European Journal of Sociology* 5:131–59.

Levy, Daniel, and Natan Sznaider. 2006. Sovereignty Transformed: A Sociology of Human Rights. *British Journal of Sociology* 57:657–77.

Libet, Benjamin. 1999. Do We Have Free Will? *Journal of Consciousness Studies* 6:47–57.

Lieberman, Matthew D. 2010. Social Cognitive Neuroscience. In Fiske, *Handbook of Social Psychology*, 1:143–93.

Lipsey, Mark W., and Francis T. Cullen. 2007. The Effectiveness of Correctional Rehabilitation: A Review of Systematic Reviews. *Annual Review of Law and Social Science* 3:297–320.

Liska, Allen E., and Steven F. Messner. 1999. *Perspectives on Crime and Deviance*. Upper Saddle River, NJ: Prentice Hall.

Liska, Allen E., and Barbara D. Warner. 1991. Functions of Crime: A Paradoxical Process. *American Journal of Sociology* 96:1441–63.

Loeber, Rolf, Stephanie M. Green, and Benjamin B. Lahey. 1990. Mental Health Professionals' Perception of the Utility of Children, Mothers, and Teachers as Informants on Childhood Psychopathology. *Journal of Clinical Child Psychology* 19:136–43.

Loeber, Rolf, Stephanie M. Green, Benjamin B. Lahey, and Magda Stouthamer-Loeber. 1991. Differences and Similarities between Children, Mothers, and Teachers as Informants on Disruptive Child Behavior. *Journal of Abnormal Child Psychology* 19:75–95.

Lorber, Michael F. 2006. Can Minimally Trained Observers Provide Valid Global Ratings? *Journal of Family Psychology* 20:335–38.

Loyal, Steven, and Barry Barnes. 2001. "Agency" as a Red Herring in Social Theory. *Philosophy of the Social Sciences* 31:507–24.

Ludwig, Kristin B., and Joe F. Pittman. 1999. Adolescent Prosocial Values and Self-Efficacy in Relation to Delinquency, Risky Sexual Behavior, and Drug Use. *Youth and Society* 30:461–82.

Lukes, Steven. 1973. *Emile Durkheim*. New York: Penguin Books.

Lynch, Michael J., and Raymond Michalowski. 2006. *Primer in Radical Criminology: Critical Perspectives on Crime, Power, and Identity*. Monsey, NY: Criminal Justice Press.

Lynch, Michael J., Herman Schwendinger, and Julia Schwendinger. 2006. The Status of Empirical Research in Radical Criminology. In Cullen, *Taking Stock*, 191–215.

MacDonald, John. 2010. *Measuring Crime and Criminality, Advances in Criminological Theory*. Vol. 17. New Brunswick, NJ: Transaction.

MacLean, Brian D., and Dragon Milovanovic. 1997. *Thinking Critically about Crime*. Vancouver: Collective Press.

Maasen, Sabine, Wolfgang Prinz, and Gerhard Roth. 2003. *Voluntary Action: Brains, Minds, and Sociality*. Oxford: Oxford University Press.

Madene, Kim. 2009. Race and Gender Differences in the Earnings of Black Workers. 2009. *Industrial Relations* 48:466–88.

Magura, S., and Y. Kang. 1996. Validity of Self-Reported Drug Use in High Risk Populations: A Meta-Analytical Review. *Substance Use and Misuse* 31:1131–53.

Maier-Katkin, Daniel, Daniel P. Mears, and Thomas J. Bernard. 2009. Toward a Criminology of Crimes against Humanity. *Theoretical Criminology* 13:227–55.

Marini, Margaret Mooney. 1992. The Role of Models of Purposive Action in Sociology. In *Rational Choice Theory: Advocacy and Critique*, edited by James S. Coleman and Thomas J. Fararo, 21–48. Newbury Park, CA: Sage.

Markowitz, Fred E., and Richard B. Felson. 1998. Socio-Demographic Differences in Attitudes and Violence. *Criminology* 36:117–38.

Maruna, Shadd. 2001. *Making Good: How Ex-Convicts Reform and Reclaim Their Lives.* Washington, DC: American Psychological Association Books.

Maruna, Shadd, and Heith Copes. 2005. What Have We Learned from Five Decades of Neutralization Research. *Crime and Justice* 32:221–320.

Matsueda, Ross L. 1988. The Current State of Differential Association Theory. *Crime and Delinquency* 34:277–306.

———. 1992. Reflected Appraisals, Parental Labeling, and Delinquency: Specifying a Symbolic Interactionist Theory. *American Journal of Sociology* 97:1577–1611.

Matsueda, Ross L., and Kathleen Anderson. 1998. The Dynamics of Delinquent Peers and Delinquent Behavior. *Criminology* 36:269–308.

Matsueda, Ross L., Derek A. Keager, and David Huizinga. 2006. Deterring Delinquents: A Rational Choice Model of Theft and Violence. *American Sociological Review* 71:95–122.

Matthews, Rick A., and David Kaularich. 2007. State Crimes and State Harms: A Tale of Two Definitional Frameworks. *Crime, Law, and Social Change* 48:43–55.

Matza, David. 1964. *Delinquency and Drift.* New York: John Wiley and Sons.

———. 1969. *Becoming Deviant.* Englewood Cliffs, NJ: Prentice-Hall.

McCarthy, Bill. 2002. New Economics of Sociological Criminology. *Annual Review of Sociology* 28:417–42.

McCarthy, Bill, and John Hagan. 2005. Danger and the Decision to Offend. *Social Forces* 83:1065–96.

McCrae, Robert R., Paul T. Fritz Ostendorf, Alois Angleitner, Martina Hrebickova, Maria D. Avia, Jesus Sanz, Maria L. Sanchez-Bernardos, M. Ersin Kusdil, Ruth Woodfield, Peter R. Saunders, and Peter B. Smith. 2000. Nature over Nurture: Temperament, Personality, and Life Span Development. *Journal of Personality and Social Psychology* 78:173–86.

Meier, Robert F., and Gilbert Geis. 2006. *Criminal Justice and Moral Issues.* Los Angeles: Roxbury.

Merry, Sally Engle. 2006. Anthropology and International Law. *Annual Review of Anthropology*35:99–116.

Merton, Robert. 1938. Social Structure and Anomie. *American Sociological Review* 3:672–82.

———. 1968. *Social Theory and Social Structure.* New York: Free Press.

Messerschmidt, James W. 1993. *Masculinities and Crime.* Lanham, MD: Rowman and Littlefield.

———. 2004. *Flesh and Blood.* Lanham, MD: Rowman and Littlefield.

Messner, Steven F., Marvin D. Krohn, and Allen E. Liska. 1989. *Theoretical Integration in the Study of Deviance and Crime: Problems and Prospects.* Albany: State University of New York Press.

Messner, Steven F., and Richard Rosenfeld. 2007. *Crime and the American Dream.* Belmont, CA: Wadsworth.

Messner, Steven F., Helmut Thorne, and Richard Rosenfeld. 2008. Institutions, Anomie, and Violent Crime: Clarifying and Elaborating Institutional-Anomie Theory. *International Journal of Conflict and Violence* 2:163–81.

Meyers, Lawrence S., Glenn Gamst, and A. J. Guarino. 2006. *Applied Multivariate Research.* Thousand Oaks, CA: Sage.

Meyers, Peter Alexander. 2006. Speaking Truth to Ourselves: Lukacs, "False Consciousness" and a Dilemma of Identity Politics in Democracy. *International Review of Sociology* 16:549–89.

Michael, Jerome, and Mortimer Adler. 1933. *Crime, Law, and Social Science.* New York: Harcourt, Brace.

Michalowski, Raymond J., and Ronald C. Kramer. 2007. State-Corporate Crime and Criminological Inquire. In *International Handbook of White-Collar and Corporate Crime,* edited by Henry N. Pontell and Gilbert L. Geis, 200–222. New York: Springer.

Mikhail, John. 2007. Universal Moral Grammar: Theory, Evidence, and the Future. *TRENDS in Cognitive Sciences* 11:143–52.

Milgram, Stanley. 1983. *Obedience to Authority.* New York: Harper Perennial.

Miller, Jody. 2001. *One of the Guys: Girls, Gangs, and Gender.* New York: Oxford University Press.

Mitchell, Ojmarrh. 2005. A Meta-Analysis of Race and Sentencing Research: Explaining the Inconsistencies. *Journal of Quantitative Criminology* 21:439–66.

Moffitt, Terrie E., Avshalom Caspi, Michael Rutter, and Phil A. Silver. 2001. *Sex Differences in Antisocial Behavior.* Cambridge: Cambridge University Press.

Morash, Merry. 2006. *Understanding Gender, Crime, and Justice.* Thousand Oaks, CA: Sage.

Mosher, Clayton J., Terrance D. Miethe, and Dretha M. Philips. 2002. *The Mismeasure of Crime.* Thousand Oaks, CA: Sage.

Mullis, Ronald L., Ann K. Mullis, Thomas A. Cornille, Mary Ann Kershaw, Adela Beckerman, and Daniel Perkins. 2005. Young Chronic Offenders: A Case Study of Contextual and Intervention Characteristics. *Youth Violence and Juvenile Justice* 3:133–50.

Nagin, Daniel S. 1998. Criminal Deterrence Research at the Outset of the Twenty-First Century. *Crime and Justice: A Review of Research* 23:1–42.

———. 2007. Moving Choice to Center Stage in Criminological Research and Theory. *Criminology* 45:259–72.

Nelson, Todd D. 2009. *Handbook of Prejudice, Stereotyping, and Discrimination.* New York: Psychology Press.

Neuberg, Steven L., Douglas T. Kenrick, and Mark Schaller. 2010. Evolutionary Social Psychology. In Fiske, *Handbook of Social Psychology,* vol. 2, 761–96.

Nisbett, Richard E. 2009. *Intelligence and How to Get It.* New York: W. W. Norton.

Noller, Patricia, and Victor J. Callan. 1988. Understanding Parent-Adolescent Interactions: Perceptions of Family Members and Outsiders. *Developmental Psychology* 24:707–14.

Normand, Roger, and Sarah Zaidi. 2008. *Human Rights at the UN: The Political History of Universal Justice.* Bloomington: Indiana University Press.

Nutt, David, Leslie A. King, William Saulsbury, and Colin Blakemore. 2007. Development of a Rational Scale to Assess the Harm of Drugs. *Lancet* 369:1047–53.

Office of Justice Programs. 2007. *One in Every 31 U.S. Adults Were in Prison or Jail or on Probation or Parole in 2007.* Press Release, Office of Justice Programs, U.S. Department of Justice.

Office of the United Nations High Commissioner for Human Rights. 2008. *Frequently Asked Questions on Economic, Social and Cultural Rights, Fact Sheet No. 33.* Geneva: Office of the United Nations High Commissioner for Human Rights.

Offord, David R., Michael H. Boyle, Yvone Racine, Peter Szatmari, Jan E. Fleming, Mark Sanford, and Ellen L. Lipman. 1996. Integrating Assessment Data from Multiple Informants. *Journal of the American Academy of Child and Adolescent Psychiatry* 35:1078–85.

Ogle, Robbin S., and Candice Batton. 2009. Revisiting Patriarchy: Its Conceptualization and Operationalization in Criminology. *Critical Criminology* 17:159–82.

Osgood, Wayne D., Janet K. Wilson, Patrick M. O'Malley, Jerald G. Bachman, and Lloyd D. Johnston. 1996. Routine Activities and Individual Deviant Behavior. *American Sociological Review* 61:635–55.

Otten, Sabine, Kai Sassenberg, and Thomas Kessler. 2009. *Intergroup Relations.* New York: Psychology Press.

Overbye, Dennis. 2007. Free Will: Now You Have It, Now You Don't. *New York Times,* January 2, D1, 4.

Pager, Devah, and Lincoln Quillian. 2005. Walking the Talk? What Employers Say versus What They Do. *American Sociological Review* 70(3): 355–80.

Passas, Nikos, and Neva Goodwin. 2004a. Introduction. In Passas, *It's Legal but It Ain't Right,* 1–27.

———, eds. 2004b. *It's Legal but It Ain't Right: Harmful Social Consequences of Legal Industries.* Ann Arbor: University of Michigan Press.

Patterson, Gerald R., John B. Reid, and Thomas J. Dishion. 1992. *Antisocial Boys.* Eugene, OR: Castalia.

Peets, Katlin, and Eve Kikas. 2005. Aggressive Strategies and Victimization during Adolescence: Grade and Gender Differences, and Cross-Informant Agreement. *Aggressive Behavior* 32:68–79.

Pemberton, Simon. 2004. A Theory of Moral Indifference: Understanding the Production of Harm by Capitalist Society. In Hillyard, *Beyond Criminology,* 67–83.

———. 2007. Social harm future(s): Exploring the Potential of the Social Harm Approach. *Crime, Law and Social Change* 48:27–41.

Pettigrew, Thomas P., and Linda R. Tropp. 2006. A Meta-Analytic Test of Intergroup Contact Theory. *Journal of Personality and Social Psychology* 90:751–83.

Pinker, Steven. 2002. *The Blank Slate: The Modern Denial of Human Nature.* New York: Viking.

———. 2004. Why Nature and Nurture Won't Go Away. *Daedalus* 133(4): 5–18.

———. 2006. The Blank Slate. *General Psychologist* 41(1): 1–8.

———. 2008. The Moral Instinct. *New York Times Magazine,* January 13, 32–37, 52, 55, 56, 58.

Piquero, Alex R. 2008. Measuring Self-Control. In *Out of Control: Assessing the General Theory of Crime,* edited by Erich Goode,. 26–37. Stanford, CA: Stanford University Press.

Piquero, Alex, and Paul Mazerolle. 2001. *Life-Course Criminology.* Belmont, CA: Wadsworth.

Piquero, Alex R., and Stephen G. Tibbetts. 2002. *Rational Choice and Criminal Behavior.* New York: Routledge.

Piquero, Nicole Leeper, Stephanie Carmichael, and Alex R. Piquero. 2008. Assessing the Perceived Seriousness of White-Collar and Street Crimes. *Crime and Delinquency* 54:291–312.

Pogarsky, Gregg. 2002. Identifying "Deterrable" Offenders: Implications for Research on Deterrence. *Justice Quarterly* 19:431–52.

Polizzi, David. Forthcoming. Agnew's General Strain Theory Reconsidered: A Phenomenological Perspective. *International Journal of Offender Therapy and Comparative Criminology*.<AU: volume and page numbers?>

Pratt, Travis C., and Francis Cullen. 2000. The Empirical Status of Gottfredson and Hirschi's General Theory of Crime. *Criminology* 38:931–64.

———. 2005. Assessing Macro-Level Predictors and Theories of Crime: A Meta-Analysis. *Crime and Justice: A Review of Research* 32:373–450.

Pratt, Travis C., Francis T. C, Kristie R. Blevins, Leah H. Daigle, and Tamara D. Madensen. 2006. The Empirical Status of Deterrence Theory: A Meta-Analysis. In Cullen, *Taking Stock*, 367–96.

Pratt, Travis C., and Christopher T. Lowenkamp. 2002. Conflict Theory, Economic Conditions, and Homicide. *Homicide Studies* 6:61–83.

Pratt, Travis C., Michael G. Turner, and Alex R. Piquero. 2004. Parental Socialization and Community Context: A Longitudinal Analysis of the Structural Sources of Low Self-Control. *Journal of Research in Crime and Delinquency* 41:219–43.

Presser, Lois. 2009. The Narratives of Offenders. *Theoretical Criminology* 13:177–200.

Prinz, Wolfgang. 2003. How Do We Know about Our Own Actions? In Maasen, *Voluntary Action*, 21–33.

Purdie-Vaughns, Valerie, and Richard P. Eibach. 2008. Intersectional Invisibility: The Distinctive Advantages and Disadvantages of Multiple Subordinate-Group Identities. *Sex Roles* 59:377–91.

Quillian, Lincoln. 2006. New Approaches to Understanding Racial Prejudice and Discrimination. *Annual Review of Sociology* 32:299–328.

Quinney, Richard. 1977. *Class, State, and Crime*. New York: Longman.

Rafter, Nicole. 2010. Silence and Memory in Criminology. *Criminology* 48:339–56.

Raine, Adrian. 1993. *The Psychopathology of Crime*. San Diego, CA: Academic Press.

Reiman, Jeffrey. 2006. Review of *Beyond Criminology: Taking Harm Seriously* by Paddy Hillyard, Christina Pantazis, Steve Tombs, and Dave Gordon. *British Journal of Criminology* 46:362–64.

Reiman, Jeffrey, and Paul Leighton. 2010. *The Rich Get Richer and the Poor Get Prison*. Boston: Allyn and Bacon.

Reiss, Albert J. Jr., and Jeffrey A. Roth. 1993. *Understanding and Preventing Violence*. Washington, DC: National Academy Press.

Renk, Kimberly. 2005. Cross-Informant Ratings of the Behavior of Children and Adolescents: The "Gold Standard." *Journal of Child and Family Studies* 14:457–68.

Renk, Kimberly, Reesa Donnelly, Cliff McKinney, and Elizabeth Baksh. 2007. Do Schacter's Seven Sins of Memory Apply to Ratings of Children's Emotional and Behavioral Functioning? *Journal of Child and Family Studies* 16:297–306.

Richters, John E. 1992. Depressed Mothers as Informants about Their Children: A Critical Review of the Evidence for Distortion. *Psychological Bulletin* 112:485–99.

Ridley, Matt. 2004. The DNA behind Human Nature: Gene Expression and the Role of Experience. *Daedalus* 133(4): 89–99.

Roberts, Julian V., Loretta J. Stalans, David Indermaur, and Mike Hough. 2003. *Penal Populism and Public Opinion*. Oxford: Oxford University Press.

Robinson, Matthew B., and Kevin M. Beaver. 2009. *Why Crime? An Interdisciplinary Approach to Explaining Criminal Behavior.* Durham, NC: Carolina Academic Press.

Roscigno, Vincent J. 2007. *The Face of Discrimination.* Lanham, MD: Rowman and Littlefield.

Rosenstein, Judith E. 2008. Individual Threat, Group Threat, and Racial Policy: Exploring the Relationship between Threat and Racial Attitudes. *Social Science Research* 37:1130–46.

Rothe, Dawn, and Christopher W. Mullins. 2006. The International Criminal Court and United States Opposition. *Crime, Law, and Social Change* 45:202–26.

Rothe, Dawn L., Jeffrey Ian Ross, Christopher W. Mullins, David Friedrichs, Raymond Michalowski, Gregg Barak, David Kauzlarich, and Ronald C. Kramer. 2009. That Was Then, This Is Now, What About Tomorrow? Future Directions in State Crime Studies. *Critical Criminology* 17:3–13.

Rothenberg, Paula S. 2007. *Race, Class, and Gender in the United States.* New York: Worth.

Rowe, David C., and Denise Kandel. 1997. In the Eye of the Beholder? Parental Ratings of Externalizing and Internalizing Symptoms. *Journal of Abnormal Child Psychology* 25:265–75.

Rummel, R. J. 1994. Democide in Totalitarian States: Mortocracies and Megamurders. In *Genocide: A Critical Bibliographic Review*, vol. 3, edited by W. I. Charny, 229–63. New Brunswick, NJ: Transaction.

Rutter, Michael. 1985. Resilience in the Face of Adversity: Protective Factors and Resistance to Psychiatric Disorder. *British Journal of Psychiatry* 147: 598–611.

Rutter, Michael, Terrie E. Moffitt, and Avshalom Caspi. 2006. Gene-Environment Interplay and Psychopathology: Multiple Varieties but Real Effects. *Journal of Child Psychology and Psychiatry* 47 (3/4): 226–61.

Sampson, Robert J., and John H. Laub. 1993. *Crime in the Making.* Cambridge, MA: Harvard University Press.

Sampson, Robert J., Stephen Raudenbush, and Felton Earls. 1997. Neighborhoods and Violent Crime: A Multilevel Study of Collective Efficacy. *Science* 227:918–24.

Savage, Joanne, Richard R. Bennett, and Mona Danner. 2008. Economic Assistance and Crime: A Cross-National Investigation. *European Journal of Criminology* 5:217–38.

Schaffer, Megan, Stephanie Clark, and Elizabeth L. Jeglie. 2009. The Role of Empathy and Parenting Style in the Development of Antisocial Behaviors. *Crime and Delinquency* 55:586–99.

Schaller, Marc, and Steven l. Neuberg. 2008. Intergroup Prejudices and Intergroup Conflicts. In Crawford, *Foundations of Evolutionary Psychology*, 401–14.

Schmitt, David P. 2008. Evolutionary Psychology Research Methods. In Crawford, *Foundations of Evolutionary Psychology*, 215–36.

Schwartz, Martin D., and Suzanne E. Hatty. 2003. *Controversies in Critical Criminology.* Cincinnati, OH: Anderson.

Schwarz, J. Conrad, Marianne L. Barton-Henry, and Thomas Pruzinsky. 1985. Assessing Child-rearing Behaviors: A Comparison of Ratings Made by Mother, Father, Child, and Sibling on the CRPBI. *Child Development* 56:462–79.

Schwendinger, Herman, and Julia Schwendinger. 1970. Defenders of Order or Guardians of Human Rights? *Issues in Criminology* 5:123–57.

———. 2001. Defenders of Order or Guardians of Human Rights? In Henry, *What Is Crime?*, 65–98.

Sellin, Thorsten. 1938. *Culture Conflict and Crime*. New York: Social Science Research Council.

Semyonov, Moshe, and Noah Lewin-Epstein. 2009. The Declining Racial Earnings Gap in United States: Multiple-level Analysis of Males' Earnings: 1960–2000. *Social Science Research* 38:296–311.

Sessa, Frances M., Shelli Avenevoli, Laurence Steinberg, and Amanda S. Morris. 2001. Correspondence among Informants on Parenting: Preschool Children, Mothers, and Observers. *Journal of Family Psychology* 15:53–68.

Sewell, William H. 1992. A Theory of Structure: Duality, Agency, and Transformation. *American Journal of Sociology* 98:1–29.

Shapland, Joanna, and Matthew Hall. 2007. What Do We Know about the Effects of Crime on Victims? *International Review of Victimology* 14:175–217.

Sherman, Lawrence W. 1993. Defiance, Deterrence, and Irrelevance: A Theory of the Criminal Sanction. *Journal of Research in Crime and Delinquency* 30:445–73.

Sherman, Lawrence W., Denise Gottfredson, Doris MacKenzie, John Eck, Peter Reuter, and Shawn Bushway. 2002. *Evidence-Based Crime Prevention*. London: Routledge.

Sherman, Lawrence W., and Heather Strang. 2007. *Restorative Justice: The Evidence*. London: Smith Institute.

Short, James F. Jr. 1998. The Level of Explanation Problem Revisited. *Criminology* 36:3–36.

Short, James F. Jr., and Fred L. Strodtbeck. 1965. *Group Process and Gang Delinquency*. Chicago: University of Chicago Press.

Shover, Neal. 1996. *Great Pretenders: Pursuits and Careers of Persistent Thieves*. Boulder, CO: Westview.

Shover, Neal, and Andy Hochstetler. 2006. *Choosing White-Collar Crime*. New York: Cambridge University Press.

Shweder, Richard A., Manamohan Mahapatra, and Joan G. Miller. 1987. Culture and Moral Development. In *The Emergence of Morality in Young Children*, edited by Jerome Kagan and Sharon Lamb, 1–83. Chicago: University of Chicago Press.

Siegel, Larry J. 2006. *Criminology*. Belmont, CA: Thomson Wadsworth.

Simpson, Sally S., and David Weisburd. 2010. *The Criminology of White-Collar Crime*. New York: Springer.

Sims, Barbara. 2003. The Impact of Causal Attribution on Correctional Ideology: A National Study. *Criminal Justice Review* 28:1–25.

Singer, Peter. 1981. *The Expanding Circle: Ethics and Sociobiology*. New York: Farrar, Straus and Giroux.

———. 2000. *A Darwinian Left*. New Haven, CT: Yale University Press.

Sloan, Frank A., Jan Ostermann, Gabriel Picone, Christopher Conover, and Donald H. Taylor Jr. 2004. *The Price of Smoking*. Cambridge, MA: MIT Press.

Smith, Cindy. 2006. What Is the Role of Criminology in Informing United Nations Public Policy? *Criminologist* 31(6): 1, 3–5.

Snyder, Mark, and Seymour W. Uranowitz. 1978. Reconstructing the Past: Some Cognitive Consequences of Person Perception. *Journal of Personality and Social Psychology* 36:941–50.

Social Justice, 1999. 25th Anniversary Edition of *Social Justice* 26(2).

Spohn, Cassie C., and D. Holleran. 2000. The Imprisonment Penalty Paid by Young, Unemployed, Black and Hispanic Male Offenders. *Criminology* 38:281–306.

Steffensmeier, Darrell, and Emilie Allan. 1996. Gender and Crime: Toward a Gendered Theory of Female Offending. *Annual Review of Sociology* 22:459–87.

Steffensmeier, Darrell, Jeffrey Ulmer, and J. Kramer. 1998. The Interaction of Race, Gender, and Age in Criminal Sentencing: The Punishment Cost of Being Young, Black, and Male. *Criminology* 36:763–97.

Stone, Catriona H., and Richard J. Crisp. 2007. Superordinate and Subgroup Identification as Predictors of Intergroup Evaluation in Common Ingroup Contexts. *Group Processes and Intergroup Relations* 10:493–513.

Stylianou, Stelios. 2003. Measuring Crime Seriousness Perceptions: What Have We Learned and What Do We Want to Know. *Journal of Criminal Justice* 31:37–56.

Surette, Ray, and Charles Otto. 2001. The Media's Role in the Definition of Crime. In Henry, *What Is Crime?*, 139–54.

Sutherland, Edwin H. 1939. *Principles of Criminology*. Philadelphia: J. B. Lippincott.

———. 1940. White-Collar Criminality. *American Sociological Review* 5:1–12.

———. 1944. Is "White-Collar Crime" Crime? *American Sociological Review* 10: 132–39.

Sutherland, Edwin H., Donald R. Cresset, and David F. Luckenbill. 1992. *Principles of Criminology*. Dix Hills, NY: General Hall.

Sykes, Gresham M., and David Matza. 1957. Techniques of Neutralization: A Theory of Delinquency. *American Sociological Review* 22:664–70.

Talaska, Cara A., Susan T. Fiske, and Shelly Chaiken. 2008. Legitimating Racial Discrimination: Emotions, Not Beliefs, Best Predict Discrimination in a Meta-Analysis. *Social Justice Research* 21:263–96.

Tancredi, Laurence R. 2005. *Hardwired Behavior: What Neuroscience Reveals about Morality*. New York: Cambridge University Press.

Tappan, Paul W. 1947. Who is the Criminal? *American Sociological Review* 12:96–112.

Tashakkori, Abbas, and Charles Teddlie. 2003. *Handbook of Mixed Methods in Social and Behavioral Sciences*. Thousand Oaks, CA: Sage.

Taylor, Ian, Paul Walton, and Jock Young. 1973. *The New Criminology: For a Social Theory of Deviance*. London: Routledge and Kegan Paul.

Tein, Jenin-Yun, Mark W. Roosa, and Marcia Michaels. 1994. Agreement between Parent and Child Reports on Parental Behaviors. *Journal of Marriage and the Family* 56:341–55.

Thoits, Peggy A. 2006. Personal Agency in the Stress Process. *Journal of Health and Social Behavior* 47:309–23.

Thornberry, Terence P. 1987. Toward an Interactional Theory of Delinquency. *Criminology* 25:863–91.

Tift, Larry L., and Dennis C. Sullivan. 2001. A Needs-Based, Social Harms Definition of Crime. In Henry, *What Is Crime?*, 179–203.

Tittle, Charles R. 1995. *Control Balance: Toward a General Theory of Deviance*. Boulder, CO: Westview.

Tittle, Charles R., and Raymond Paternoster. 2000. *Social Deviance and Crime*. Los Angeles: Roxbury.

Toby, Jackson. 1979. The New Criminology Is the Old Sentimentality. *Criminology* 16:516–26.

Tomasello, Michael. 2009. *Why We Cooperate*. Cambridge, MA: MIT Press.

Tonry, Michael. 2008. Learning from the Limitations of Deterrence Research. *Crime and Justice* 37: 279–308.

Topalli, Volkan. 2005. When Being Good Is Bad: An Expansion of Neutralization Theory. *Criminology* 43:797–836.

Tremblay, Richard E. 2006. Tracking the Origins of Criminal Behavior: Back to the Future. *The Criminologist* 31(1): 1, 3–7.

Turk, Austin T. 1982. Legal, Polemical, and Empirical Definitions of Criminality. In Elliston, *Ethics, Public Policy, and Criminal Justice,* 5–17.

United Nations. 2010. Convention on the Elimination of All Forms of Discrimination against Women. www.un.org/womenwatch/daw/cedaw/

Unnever, James D., Michael L. Benson, and Francis T. Cullen. 2008. Public Support for Getting Tough on Corporate Crime. *Journal of Research in Crime and Delinquency* 45:163–90.

Unnever, James D., and Francis T. Cullen. 2007. The Racial Divide in Support for the Death Penalty: Does White Racism Matter? *Social Forces* 85:1281–1301.

Unnever, James D., Francis T. Cullen, Scott Mathers, Timothy McClure, and Marissa Allison. 2009. Racial Discrimination and Delinquent Involvement: Revisiting Hirschi's Criminological Classic. *Justice Quarterly* 26:377–409.

Useem, Bert, and Anne Morrison Piehl. 2008. *Prison State: The Challenge of Mass Incarceration.* New York: Cambridge University Press.

van der Valk, J. C., E. J. C. G. van den Oord, F. C. Verhulst, and D. I. Boomsma. 2001. Using Parental Ratings to Study the Etiology of Three-year-Old Twins' Problem Behaviors: Different Views or Rater Bias? *Journal of Child Psychology and Psychiatry* 42:921–31.

Vignoles, Vivian L., and Natalie J. Moncaster. 2007. Identity Motives and In-Group Favouritism: A New Approach to Individual Differences in Intergroup Discrimination. *British Journal of Social Psychology* 46:91–113.

Vold, George B., Thomas J. Bernard, and Jeffrey B. Snipes. 2002. *Theoretical Criminology.* New York: Oxford University Press.

Walton, Paul, and Jock Young. 1998. *The New Criminology Revisited.* New York: St. Martin's Press.

Ward, David A., Mark C. Stafford, and Louis N. Gray. 2006. Rational Choice, Deterrence, and Theoretical Integration. *Journal of Applied Social Psychology* 36:571–85.

Ward, Tony. 2004. State Harms. In Hillyard, *Beyond Criminology,* 84–100.

Waters, Tony. 2007. *When Killing Is a Crime.* Boulder, CO: Rienner.

Wegner, Daniel M. 2004. Precis of the Illusion of Conscious Will. *Behavioral and Brain Sciences* 27:649–92.

Weisburd, David, and Alex R. Piquero. 2008. How Well Do Criminologists Explain Crime? Statistical Modeling in Published Studies. *Crime and Justice: An Annual Review of Research* 37:453–502.

Welsh, Brandon C., David P. Farrington, and Lawrence W. Sherman. 2001. *Costs and Benefits of Preventing Crime.* Boulder, CO: Westview.

Western, Bruce. 2006. *Punishment and Inequality in America.* New York: Russell Sage Foundation.

White, Rob. 2008. *Crimes against Nature.* Devon, England: Willon.

Whitt, J. Allen. 1993. Toward a Class-Dialectical Model of Power. In Chambliss, *Making Law,* 261–89.

Wiener, Jon. 2005. Working-Class Republicans and "False Consciousness." *Dissent* 52(2): 55–58.

Wikman, Anders. 2006. Reliability, Validity, and True Values in Surveys. *Social Indicators Research* 78:85–110.

Wikstrom, Per-Olof H. 2005. The Social Origins of Pathways in Crime: Toward a Developmental Ecological Action Theory of Crime Involvement and Its Changes. In *Integrated Developmental and Life-Course Theories of Offending*, edited by David P. Farrington, 211–45. New Brunswick, NJ: Transaction.

Williams, Tannis MacBeth. 1986. *The Impact of Television: A Natural Experiment in Three Communities*. Orlando, FL: Academic Press.

Wilson, James Q. 1975. *Thinking About Crime*. New York: Vintage Books.

———. 1993. *The Moral Sense*. New York: Free Press.

World Health Organization. 2008. *WHO Report on the Global Tobacco Epidemic, 2008*. Geneva: World Health Organization.

Wrangham, Richard. 2004. Killer Species. *Daedalus* 133(4): 25–36.

Wrangham, Richard, and Dale Peterson. 1996. *Demonic Males: Apes and the Origins of Human Violence*. Boston: Mariner Books.

Wright, Bradley R. E., Avshalom Caspi, Terrie E. Moffitt, Richard A. Meich, and Phil A. Silver, 1999. Reconsidering the Relationship between SES and Delinquency: Causation but Not Correlation. *Criminology* 37:175–94.

Wright, Bradley R. E., Avshalom Caspi, Terrie E. Moffitt, and Ray Paternoster. 2004. Does the Perceived Risk of Punishment Deter Criminally Prone Individuals? Rational Choice, Self-Control, and Crime. *Journal of Research in Crime and Delinquency* 41:180–213.

Wright, John Paul, and Kevin Beaver. 2005. Do Parents Matter in Creating Self-Control in their Children? *Criminology* 43:1169–1202.

Wright, John Paul, Stephen G. Tibbetts, and Leah E. Daigle. 2008. *Criminals in the Making: Criminality across the Life Course*. Thousand Oaks, CA: Sage.

Wrong, Dennis H. 1961. The Oversocialized Conception of Man in Modern Sociology. *American Sociological Review* 26:183–93.

———. 1979. *Power: Its Forms, Bases and Uses*. New York: Harper and Row.

Yamagishi, Toshio, and Nobuhiro Mifune. 2009. Social Exchange and Solidarity: In-Group Love or Out-Group Hate? *Evolution and Human Behavior* 30:229–37.

Young, Jock. 1999. *The Exclusive Society*. London: Sage.

Young, Jock, and Roger Matthews. 1992. *Rethinking Criminology: The Realist Debate*. London: Sage.

Yzerbyt, Vincent, and Stephanie Demoulin. 2010. Intergroup Relations. In Fiske, *Handbook of Social Psychology*, vol. 2, 1024–83.

Zagefka, Hanna, Rupert Brown, Murielle Broquard, and Sibel Leventoglu Martin. 2007. Predictors and Consequences of Negative Attitudes toward Immigrants in Belgium and Turkey: The Role of Acculturation Preferences and Economic Competition. *British Journal of Social Psychology* 46:153–69.

Zahn, Margaret. 2009. *The Delinquent Girl*. Philadelphia, PA: Temple University Press.

Zahn-Waxler, Carolyn, Marian Radke-Yarrow, and Elizabeth Wagner. 1992. Development of Concern for Others. *Developmental Psychology* 28:126–36.

Name Index

Aberson, Christopher, 117, 134n5
Achenbach, Thomas, 171, 171n2, 171n3, 172, 175, 177n6, 177, 178n9
Adler, Freda, 14
Agnew, Robert, vii, 4n1, 5, 28, 45, 45n2, 46n3, 47, 48n4, 51, 52, 54n10, 56, 57, 57n14, 58, 59, 59n15, 61, 61n16, 62, 64, 65, 65n19, 66, 67, 68, 70n21, 71, 75n4, 76, 76n5, 77, 77n6, 78, 78n7, 80, 81, 82, 83, 93, 100, 112, 114, 122, 124, 124n3, 127, 128, 133, 135n6, 136, 142, 143, 143n10, 144, 144n11, 146n12, 152, 156, 161, 162, 164, 168, 170, 176, 180, 187, 188, 200, 201
Ajzenstadt, Mimi, 48, 149
Akers, Ronald, 3, 48n4, 74n2, 75, 77, 77n6, 82, 83, 83n10, 118n1, 120n2, 124n3, 135n6, 145, 187n15
Alder, Mortimer, 13n1, 15
Allan, Emily, 3
Amnesty International, 23n10, 131
Anderson, Elijah, 59m15, 83, 114, 125, 145, 178, 180, 187n15
Anderson, Karen, 175n5, 177n6
Anderson, Linda, 116
Andrews, D. A., 73, 199
Arrigo, Bruce, 4, 124n3
Auerhahn, Kathleen, 15, 16, 110, 125

Baker, Laura, 105n23, 106n26, 106n27
Bandura, Albert, 45n1, 52n7, 53, 53n9, 54n10, 56, 56n12, 57, 57n14, 58, 65, 85, 96n16, 105, 106, 116, 116n32, 151
Barak, Gregg, 3, 15n2, 19n5, 22n8, 23n9, 24, 142, 142n9, 144n11
Bargh, John, 55, 93, 94, 173
Barkan, Steven, 124n3, 130n4, 141n8, 142n9, 144n11

Barnes, Barry, 52n7, 56n12, 59
Bateson, Patrick, 106n26
Batson, Daniel, 91
Batton, Candice, 124n3, 153
Baumeister, Roy, 92, 98
Baumer, Eric, 144n11
Bayer, U., 54n10, 56n12
Beaver, Kevin, 105n23, 105n24, 106n26, 106n27, 122, 143
Beck, Sarah, 134n5, 155n21
Beckett, Katherine, 15, 51
Beirne, Piers, 45n2, 46
Bennett, William, 50
Benson, Michael, 163
Berkowitz, Leonard, 94
Bernard, Thomas, 1, 5, 74, 79, 118n1, 119, 120n2, 124, 124n3, 127, 135n6, 145, 191, 201
Bernburg, Jon, 28
Bertelsen, Preben, 52n7, 53, 59n10, 57
Betsinger, Sara, 142n9, 151
Bijleveld, Catrien, 14
Blakemore, Sarah-Jayne, 105n24
Blau, Judith, 23, 23n10, 23n11, 24, 24n12, 26, 32, 32n18, 33, 34, 39
Blazak, Randy, 146n12, 154n17
Bloom, Paul, 72, 99, 99n18
Bobbitt-Zeher, Donna, 129
Bobo, Lawrence, 124n3, 127, 128, 151n16
Bolzendahl, Catherine, 127, 137
Bonczar, Thomas, 28
Bonger, Willem, 116, 120, 132, 162
Bottoms, Anthony, 199
Bouchard, Thomas, 105n23, 107
Boudon, Raymond, 74n1, 93, 93n13
Bowleg, Lisa, 130
Bowles, Samuel, 103n20, 104
Bowling, Benjamin, 49n5, 53n9, 55n11

Box, Steven, 16n3, 17, 17n4, 18, 19n5, 20, 21n7, 25, 25n14, 27n16, 41, 124n3
Braithwaite, John, 41, 68, 70n21, 78
Brewer, Marilynn, 92, 98, 116
Brezina, Timothy, 146n12
Bronitt, Simon, 18, 25n13
Brooks, Thom, 23n10, 23n11, 24, 24n12
Brown, Donald, 17, 87, 96, 97
Buckler, Kevin, 141n8, 151
Building Blocks for Youth, 134
Bunkley, Nick, 118
Burgess-Proctor, Amanda, 124n3, 130n4
Burns, Tom, 52n7, 53n9

Calkins, Susan, 100n19
Callan, Victor, 175n4, 176
Callaway, Rhonda, 23n10, 23n11, 24n12
Carmichael, Stephanie, 93
Carter, Scott, 127, 137, 156
Caspi, Avshalom, 100n19, 105n23, 106n27, 178n8
Chambliss, William, 3, 15, 16n3, 18, 20, 21n7, 65, 118n1, 120n2, 124n3, 125, 126, 129, 136
Chamlin, Mitchell, 141n8, 156
Chartrand, Tanya, 55, 93, 94, 173
Cheatwood, Derral, 200
Clarke, Ronald, 48, 48n4, 49, 50, 55, 56n12, 74, 74n1, 74n2, 75n3, 77, 78, 94n14
Clear, Todd, 28
Cloninger, Robert, 100n19, 105n23
Cloward, Richard, 78n7, 79, 81n9
Cocharn, John, 70n20
Cohen, Albert, 78, 79, 81n9, 146n12
Cohen, Mark, 15
Cohen, Stanley, 25n14
Collins, Randall, 79, 80
Colvin, Mark, 3, 5n2, 133, 135n6, 143n10, 144, 144n11, 161
Conger, Rand, 65, 66
Cook, William, 177n6, 177n7
Cooper, Jonathan, 5
Copes, Heath, 116n32
Cornish, Derek, 48, 48n4, 49, 55, 56n12, 74, 74n1, 74n2, 75n3, 77, 94n14

Crawford, Charles, 103n20
Crisp, Richard, 134n5, 155n21
Cropley, David, 66
Cullen, Francis, 27n16, 36, 46n3, 47, 51, 59, 70n21, 75n4, 77, 122, 124n3, 135, 135n6, 141n8, 142, 144, 144n11, 148, 160, 161, 180, 186, 188, 199
Currie, Elliott, 3, 116, 124n3, 132, 133, 135, 143n10

Dabney, Dean, 178n10, 183n13
Davies, Alastair, 155n22
Davis, Nancy, 153, 156
Daynard, Richard, 25, 26
Decker, Scott, 114
De Coster, Stacy, 188
De Dreu, Carsten, 154n18, 155n21
Degnan, Kathryn, 100n19
DeKeseredy, Walter, 2, 34, 124n3, 135n6
De Los Reynes, Andres, 171n2, 171n3, 172, 174, 175, 189
De Mesquinta, Bruse, 86
Demoulin, Stephanie, 154n18
Demuth, Stephen, 171n2
De Pauw, Sarah, 100, 100n19
Desimone, Laura, 171n2
De Waal, Frans, 102, 103, 106
Dick, Danielle, 105n23, 106n26
Dietz, Thomas, 52n7
Dijksterhuis, Ap, 53, 94, 173
Dillon, Michelle, 124, 127, 130n4, 138, 145, 146n13, 158, 178n10
Dodge, Kenneth, 174
Dodson, Lisa, 182n13
Doerner, Jill, 142, 142n9, 159
Dombrink, John, 136
Domhoff, G. William, 126, 128, 129, 137, 138, 140
Dovidio, John, 117, 154n18, 155n19
Dowdall, George, 126
Dunbar, Robin, 89n11, 92n12, 99n18, 103n20, 104n22, 106n26
Duntley, Joshua, 103n20
Dye, Thomas, 138

Eck, John, 50
Eibach, Richard, 152, 158, 159
Einstadter, Werner, 24, 26n15, 74n1, 78n7,
    81, 118n1, 120n2, 124n3, 127, 161, 169n1,
    178n10, 188
Eitle, David, 134, 141n8
Elder, Glenn, 52n7, 53n9, 60, 65n18
Elder-Vass, Dave, 52n7, 54n10, 55n11, 57,
    57n14, 65n18
Elliott, Delbert, 5n2
Elster, John, 74n1, 93n13
Emirbayer, Mustafa, 52n7, 54n10, 55n11,
    56n12, 57n14, 59, 65n18

Fagan, Andrew, 22, 26, 34n19
Farr, Kathryn, 12, 16
Farrall, Stephen, 49n5, 53n9, 55n11
Farrington, David, 47, 68, 78, 113, 124,
    178n8
Fehr, Ernst, 86, 89n11, 92n12, 93, 93n13,
    103n20
Felson, Marcus, 50, 60, 67, 78, 200
Felson, Richard, 136, 200
Feminist Majority Foundation, 131
Ferdinand, Robert, 188
Ferrell, Jeff, 3, 175, 177, 178n10, 180,
    182n13
Fischbacher, Urs, 89n11, 92n12, 103n20
Fiske, Susan, 151, 161n1
Fletcher, George, 25, 25n13, 36
Foglia, Wanda, 70n20
Freund, Peter, 114
Friedrichs, David, 23n9
Friedrichs, Jessica, 23n9

Gabbidon, Shaun, 124n3, 127, 128, 145
Gaertner, Samuel, 117, 154n18, 155n19
Galliher, John, 15, 16, 20, 22n8
Garcia, Marie, 15
Gazzaniga, Michael, 52n7, 53n8, 93n13,
    94n15, 95, 98n17, 99n18, 103, 103n20,
    105n25, 173, 175
Geis, Gilbert, 15, 16, 20, 125
Gert, Bernard, 98n17
Gettleman, Jeffrey, 84

Gibbons, Don, 13n1, 116
Gintis, Herbert, 86, 89n11, 92n12, 93, 93n13,
    103n20, 103n21, 104, 105n25
Giordano, Peggy, 3, 9, 49, 49n5, 50, 56, 71,
    182n14
Goldhagen, Daniel, 84
Goldkamp, John, 46, 46n3, 48, 49
Goldstein, Michael, 177n6, 177n7
Gonzales, Nancy, 175m4, 177
Goode, Erich, 21, 26, 26n15, 27
Goodwin, Neva, 19, 21n7, 22n8, 23n9, 24,
    25, 34n19, 39, 43n22
Gopnik, Alison, 99n18
Goschke, Thomas, 53, 54n10, 55n11, 56
Gottfredson, Michael, 4n1, 9, 46, 46n3,
    48n4, 74, 75, 75n3, 76, 76n5, 113, 122
Green, Penny, 19, 21n7, 22n8, 23n9, 24,
    28n17, 29, 39, 43n22
Greenberg, David, 9n3, 76n5, 77, 124n3, 127,
    141n8, 145, 146n12
Greene, Joshua, 94, 97, 105n25
Greenwood, Peter, 78, 124
Greer, Scott, 13n1, 15n2, 23n10, 23n11, 29,
    28n17
Groves, Robert, 175, 182n13
Guo, Gang, 106n26
Gustafson, Regan, 144n11

Haag, Sarah, 117, 134n5
Haederle, Michael, 44
Hagan, Frank, 14
Hagan, John, 15, 15n1, 15n2, 23n9, 23n10,
    23n11, 24, 28, 28n17, 29, 30, 35, 37, 43,
    124n3, 139, 142, 158, 182n14, 200
Haidt, Jonathan, 93n13, 94, 94n15, 96, 97,
    98n17, 103n20, 105n25
Hall, Matthew, 15
Hamilton, David, 154n18
Hamilton, Richard, 103n20
Hancock, Ange-Marie, 158
Harkness, Allan, 182n12
Harrelson-Stephens, Julie, 23n10, 23n11,
    24n12
Harris, Judith, 92
Hatty, Suzanne, 9n3, 124n3

Liska, Allan, 15, 25n15, 118n1, 120n2, 141n8, 169n1, 178n10, 180
Loeber, Rolf, 64, 171n2, 172, 174, 178n8, 182n12
Long, Charisse, 52n7, 58, 59n15
Lorber, Michael, 176, 178n9
Lowenkamp, Christopher, 144n11
Loyal, Steven, 52n7, 56n12, 59
Ludwig, Kristin, 65, 66, 67
Lukes, Steven, 146n14
Lynch, Michael, 3, 15n2, 16n3, 19n5, 118n1, 124n3, 129, 135n6, 140n7, 141n8, 142n9, 143n10, 144, 144n11, 145

Maasen, Sabine, 52n7
MacDonald, John, 177
MacLean, Brian, 2, 9n3, 124n3
Madene, Kim, 159
Magura, S., 172
Maier-Katkin, Daniel, 19, 23n9, 24, 131
Marini, Margaret, 74n1, 74n2, 93, 93n13
Markowitz, Fred, 136
Martin, George, 114
Maruna, Shadd, 49, 49n5, 50, 58, 71, 96n16, 116n32
Matsueda, Ross, 28, 74n1, 77n6, 82, 94n14, 175n5, 177n6
Matthews, Rick, 21n6, 21n7, 23n9, 28n17
Matthews, Roger, 3, 17, 124n3
Matza, David, 45n2, 48, 54, 61, 62, 83, 96n16, 116n32, 151, 187n15
Mazerolle, Paul, 200
McCarthy, Bill, 74n1, 77n6, 94n14, 182n14, 200
McCrae, Robert, 100n19, 105n23
Meier, Robert, 15, 16, 20, 125
Merry, Sally, 23n10, 32n8
Merton, Robert, 78, 80
Messerschmidt, James, 114, 146n12, 200
Messner, Steven, 5, 26n15, 116, 118n1, 120n2, 132, 141n8, 144n11, 162, 169n1, 178n10, 180, 199, 201
Meyers, Daniel, 127
Meyers, Lawrence, 177n6
Meyers, Peter, 153
Michael, Jerome, 13n1, 15

Michalowski, Raymond, 3, 14, 15n2, 16n3, 19n5, 22n8, 23n9, 118n1, 124n3, 126, 129, 140n7, 141n8, 142n9, 143n10, 144, 144n11, 145, 146n13
Mifune, Nobuhiro, 155n19
Mikhail, John, 94n15, 95, 96
Milgram, Stanley, 115
Miller, Jody, 114, 180
Milovanovic, Dragon, 2, 9n3, 124n3
Mische, Ann, 52n7, 54n10, 56n12, 57n14, 59
Mitchell, Ojmarrh, 142n9
Moffitt, Terrie, 123, 144
Monahan, Susanne, 134, 141n8
Moncada, Alberto, 23, 23n10, 23n11, 24, 24n12, 26, 32, 32n18, 33, 34, 39
Moncaster, Natalie, 155n21
Moore, E., 163
Morash, Merry, 48n4, 125, 127, 130n4, 133, 134, 139, 142, 145, 146n13, 151, 153, 156, 157, 158, 178n10
Mosher, Clayton, 35, 176, 177
Mullins, Christopher, 24
Mullis, Ronald, 24, 66
Myers, Daniel, 137

Nagin, Daniel, 48, 70, 74n2, 93n13, 94n14
Nelson, Todd, 135n5, 154n18
Neuberg, Steven, 103n20, 103n21, 104, 154n18, 155n19, 155n22
Nisbett, Richard, 106n26
Noller, Patricia, 175n4, 176
Normand, Roger, 23n10, 23n11, 24, 24n12, 26, 33, 34
Nutt, David, 34n19

Office of Justice Programs, 27
Office of the United Nations High Commissioner for Human Rights, 23n10, 32, 34, 34n19, 35n20
Offord, David, 172
Ogle, Robin, 124n3, 153
Ohlin, Lloyd, 78n7, 79, 81n9
Osgood, Wayne, 187n15
Otten, Sabine, 134n5, 154n18, 155n19, 155n21
Otto, Charles, 27n16
Overbye, Dennis, 52

Pager, Devah, 176
Passas, Nikos, 19, 21n7, 22n8, 23n9, 24, 25, 34n19, 39, 43n22
Paternoster, Raymond, 21, 22, 26, 26n15, 27, 38n21
Patterson, Gerald, 172, 176, 178n8, 185
Peets, Katlin, 174
Pemberton, Simon 3, 12, 22n8, 25n14
Peterson, Dale, 88, 101
Pettigrew, Thomas, 117
Piehl, Anne, 51, 77
Pinker, Steven, 17, 47, 52n7, 74, 79, 82, 86, 89n11, 92n12, 94n15, 97, 98n17, 103n20, 103n21, 105n23, 105n24, 105, 105n25, 106, 106n26, 116, 155n22, 175n4, 200
Piquero, Alex, viii, 5, 15, 47, 74n2, 75n3, 93, 93n13, 94n14, 136, 186, 201
Pittman, Joe, 65, 66, 67
Pogarsky, Gregg, 70n20, 71
Polizzi, David, 178n10
Pratt, Travis, 122, 143, 144n11, 161, 186, 199
Presser, Lois, 170, 178n12
Prinz, Wolfgang, 53, 53n8, 55
Purdie-Vaughns, Valerie, 152, 158, 159

Quillian, Lincoln, 137, 139, 140, 140n7, 151, 152, 173, 176
Quinney, Richard, 124n5

Rafter, Nicole, 3, 45n2, 169n1
Raine, Adrian, 73, 199
Reiman, Jeffrey, 13, 15n2, 17, 18, 19, 21n7, 25, 25n13, 25n14, 26, 27, 27n16, 34n19, 35, 26, 41, 43n22, 124n3, 140n7, 142, 142n9, 144n11, 151, 153
Renk, Kimberly, 173, 175, 177n6, 182n12, 184
Richters, John, 174
Ridley, Matt, 105n23, 106n26
Roberts, Julian, 27n16
Robinson, Matthew, 105n22, 105n24, 106n26, 106n27
Robinson, Robert, 153, 156
Roscigno, Vincent, 140, 140n7
Rosenfeld, Richard, 116, 132, 162, 199
Rosenstein, Judith, 140, 141n8, 151n16

Rothe, Dawn, 24, 126, 146n13
Rothenberg, Paula, 140n7
Rowe, David, 177n7, 178n8, 182n12
Rummel, R. J., 19
Rutter, Michael, 177n7, 178n8, 182n12

Sampson, Robert, 3, 9, 49n5, 50, 75n4, 182n14, 199
Sasson, Theodore, 15, 51
Savage, Joanne, 144n11, 148
Schaffer, Megan, 113
Schaller, Marc, 104, 154n18, 155n19, 155n22
Schmitt, David, 89
Schnabel, Albrecht, 24n12, 32n18,
Schwartz, D., 174, 175n4
Schwartz, Martin, 9n3, 124n3
Schwarz, J., 174
Schwendinger, Herman, 13n1, 15n2, 16n3, 17, 22, 23, 43
Schwendinger, Julia, 13n1, 15n2, 16n3, 17, 22, 23, 43
Sellers, Christine, 3, 118n1, 120n2, 124n3, 135n6, 145
Sellin, Thorsten, 15n2, 16, 27, 28n17
Semyonov, Moshe, 140
Sessa, Frances, 177
Sewell, William, 45n1, 52n7, 53n9, 55n11, 59, 65n18
Shackelford, Todd, 103n20, 155n22
Shapland, James, 15
Sherman, Lawrence, 70n21, 78, 152
Short, James, 78, 114, 200
Shover, Neal, 49n5, 132
Siegel, Larry, 14
Simpson, Sally, 3, 134
Sims, Barbara, 50
Singer, Peter, 110, 115, 116
Sloan, Frank, 26, 134n19
Smith, Cindy, 35
Snipes, Jeffrey, 1, 5, 191, 201
Snyder, Mark, 175
Social Justice, 3
Spohn, Cassie, 142
Steffensmeier, Darrell, 3, 142, 159
Stone, Catriona, 155n19
Strang, Heather, 78

Subject Index

Definition of crime (*continued*): and controlling crime, 41; core characteristics of crime, 31- 41; and essentialist approach, 26, 29; and human nature, 109-110; and human rights, 21-24, 32-35; integrated definition, 30- 43; legal definition, 13-20; prism of crime, 29-30; pyramid of crime, 28-29; as sanctioned acts, 26-30, 37. *See also* Agency; Constructionist approach; Critical criminology; Mainstream criminology

Determinism, 6, 44-71, 195-196; and controlling crime, 47; and human nature, 110-111; *See also* Agency, Integrated theory of bounded agency, Positivistic approach.

Deterrence theory, 50-51, 75-78, 170

Differential association theory, 82-83

Evolutionary psychology, 88-89, 103-105. *See also* Blank Slate; Human nature; Self-interest; Social concern

Experiments: and desire to help others, 91-92; examining human nature, 86-87, 89-94; and inclination to conform, 92; and in-group bias, 92; and rationality, 92-93; and self-interest, 89-91; and social concern, 89-91. *See also* Blank slate; Human nature; Rational choice; Self-interest; Social concern

Feminist criminology, 126-127, 133, 138-139; and agency, 48

Free will. *See* Agency

Game studies. *See* Experiments

Gender, 123, 126-127, 130, 133-134, 137, 140, 151-154, 158-159

Human nature, 7, 72-117, 196-197; and agency, 110-111; and causes of crime, 111-115; and control of crime, 115-117; definition, 73; and definition of crime, 109-110; evidence on, 84-106; integrated view of, 106-117; views of, 72-84. *See also* Blank slate; Biological research;

Evolutionary psychology; Experiments; Human universals; Infant studies; Moral dilemmas; Moral principles; Primate studies; Rational choice; Self-interest; Social concern

Human rights, 22-24, 31-35. *See also* Definition of crime

Human universals, 87-88, 97-98. *See also* Blank slate; Human nature; Self-interest; Social concern

Infant studies, 88, 99-101. *See also* Blank slate; Human nature; Self-interest; Social concern

Integrated theories, vii-viii, 5, 111-112, 191-202

Integrated consensus/conflict perspective, 145-166; and agency, 164; and causes of crime, 160-164; and controlling crime, 164-165; real and perceived conflict, 153-154; types of consensus and conflict, 147-153; variation in consensus/conflict, 154-157

Integrated theory of bounded agency, 52-71; and causes of crime, 65-68; and consensus/conflict, 164; and control of crime, 68-70; and variation in crime, 61-65. *See also* Agency; Determinism

Intersectionality, 130, 158-160

Labeling theory, 188-189

Latent variables, 177-178, 183-184. *See also* Reality

Life-course criminology, and agency, 49

Mainstream criminology, 2-11, and definition of crime, 13- 20; and determinism, 45-46. *See also* Critical criminology

Marxist criminology, 126-130. *See also* Critical criminology

Mixed methods approach, 182

Moral dilemmas, 94-97. *See also* Blank slate; Human nature; Self-interest, Social concern

Moral principles, 96-98

About the Author

ROBERT AGNEW is Samuel Candler Dobbs Professor of Sociology at Emory University and author of many books, including *Criminological Theory: Past to Present*; *Juvenile Delinquency: Causes and Control*; *Pressured into Crime: An Overview of General Strain Theory*; and *Why Do Criminals Offend: A General Theory of Crime and Delinquency*. He is a Fellow of the American Society of Criminology and President Elect of that organization.